Generations of Faith

Resource Manual

Lifelong Faith Formation for
the Whole Parish Community

Generations
of Faith
Resource Manual

Lifelong Faith Formation for the Whole Parish Community

JOHN ROBERTO
with Mariette Martineau

TWENTY
THIRD *23rd*
PUBLICATIONS

The research and development of the *Generations of Faith Resource Manual: Lifelong Faith Formation for the Whole Parish Community* has been funded by a generous grant from the Lilly Endowment.

First published by:
Center for Ministry Development
P.O. Box 699
Naugatuck, CT 06770

Cover art: "One Sacred Community" by Mary Southard, CSJ.
Courtesy of www.ministryofthearts.org

Twenty-Third Publications
A Division of Bayard
P.O. Box 180
Mystic, CT 06355
(860) 437-3012 or (800) 321-0411
www.23rdpublications.com
ISBN:1-58595-399-7

Library of Congress Catalog Card Number: 2004117342
Printed in the U.S.A.

Contents

Introduction

Background and History

The *Generations of Faith Resource Manual: Lifelong Faith Formation for the Whole Parish Community* has grown out of ten years of research, development, and direct work with parishes across North America by the Center for Ministry Development. The Generations of Faith Project seeks to translate the catechetical vision of the Catholic Church into reality in parish life. The *General Directory for Catechesis* (1997) calls for a lifelong approach to faith formation with the parish community at the center of catechesis. Generations of Faith provides this by developing an events-centered approach to faith formation, focusing on the events of Church life: Church year feasts and seasons, sacraments and Church rituals, justice and service, prayer and spirituality, and community life.

The Generations of Faith approach includes intergenerational catechetical programs for all ages and resources for home faith-sharing and learning. Generations of Faith is not a program; rather, it is an approach to creating lifelong, intergenerational, events-centered faith formation. Parishes of all sizes and cultures have found the Generations approach works in their parish community. The key to the Generations approach is that it builds on the strengths of a parish's current catechetical programming, while creating a lifelong faith formation plan and intergenerational learning programs that gather people of all ages and stages of life to learn together. Parishes customize the Generations approach to their parish community—to the mission of the parish, the needs of their people, the cultures in the parish, and the resources and facilities of the parish.

In 2001, the Center for Ministry Development received a multi-year grant from the Lilly Endowment to work with parishes across North America in implementing a lifelong, intergenerational, events-centered approach to faith formation. Through the Generations of Faith Project, the Center has created workshops, online resources, and publications to support parishes in their work. As of January 2005, over 1000 parishes across the United States and Canada are working to incorporate lifelong, intergenerational, events-centered learning into their parish catechetical curriculum.

About the Resource Manual

This manual is the first of two publications from the Generations of Faith Project. Research and development for both books has been funded by the Lilly Endowment. The second publication, the Sourcebook, will be published in 2006. It will contain expanded coverage of the foundations of the Generations of Faith vision and practices and results of the research from parishes that have been participating in the Generations of Faith Project since 2001.

The manual is designed as a planning guide and workbook to help the parish community embrace the vision and practices of Generations of Faith. *The Resource Manual* provides detailed processes and tools to move from vision to reality and is supported by the practical tools, resources, and parish examples available through Generations of Faith Online (www.generationsoffaith.org). Throughout the book you will find suggestions to go online to find more information and download practical tools for your work.

Here is a brief overview of the manual:

- Chapter 1: Vision and Practice is an essay describing the vision and seven practices of the Generations approach.
- Chapter 2: Fashioning a Lifelong Curriculum provides the rationale, process, instructions, and tools for creating a six-year curriculum plan for your parish.
- Chapter 3: Implementing the Curriculum provides practical advice and tools for scheduling, determining budgets and fees, and developing promotional and registration materials.
- Chapter 4: Developing Leadership provides the rationale for developing an empowerment mindset, as well as the processes, suggestions, and tools for inviting people into leadership, preparing and training leaders, and supporting them.
- Chapter 5: Designing a Learning Plan guides you through the process of developing a learning plan for an event:
  1. creating alignment of learning for all ages
  2. designing parish learning programs, in particular, intergenerational learning
  3. designing home activities
  4. designing reflection activities.
- Chapter 6: Planning and Facilitating Meetings is designed for the team leader who is facilitating the planning meetings. It provides strategies and tools for facilitating meetings, as well as detailed meeting outlines for the work of Chapters 1-5.

Before You Begin

The most important task in facilitating the Generations of Faith approach is to gather a core team. You cannot plan and implement this approach without a team and the support of key parish leadership, especially the pastor. A core team broadens the base of input into the planning process and increases support for the plan. The team approach emphasizes collaboration and shared decision-making, which builds a strong sense of *ownership* among team members. This ownership extends the responsibility for the faith formation beyond the director of religious education to the parish leadership, and eventually to the parish community.

The core team guides the process of fashioning, implementing, and evaluating a curriculum for Generations of Faith. As such, their major tasks include:

- fashioning the lifelong faith formation curriculum;
- developing the implementation procedures for the curriculum—scheduling, promotion, budgeting, and so on;
- developing leadership—recruiting, training, and providing support—for learning programs and other important areas of the curriculum;

- coordinating the work of the design team—who designs learning programs and home resources—and the implementation team—who conducts learning programs;
- monitoring the progress of the curriculum throughout the year;
- evaluating the curriculum at the end of the year and planning for the next year.

The core team is drawn from the parish staff, parish leadership, and faith formation leaders, both paid and volunteer, in your parish community. These may include:

- pastor
- director of religious education
- school principal
- youth minister
- adult educator
- family minister
- liturgical minister
- music minister
- RCIA (Rite of Christian Initiation of Adults) and sacramental preparation leaders
- justice and service leaders
- small Christian community leaders
- evangelization leaders
- key faith formation leaders, such as catechists and religious board members

Change Takes Time

When you begin the process of creating a lifelong, intergenerational, events-centered faith formation plan, you are embarking on a journey of change. And change takes time! One of the most difficult realities for parish teams to accept is that a new approach to faith formation will take years to become anchored in the life of the parish. It will take years for families and individuals to embrace household faith formation. But it *will* happen!

John Kotter, a Harvard University professor and international consultant on change, says that producing change requires leadership—establishing direction, aligning, motivating, and inspiring people—as well as management—planning, budgeting, organizing, and problem-solving. From his work with profit and non-profit organizations of all sizes, he has indentified eight steps in the process of initiating change:

1. establishing a sense of urgency
2. creating a guiding coalition
3. developing a vision and strategy
4. communicating the vision
5. empowering others to act on the vision
6. planning for and creating short-term wins
7. consolidating improvements and producing new change
8. anchoring new approaches in the culture.

Kotter says that the first four steps in the transformation process help an organization defrost a hardened status quo. Steps five to seven then introduce new practices. The last step grounds the change in the organizational culture and helps make it stick. Successful change of any magnitude goes through all eight stages, usually in the sequence given above. Although it is not unusual to work in multiple steps at the same time, skipping even a single step and getting too far ahead without a solid base almost always creates problems.

This manual is designed to guide you from step 1 through step 7. As for step 8, over time the changes to faith formation will become anchored in the life of the parish community and people will say: "We've always done it this way." Here are several signs that the Generations approach is becoming anchored in your parish community:

- There is a lot of "buzz" among participants who are now bringing new individuals and families to the intergenerational learning program. People who were once marginal to faith formation and parish life are starting to get involved.
- The curriculum plan moves into its third or fourth year and is now fully implemented.
- New learning models (intergenerational learning, alignment of learning across the whole parish) gain wider acceptance and participation.
- There is a wider use of home activities as evidenced through stories and evaluation.
- The job descriptions of parish staff and key leaders are modified to embrace the work of a Generations of Faith curriculum.
- Parish catechetical policies and handbooks are revised to incorporate the Generations of Faith vision and practices, as well as new learning models.
- The orientation program for new staff members includes an orientation to the Generations of Faith vision and practices.

Adopting an Innovation

The hard reality is that the adoption of change by the parish community takes time; nobody knows exactly how long it will take. Yet there are some patterns of involvement in a change that can be instructive as you begin to implement a new approach to faith formation and learning.

Everett Rogers and his colleagues have studied the process of adoption for all kinds of products, across a wide diversity of populations. Through their studies, some common patterns have emerged. First, perceptions concerning an innovation are crucial to the process of diffusing it. Characteristics that influence the adoption or rejection of an innovation include:

1. *Relative advantage*, the degree to which the innovation is perceived as being better than the idea it supersedes. (How do the benefits of the innovation outweigh the current approach and its problems?)
2. *Compatibility*, or the perception that the innovation is consistent with existing values, past experiences, and the needs of potential adopters: "Being able to connect it to a previous tradition or way of doing things is important and provides an anchor to people's meanings." (How does the innovation connect to the parish mission statement, values, etc.?)
3. *Complexity*, or the degree to which it is perceived as difficult to understand and use. (How is the innovation simpler to understand and more user-friendly?)
4. *Trialability*, or the degree to which it may be experimented with on a limited basis: "Think of the trial as a way to gradually internalize the innovation." (How do we provide people with the opportunity to experience it before they make a commitment?)

5. *Observability,* that is, the degree to which the results of an innovation are visible to others. (How do we make sure that we don't just talk about the innovation, but actually implement it so that people can see it and experience it?)

Second, it takes time for an innovation to reach critical mass, the point at which enough individuals have adopted it so that its further rate of adoption is self-sustaining. Reaching critical mass usually takes more time than most parishes are willing to commit to. Resistance may be strongest right before critical mass is achieved. Innovation, to be diffused, takes time and resources; it demands commitment from parish leadership to stay with an innovation long enough. The wise investment of resources requires an emphasis on the journey to achieve critical mass.

Third, people differ markedly in their readiness to try new ideas, concepts, and programs. People can be classified into adopter categories (see below). The adoption process is represented as a normal distribution when plotted over time. After a slow start, an increasing number of people adopt the innovation, the number reaches a peak, and then it diminishes as fewer non-adopters remain. Innovators are defined as the first 2.5% of the people to adopt a new idea; the early adopters are the next 13.5% who adopt the new idea; early majority constitute 34% of the total population. Eventually the late majority (34%) adopt the innovation. The laggards represent 16% and may or may not adopt the innovation.

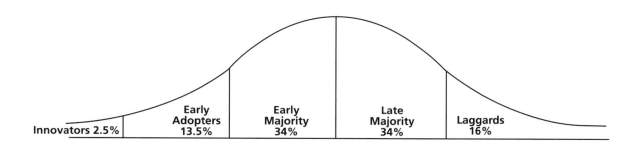

Rogers sees the five adopted groups as differing in their value orientations. *Innovators* are venturesome; they are willing to try new ideas at some risk. *Early adopters* are guided by respect; they are opinion leaders in their community and adopt new ideas early but carefully. The *early majority* are deliberate; they adopt new ideas before the average person, although they rarely are leaders. The *late majority* are skeptical; they adopt an innovation only after a majority of people have tried it. Finally *laggards* are tradition-bound; they are suspicious of changes, mix with other tradition-bound people, and adopt the innovation only when it takes on a measure of tradition itself.

It is very important that leaders focus their time and energy appropriately with each particular group of people. It is also important to note that adoption (and therefore change) moves from left to right: from innovators to early adopters to the majority. One group "evangelizes" the next group.

As more members of the parish community adopt the innovation (participate in intergenerational learning and Church life, engage in household faith-sharing), the innovation becomes anchored in the parish community. Adoption moves deliberately through these audiences over time.

A New Beginning

We are at the beginning of a widespread transformation of faith formation in the Catholic Church. To this end, the Generations of Faith approach is taking hold in parishes across the United States and Canada. Parishes large and small, urban and sub-urban, big city and small town, multi-ethnic and multi-lingual are embracing and implementing lifelong, intergenerational, events-centered faith formation. The Generations of Faith vision, solidly grounded in the *General Directory for Catechesis,* holds great promise for the future of parish and home faith formation. This manual will guide you in your journey toward making this vision a reality in your parish.

CHAPTER 1

Vision and Practice

▶ A New Approach to Faith Formation

Since the Second Vatican Council ended in 1965, the Catholic Church has offered a comprehensive and compelling vision of faith formation and lifelong learning for people of all ages and generations. This vision is firmly rooted in the life of the Church. The wonderful image of catechesis from the *General Directory for Catechesis* (#59), that "'the model for all catechesis is the baptismal catechumenate...'"(1977 Synod *Message to the People of God* [MPD]), reflects an approach to faith formation and learning that immerses people into the life of the Church.

> Finally, the concept of the baptismal catechumenate as a process of formation and as a true school of the faith offers post-baptismal catechesis dynamic and particular characteristics: comprehensiveness and integrity of formation; its gradual character expressed in definite stages; its connection with meaningful rites, symbols, biblical and liturgical signs; its constant references to the Christian community. (GDC #91)

Yet catechesis across the United States and Canada is still struggling under the burden of an outdated model of faith formation. Embracing the vision of faith formation laid out in the *General Directory for Catechesis* requires moving beyond a school paradigm to a community or "whole Church" paradigm of faith formation. This shift requires a series of significant changes:

- moving from a focus on only educating children (think of all the time, energy, and resources we still commit to children) by implementing lifelong faith formation for all ages and generations, including and especially adults;
- ending "start and stop" catechesis (think graduation at confirmation; think preparation for sacraments) by implementing lifelong and continuous faith formation, learning through involvement in the events of Church life;
- overcoming age segregation (think grade levels, youth groups, etc.) by implementing intergenerational faith formation that connects all the generations in learning programs and parish involvement;
- moving beyond a focus on textbooks as the only means of forming a curriculum by utilizing the events of Church life as the curriculum for all ages and generations, providing catechesis that prepares everyone to participate in the events of Church life;
- not blaming families for the failures of current faith formation practices, instead encouraging the faith of the family as integral to faith formation;
- implementing a more collaborative and integrated approach that involves all of the parish's ministries in faith formation and that views catechesis in its connection with liturgy, sacraments, the Church year, justice and service, and prayer.

The Generations of Faith approach equips the parish to become a community of learners by creating lifelong faith formation that is centered in the events of Church life, embraces all ages and generations, and promotes faith growth at home, through parish preparation programs, and, most importantly, through participation in Church life.

▶ A Story of Faith Formation

Imagine a parish that is embracing this vision of faith formation and preparing the entire faith community for Lent:

Lent is coming and the entire community of Holy Family Parish is preparing to immerse themselves in the lenten season through liturgy and prayer (Ash Wednesday, the Sunday liturgies, Holy Week, Stations of the Cross), justice and service (food and clothing collection, Operation Rice Bowl), and community life activities (lenten meals)—in the parish and at home.

The Holy Family catechetical ministry has designed a variety of ways to prepare all of the generations for their participation in the lenten season. Their goal is to prepare everyone in the parish community for Lent focusing on the theme for the year: "The Three Practices of Lent: Fasting, Praying, and Almsgiving." Preparation programs guide people of all ages to understand the meaning of Lent and the three practices, to appreciate the significance of Lent and the three practices in our Catholic tradition, to participate actively in the lenten season, and to live the three practices at home and in the world. When people are prepared for an event they feel confident, comfortable, and competent to participate in the events of church life.

The lenten lectionary readings will be a primary resource for preparation. The music director has selected special lenten songs, one for each week of Lent, that express musically the lenten theme. These songs will be used in parish programs and at Sunday worship.

The week before Ash Wednesday, on a Wednesday night, Friday night, or Saturday morning, all ages—from families with children through older adults, arrive at the parish center for a light dinner or continental breakfast, followed by the feature activity—learning how to live the three practices of fasting, praying, and almsgiving. The program moves through several stages of activities:

▶ Everyone gathers together for a meal—a great time to build community.

▶ The program begins with prayer and song inspired by the lenten season and the three practices.

▶ An all-ages opening experience introduces everyone to the focus of preparation—the three practices of Lent.

▶ The in-depth learning component of the program helps everyone to explore the meaning of the event through age-appropriate learning groups. Families with children explore the lenten practices through three activity centers—praying, fasting, and almsgiving/service. The adolescents explore the lenten practices and create contemporary ways to live the three practices today. A guest speaker presents an overview of the lenten lectionary and a contemporary interpretation of the lenten practices for adults.

▶ The entire group gathers again to share their learning from the in-depth sessions.

- ▶ One of the leaders reviews how to use the Lenten Home Kit, which provides resources for families and individuals to experience Lent at home: a lenten calendar with daily activities and Scripture passages; a lenten journal for teens with daily readings, prayers, and activities; a daily lenten prayer guide for adults; placemats with weekly table prayers; suggested local service projects and Operation Rice Bowl; several learning activities on lenten themes; and a copy of the parish's lenten calendar.

- ▶ In family groupings and adult groupings, everyone develops a Lenten Pledge to live the three practices at home and in the world.

- ▶ The program closes in prayer and song.

Young adults—those at home, in college, or in the military—receive, via e-mail, a special Lenten Journal with a daily lectionary reading, a reflection written by young adults, and a prayer. All of the adult faith sharing groups in the parish dedicate a session to the "Three Practices of Lent" by exploring the meaning of Lent and reflecting on the lenten lectionary readings. Each participant receives a booklet of daily lenten reflections to guide their journey through the season. All of the parish committees and councils that meet prior to or at the beginning of Lent open their meetings with a special prayer service on the lenten theme. All of the adult participants receive a Lenten Home Kit and a copy of the parish's lenten calendar.

In addition to the Lenten Home Kit, the parish's web site, Holy Family On-Line, features the parish lenten calendar, prayers and reflections for all ages on the lenten Scripture readings, and the entire Lenten Home Kit. A special bulletin insert for each week of Lent is distributed at all of the Masses.

Wherever you go in the Holy Family community people of all ages and generations are united in a common endeavor: to prepare for Lent, to experience Lent fully at home and in the parish, and to integrate their learning into their daily lives as Catholics.

Faith formation at Holy Family Parish is in the midst of a transformation. They are moving toward a curriculum that is centered on the formative events of the Church community and the participation of all ages and generations in the shared experiences of Church life. Holy Family Parish has embraced the Generations of Faith approach to faith formation.

▶ Foundations of Generations of Faith

The Generations of Faith approach is built on the Church's catechetical teachings over the past forty years and seeks to give expression to these teachings in a distinctive approach to faith formation. This section examines four important foundations for the approach, drawn from the *General Directory for Catechesis:*

- • the goals of catechesis
- • the parish as a community of learning
- • the baptismal catechumenate as the model
- • the six interrelated tasks of catechesis for all catechesis

Foundation 1: A Living Faith

The Generations of Faith approach to faith formation is guided and inspired by goals that are as old as the Church itself.

> Quite early on, the name catechesis was given to the totality of the Church's efforts to make disciples, to help men and women believe that Jesus is the Son of God so that believing they might have life in his name, and to educate and instruct them in this life, thus building up the body of Christ. (*Catechism of the Catholic Church* [CCC], #4)

> The aim of catechetical activity consists in precisely this: to encourage a living, explicit and fruitful profession of faith (cf. CCC 1229; *Christus Domini* 14l). (GDC #66)

> "The definitive aim of catechesis is to put people not only in touch, but also in communion and intimacy, with Jesus Christ."[1] All evangelizing activity is understood as promoting communion with Jesus Christ. Starting with the "initial" (*Ad Gentes* [AG] 13b) conversion of a person to the Lord, moved by the Holy Spirit through the primary proclamation of the Gospel, catechesis seeks to solidify and mature this first adherence. It proposes to help those who have just converted "to know better this Jesus to whom he has entrusted himself: to know his 'mystery,' the kingdom of God proclaimed by him, the requirements and comments contained in his Gospel message, and the paths that he has laid down for anyone who wishes to follow him" (CT 20c). (GDC #80)

1. *Catechesi Tradendae* (CT) 5; cf. CCC 426; AG 14a. In relation to this christological end of catechesis see part one, chap. I and part two, chap. I. *"Jesus Christ mediator and fullness of Revelation"* and that which is said in part two, chap. I *"Christianity of the evangelical mission."*

Discipleship is the goal of all faith formation. Guided by this goal, faith formation seeks to *inform, form,* and *transform* individuals, families, and the entire community in the Catholic faith. This threefold aim includes nurturing people's minds and hearts with the wisdom of the Catholic faith so that who they are and how they live are deeply influenced by what they "know" (inform), shaping people's identity and lifestyle through Christian discipleship (form), and empowering people to live their faith so that the world is transformed by the Christian vision (transform).

Generations of Faith provides a comprehensive approach to discipleship that is rooted in the life of the Church, equips people to participate meaningfully in the life of the Church, and empowers them to live as disciples at home and in the world.

Foundation 2: A Lifelong Learning Community

At the heart of the Generations of Faith approach is the development of the parish as a lifelong learning community, a congregation of learners. It is essential that we empower every member of our community to become both teacher and learner. In a learning community, learners are teaching, teachers are learning, and all activities—meetings, worship, service, and community events—include learning. Through this approach, parish communities can be revitalized and transformed.

> The Christian community not only gives much to those who are being catechized but also receives much from them. New converts, especially adolescents and adults, in adhering to Jesus Christ, bring to the community which receives them new religious and human wealth. Thus the community grows and develops. Catechesis not only brings to maturity the faith of those being catechized but also brings the community itself to maturity. (GDC #221)

A congregation of learners is a center for authentic Catholic learning, viewed as a life-long endeavor that grows out of the life of the community, which, in turn, strengthens the community. A congregation of learners creates a *culture of learning*.

In such a congregation, every activity of Church life is viewed as an opportunity for learning. Catechesis is seamlessly integrated with liturgy, justice and service, prayer and spirituality. Catechesis prepares people for active, conscious, meaningful participation in liturgy and in the Church year. It helps them reflect on the meaning and significance of their participation on their lives as Catholics. Catechesis prepares people for the work of justice and acts of service, and helps individuals reflect on the connection between their actions and their faith. This approach leads to a deepening of Catholic commitment and an increased Catholic practice. It contributes to the creation of a strong sense of community and develops a community's capacity to be self-renewing.

The *General Directory for Catechesis* echoes this understanding when it reminds us that catechesis is centered in the life of the entire community.

The role of the faith community

Catechesis is an essentially ecclesial act.[2] The true subject of catechesis is the Church which, continuing the mission of Jesus the Master and, therefore animated by the Holy Spirit, is sent to be the teacher of the faith. The Church imitates the Mother of the Lord in treasuring the Gospel in her heart (cf. *Lumen Gentium* [LG] 64; *Dei Verbum* [DV] 10a). She proclaims it, celebrates it, lives it, and she transmits it in catechesis to all those who have decided to follow Jesus Christ. (GDC #78)

2. As has been stated in chapter I of this part in "The transmission of Revelation by the Church, the work of the Holy Spirit" and in part II, chapter I in "The ecclesial nature of the Gospel message." Cf. *Evangelii Nuntiandi* (EN) 60 which speaks of the ecclesial nature of any evangelizing activity.

Catechesis is nothing other than the process of transmitting the Gospel, as the Christian community has received it, understands it, celebrates it, lives it and communicates it in many ways. (GDC #105)

In giving attention to the individual, it should not be overlooked that the recipient of catechesis is the whole Christian community and every person in it. If indeed it is from the whole life of the Church that catechesis draws its legitimacy and energy, it is also true that "her inner growth and correspondence with God's plan depend essentially on catechesis (CT 13)." (GDC #168)

The intimate connection between catechesis and the other ministries

To fulfill its tasks, catechesis avails of two principal means: transmission of the Gospel message and experience of the Christian life (cf. *Codex Iuris Canonici* [CIC] 773 and 778 §2). Liturgical formation, for example, must explain what the Christian liturgy is, and what the sacraments are. It must also however, offer an experience of the different kinds of celebration and it must make symbols, gestures, etc., known and loved. Moral formation not only transmits the content of Christian morality, but also cultivates active evangelical attitudes and Christian values. (GDC #87)

The Church as the primary faith formation curriculum and catechist

Catechetical pedagogy will be effective to the extent that the Christian community becomes a point of concrete reference for the faith journey of individuals. This happens when the community is proposed as a source, *locus* and means of catechesis. Concretely, the community becomes a visible place of faith-witness. It provides for the formation of its members. It receives them as the family of God. It constitutes itself as the living and permanent environment for growth in the faith (cf. AG 14; *General Catechetical Directory* [DCG] [1971], 35; CT 24). (GDC #158)

The Christian community is the origin, *locus* and goal of catechesis. Proclamation of the Gospel always begins with the Christian community and invites man to conversion and the following of Christ. It is the same community that welcomes those who wish to know the Lord better and permeate themselves with a new life. The Christian community accompanies catechumens and those being catechized, and with maternal solicitude makes them participate in her own experience of the faith and incorporates them into herself (cf. CT 24). (GDC #254)

From this perspective it becomes clear that *the Church is both curriculum and catechist.* As Maria Harris states so clearly in her book, *Fashion Me a People: Curriculum in the Church,* ". . . the Church does not have an educational program; it is an educational program."

Foundation 3: A Comprehensive Framework

The *General Directory for Catechesis* provides a comprehensive framework for catechesis that is rooted in the life of the Church.

> The duties of catechesis correspond to education of the different dimensions of faith, for catechesis is integral Christian formation, *"open to all the other factors of the Christian life* (CT 21b)." In virtue of its own internal dynamic, the faith demands to be known, celebrated, lived and translated into prayer. Catechesis must cultivate each of these dimensions. The faith, however, is lived out by the Christian community and proclaimed in mission: it is a shared and proclaimed faith. These dimensions must also be encouraged by catechesis. The Second Vatican Council expresses these duties as follows: ..."catechetical instruction, which illumines and strengthens the faith develops a life in harmony with the Spirit of Christ, stimulates a conscious and fervent participation in the liturgical mystery and encourages men to take an active part in the apostolate (*Gravissimum Educationis* 4; cf. *Rite of Christian Initiation of Adults* [RCIA] 19, CIC 788.2)." (GDC #84)

The comprehensive vision proposed by the *General Directory for Catechesis* includes six essential and interrelated tasks for catechesis (see GDC #85):

- *Promoting knowledge of the faith.* Catechesis fosters "'the gradual grasping of the whole truth ... '" through a study of Tradition and Scripture. This task is realized by deepening one's knowledge of the Creed, "...a compendium of Scripture and of the faith of the Church ...."
- *Liturgical education.* Catechesis teaches the meaning of the liturgy and sacraments, aiming to bring the faith to a "...full, conscious, and active participation ...."
- *Moral formation.* Catechesis fosters conversion of life by transmitting the spirit of the beatitudes and values of the Decalogue, and witnesses to "...the social consequences of the demands of the Gospel."
- *Teaching to pray.* Catechesis calls the disciples to pray with sentiments of Jesus' prayer: "...adoration, praise, thanksgiving, filial confidence, supplication, and awe...." The Our Father is a "...summary of the entire Gospel ..." and handing it on is "...a true act of catechesis."
- *Education for community life.* By means of an apprenticeship (the catechumenate) that witnesses to 1) a spirit of simplicity and humility, 2) solicitude for "the least," 3) concern for alienated, 4) fraternal correction, and 5) mutual forgiveness.
- *Missionary initiation.* By equipping the faithful, especially the laity, "...to be present as Christians in society through their professional, cultural and social lives." (*Sowing the Seeds,* 24–25)

The *Directory* emphasizes that all of these tasks are essential.

> The tasks of catechesis, consequently, constitute a totality, rich and varied in aspect. ..."All of these tasks are necessary. As the vitality of the human body depends on the proper function of all of its organs, so also the maturation of the Christian life requires that it be cultivated in all its dimensions: knowledge of the faith, liturgical life, moral formation, prayer, belonging to community, missionary spirit. When catechesis omits one of these elements, the Christian faith does not attain full development." (GDC #87)

In *Fashion Me a People,* Maria Harris presents a similar, comprehensive understanding of faith formation that is rooted in the life of the Church. She writes,

> Throughout history, reaching back to Acts 2:42–47, the Church's educational ministry has been embodied and lived in five classical forms: *didache, koinonia, kerygma, diakonia, leiturgia.* If we would educate *to* all of these forms, as well as *through* all of them, then attending only to any one of them, simply would not do. The fullness of the pastoral vocation demands that any ecclesial education must be one that educates:
>
> • to *koinonia* (community and communion) by engaging in the forms of community and communion;
>
> • To *leiturgia* (worship and prayer) by engaging in the forms of prayer and worship and spirituality;
>
> • to *kerygma* (proclaiming the Word of God) by attention to and practicing and incarnating the kerygma, "Jesus is Risen," in the speech of our own lives, especially the speech of advocacy;
>
> • to *diakonia* (service and outreach) by attending to our own service and reaching out to others, personally and communally, locally and globally;
>
> • to *didache* (teaching and learning) by attention to the most appropriate forms of teaching and learning in our own communities.
>
> Should any of these be left out as full partners in the educational work of ministry; should any of these be downplayed; should any of these be exalted to the denigration of others, we will not be able to educate fully. All are needed. (Harris 43–44)

The Generations of Faith approach utilizes all six interrelated tasks of catechesis by centering faith formation in the events of Church life.

Foundation 4: A Model of Catechizing Activity

The *General Directory for Catechesis* presents the baptismal catechumenate as the model for all the Church's catechizing activity.

> Given that the *missio ad gentes* is the paradigm of all the Church's missionary activity, the baptismal catechumenate, which is joined to it, is the model of its catechizing activity (cf. MPD 8; EN 44; *Chrisifideles Laici* 61). It is therefore helpful to underline those elements of the catechumenate which must inspire contemporary catechesis and its significance. (GDC #90)

The *Directory* highlights elements of the ancient catechumenate that "...must inspire contemporary catechesis ...." In view of the "fundamental difference" between catechizing individuals not yet baptized (catechumens) and catechizing individuals already baptized, the *Directory* outlines elements as they apply to post-baptismal catechesis (#91).

- The baptismal catechumenate constantly reminds the whole Church of the fundamental importance of the function of initiation and the basic factors which constitute it: catechesis and the sacraments of Baptism, Confirmation, and Eucharist.
- The baptismal catechumenate is the responsibility of the entire Christian community....
- The baptismal catechumenate is also completely permeated by the *mystery of Christ's Passover*. For this reason, "all initiation must reveal clearly its paschal nature" (RCIA 8). The Easter Vigil, focal point of the Christian liturgy, and its spirituality of Baptism inspire all catechesis.
- The baptismal catechumenate is also an initial locus of inculturation....the Church receives catechumens integrally, together with their cultural ties. All catechetical activity participates in this function of incorporating into the catholicity of the Church, authentic "seeds of the word," scattered through nations and individuals (cf. CT 53).
- Finally, the concept of the baptismal catechumenate *as a process of formation and as a true school of the faith* offers post-baptismal catechesis dynamic and particular characteristics: comprehensiveness and integrity of formation; its gradual character expressed in definite stages; its connection with meaningful rites, symbols, biblical and liturgical signs; its constant references to the Christian community.

Viewing the baptismal catechumenate as the model for all the Church's catechizing activity has two important implications for faith formation.

1. This view reinforces an events-centered approach to faith formation that immerses people into the life of the faith community, providing the opportunities to learn by participating and experiencing. Craig Dykstra observes, "The process of coming to faith and growing in the life of faith is fundamentally a process of participation. We come to recognize and live in the Spirit as we participate more and more broadly and deeply in communities that know God's love, acknowledge it, express it, and live their lives in the light of it." (*Growing in the Life of Faith: Education and Christian Practices,* 40)

2. This view places an emphasis on engaging people in the practices of the faith community: learning by studying, practicing, performing, and reflecting, and most importantly learning by doing the activity. People come to faith and grow in faith, and in the life of faith, by participating in the practices of the Christian community, and the practices of the whole Church. It is not enough simply to know about these practices or think about them or observe other people engaging in them. Each of us must actually pray, read, interpret the Scriptures, and provide hospitality to strangers.

Why is faith formation centered on the practices of the faith community so important? Craig Dykstra writes,

> These are the kinds of practices that the Church's people engage in over and over again, because they are practices that constitute being the Church, practices to which God call us as Christians. They are, likewise, practices that place people in touch with God's redemptive activity, that put us where life in Christ may be made known, recognized, experienced, and participated in. They are means of grace, the human places in which and through which God's people come to faith and grow in maturity in the life of faith. From its own history and experience, the Church knows that such practices enable the community and its people as individuals to continue their experience with God made present in Word, in sacrament, in prayer, and in the community's life in obedience to its vocation in the world. (*Growing in the Life of Faith,* 43)

The Generations of Faith approach is designed to immerse people more deeply in the life of the Church so that they may learn by participating and experiencing. By so doing, people of all ages are engaged in the practices of the Catholic faith, practices that can become integral to each person's life.

▶ Practices of Generations of Faith

The *General Directory for Catechesis* calls for a lifelong approach to faith formation with the Church as the center of catechesis—as the curriculum for lifelong catechesis, as the content for learning, and as the catechist or teacher of the faith. The Generations of Faith approach has seven defining features, or key practices, that guide the development of faith formation in a parish community.

Practice 1: Events-centered Catechesis

With Generations of Faith, faith formation is *events-centered*. The lifelong curriculum and individual learning experiences are developed around the *events* of our shared life as a Church: Church year feasts and seasons, sacraments and liturgy, prayer and spirituality, justice and service, and community life. These events hold tremendous educative and transformative power.

The *General Directory for Catechesis* reminds us, "…it is from the whole life of the Church that catechesis draws its legitimacy and energy…" (GDC #168). The beliefs and practices for living the Catholic faith are embedded in the events of Church life. Events-centered catechetical programs prepare people of all ages and generations to understand the meaning of Church events and participate more actively in the life of the Church. If parishioners are not prepared to participate in the events of Church life, they cannot learn through their participation. The key is to unlock the power of these events through catechesis.

If the Church itself is the curriculum, then the events of Church life are learning experiences. To uncover the curriculum already present in the life of the faith community, we need only look to the communal events which shape the life of our parish community and embody the story, the beliefs, and the practices of the Catholic faith. In *Educating Congregations,* Charles Foster describes the significance and power of these communal events for faith formation.

> The gospel originated in acts of God experienced as events by communities of people. Robert MacAfee Brown has observed that all discussions of faith have some relationship to certain events in the past….Something happened long ago in the life, death, and resurrection of Jesus Christ that transformed perspectives, commitments, and ways of living among a small band of people in a small Mediterranean country. The stories of that event have gathered people into its possibilities for centuries, shaping and transforming their lives and culminating in communities of memory and transformation.
>
> Subsequent events…(in the history of the Church)…refine and particularize the meaning of the incarnation in our times and places. Events in our congregations and local communities further refine and refocus our faith experience.
>
> Our relationship to these communal events has an educative character. If they are to become important to us, we must be familiar with them. If we are to participate in them, we must learn how to do so. If we are to be agents of their meanings, we must develop sensibilities for the roles and responsibilities need-

ed to fulfill that task. As we try to understand these events we begin to link ideas and actions, to discover new possibilities for living. As these events become increasingly important to us, we find ourselves developing skills to interpret other experiences through their categories and concepts. As we encounter their limits to be gospel in our ever-changing situation, we find ourselves searching underneath and from the margins of their interpretation for new insights. In these activities certain events begin to inform our consciousness, and we find ourselves living increasingly into their meanings and out of their possibilities.

We begin to identify with them. We take on their character....We discover ourselves in a community of people identified with that event. We begin to see the world through the perspective of the community originating in and shaped by that event....These events not only tell us who we are, but also to whom we belong. They provide us with clues about how we are to relate to others and to participate in the world around us.

We can discern five distinct patterns of events in the life of the parish community, around which we can fashion a curriculum. These patterns are present in every community, and they are remarkably predictable from year to year. (Look back at the parish calendar over the past several years to determine the patterns.) They provide the clearest and most consistent structure for the education of a parish community as well as a regular ordering of Church life.

- *Church year.* The pattern of the parish's celebration of the seasons and feasts of the Church year provides a variety of events around which one may build Church-centered faith formation.
- *Sacraments and life-cycle rituals.* The celebrations of the sacraments throughout the year provide a second source for an events-centered approach. Life-cycle rituals, such as funerals, birthdays, anniversaries, and graduations, also have an educative power.
- *Prayer and spirituality.* The Church's prayer practices (e.g., the rosary, the Stations of the Cross), spiritual traditions (e.g., mysticism, contemplation), and devotions (e.g., Eucharistic adoration) provide a third source for an events-centered approach.
- *Justice and service.* The Church's work of justice and acts of service, locally and globally, provide a fourth set of events around which to build faith formation.
- *Community life.* The Church's community life—seasonal and ethnic festivals, social events, dinners, parish anniversaries, and other settings where the community gathers—provide a fifth set of events.

Practice 2: Lifelong and Systematic Catechesis

Faith formation is *systematic, cyclic, episodic,* and *continuous.* It is formed around the natural rhythm and pattern of the faith community's life as experienced throughout the year. The events of Church life form a spiral curriculum (think Church year) that immerses people more deeply each year into the faith of the Church. The events of Church life are so theologically rich that it will take years to immerse people in their meaning and practice (think of the theological themes embedded in Lent). Our catechetical task is to continually deepen their understanding and practice.

Fashioned around the life of the Church, the Generations of Faith curriculum provides a multi-year plan of events that continues to spiral more deeply into Church events on a regular basis (every six years). A multi-year curriculum plan outlines the scope (content) and sequence (timing) of your lifelong curriculum.

This lifelong curriculum of Church events systematically and comprehensively presents the Gospel message and Catholic tradition through six major content areas: Church year feasts and seasons, sacraments, justice and service, morality, prayer and spirituality, and the Creed (see GDC #84–87, 97–115.). The *General Directory for Catechesis* (#115) identifies the significance of these major aspects and dimensions of the Christian message for catechesis.

- *Church year feasts and seasons.* "The history of salvation, recounting the 'marvels of God' (*mirabilia Dei*), what He has done, continues to do and will do in the future for us, is organized in reference to Jesus Christ, the 'center of salvation history' (DCG [1971] 43)." (GDC #115) (See also GDC #85, 97–98, 101–102, 105, 108.)

- *Sacraments.* "The sacraments, which, like regenerating forces, spring from the paschal mystery of Jesus Christ, are also a whole. They form 'an organic whole in which each particular sacrament has its own vital place' (CCC 1211). In this whole, the Holy Eucharist occupies a unique place to which all of the other sacraments are ordained. The Eucharist is to be presented as the 'sacrament of sacraments' (*ibidem*)." (GDC #115) (See also GDC #85, 108.)

- *Justice and service.* "Jesus, in announcing the Kingdom, proclaims the justice of God: he proclaims God's judgment and our responsibility. ...The call to conversion and belief in the Gospel of the Kingdom—a Kingdom of justice, love and peace, and in whose light we shall be judged—is fundamental for catechesis." (GDC #102) (See also GDC #86, 102-104, 108.)

- *Prayer and spirituality.* "The Our Father gathers up the essence of the Gospel. It synthesizes and hierarchically structures the immense riches of prayer contained in Sacred Scripture and in all of the Church's life." (GDC #115) (See also GDC #85, 108.)

- *Creed.* "The Apostles' Creed demonstrates how the Church has always desired to present the Christian mystery in a vital synthesis. This Creed is a synthesis of and a key to reading all of the Church's doctrine, which is hierarchically ordered around it.[3]" (GDC #115) (See also GDC #85, 99–100, 108.)

3. St. Cyril of Jerusalem affirms with regard to the Creed: "This synthesis of faith was not made to accord with human opinions but rather what was of the greatest importance was gathered from all the Scriptures, to present the one teaching of the faith in its entirety. And just as a mustard seed contains a great number of branches in a tiny grain, so too the summary of faith encompassed in a few words the whole knowledge of the true religion contained in the Old and New Testaments."

- *Morality.* "The double commandment of love of God and neighbor is—in the moral message—a hierarchy of values which Jesus himself established. 'On these two commandments depend all the Law and the Prophets' (Mt 22:40). The love of God and neighbor, which sum up the Decalogue, are lived in the spirit of the Beatitudes and constitute the *magna carta* of the Christian life proclaimed by Jesus in the Sermon on the Mount.[4]" (GDC #115) (See also GDC #85, 97, 104, 108.)

4. St. Augustine presents the Sermon on the Mount as "the perfect charter of the Christian life and contains all the appropriate precepts necessary to guide it" (*De Sermone Domini in Monte* I, 1; *Patrologiae Cursus completus, Series Latina* 34, 1229-1231); cf. EN 8.

Practice 3: Emergent Catechetical Content

Faith formation is *emergent*. The beliefs and practices for living as a Catholic today emerge from the life, events, and practices of the faith community. Our catechetical task is to uncover the theological and doctrinal message within each event and shape the curriculum accordingly.

The content that emerges from a multi-year, events-centered curriculum provides the foundations of the Catholic faith. Consider the themes embedded in Lent: baptism, salvation, sin and repentance, conversion, cross, Jesus Christ (Messiah and suffering servant), justice, moral life, paschal mystery, and the three lenten practices (fasting, praying, and almsgiving). A cyclic curriculum moves through these themes over multiple years, immersing people more deeply into the lenten experience. While every event in the Church year is not as rich in content as Lent, each event brings its own particular aspect of the foundations of the Catholic faith to the process.

The beliefs and practices of the Catholic faith are not abstractions, but integrated into the life and events of our faith communities. These beliefs and practices emerge from the event, rather than being imposed on it. For example:

- To identify the content in a Church year season (Advent, Christmas, Lent, Easter), we explore the lectionary readings for the season, the liturgies and rituals, the key symbols for the Sundays, and major celebrations within the season.

- To discover the content in a sacramental celebration, we explore the Rite or order of service, the introduction to the Rite (the theological foundation), the lectionary readings, symbols, prayer texts, and ritual actions.

- To discover the content in a justice or service event, we explore the focus and design of the project, the social issues being addressed and their impact on people, the causes of the situation, the reason for addressing the situation, the audience being served, and the specific actions of those who are working for justice or serving those in need.

- To discover the content in prayer and spirituality events, we explore the history of the event or spiritual tradition, the prayer practices in the event, connection to a saint or Church tradition, and order of service.

Practice 4: Connected Catechesis: Prepare, Engage, Reflect/Apply

Faith formation *prepares* people of all ages and all generations for meaningful participation in Church events through intergenerational learning, *engages* all ages and generations in Church events, and guides them in *reflecting on* and *applying* the significance and meaning of the events to their lives as Catholics. It is *connected catechesis*: the catechetical program leads directly to participation in Church life. Learning programs draw their content from Church events and lead people toward active, conscious, meaningful participation in Church events. The event is the centerpiece of the learning process.

Preparing for an Event

Experiencing the Event

Reflecting on the Event Applying Its Meaning to Daily Life

Preparation empowers people to participate meaningfully in the Church event, engaging them in its dynamic and providing the activities and resources that help people participate fully in the event. Preparation programs and activities are designed to help people of all ages and generations develop:

- *know-what,* that is, an understanding of the meaning of the event and its scriptural, doctrinal, and theological foundation;
- *know-why,* the ability to appreciate and value the meaning and significance of the event for their lives;
- *know-how,* the ability to participate competently in the event and then live out its meaning and significance.

The second movement in the events-centered methodology involves our *engagement* in the event. Events are at the heart of the learning process. By actively participating in the event, people transform their lives and they learn.

The events-centered methodology comes full circle with *reflection* on the meanings people draw from their engagement with the event, using the structure of the event and the preparation content and activities as guides. It also includes *application* of the learning to one's life as a Catholic today. Reflection and application activities and strategies are often packaged in kits for use by individuals and families at home.

Reflection helps people to

- *share* their experience of the event (storytelling);
- *assess* the significance or meaning they draw from their engagement in the event and connect it to the Scriptures and Catholic tradition (theological reflection);
- *apply* the meaning (beliefs, practices) to their daily lives (transfer of learning);
- *report* or "publish" their learning for others in the parish community (feedback).

Practice 5: Intergenerational Catechesis

Faith formation is *intergenerational*. It provides events-centered catechetical programs for all ages and generations in the parish community. The *General Directory for Catechesis* reminds us, "…it should not be overlooked that the recipient of catechesis is the whole Christian community and every person in it" (GDC #168). Intergenerational learning provides an opportunity to gather the whole parish to learn, pray, celebrate, and share. It has tremendous benefits for the parish and for individuals. Intergenerational learning

- builds community and meaningful relationships across all the generations in a parish;
- provides a setting for each generation to share and learn from the other generations;
- provides an environment where new ways of living one's faith can be practiced;
- provides adult role models for children and youth;
- promotes understanding of shared values and a common faith, as well as respect for individuals in all stages and ages of life;
- helps to overcome the age-segregated nature of our society and Church programs.

Practice 6: Alignment of Catechesis for All Ages

Faith formation provides *alignment* of learning through common events and themes that are experienced and explored by all ages and all generations in the faith community. The key in events-centered learning is that the whole parish is focused. Everyone prepares for the same event with the same theological focus, creating parish-wide synergy.

All too often, parish faith formation provides little generational convergence. In the schooling and programmatic approaches, different age groups or interest groups study topics appropriate to their age or group. Scope and sequence charts and curriculum guidelines do a fine job of describing the unique content for each age group in childhood and adolescent catechesis, but do little to indicate points of convergence. Most of the time, people are learning in parallel tracks. Family members rarely explore the same theme at the same time, minimizing opportunities for mutual sharing and activities. As a result, little of what is learned gets put into practice.

The Generations of Faith approach provides a support system for learning in the parish and at home by focusing on common events and themes that engage the whole parish community. The fundamental unity of the parish and of faith formation is strengthened by establishing common events and themes that are explored by all members of the community at home and through parish faith formation programs. Establishing a common event or theme, which members of the congregation explore at their appropriate level, makes cross-generational conversations more feasible and potent in the parish and at home.

Practice 7: Home Faith Formation

Faith formation is *empowering*. Empowering and enabling individuals and families to live their faith at home and in the world is constitutive of lifelong faith formation. The lifelong, events-centered approach of common events and themes provides a focus and support structure to build a partnership between the home and parish. It overcomes the isolation many families and individuals feel when asked to engage in home-based activities and faith-sharing. The parish-wide support structure enhances faith sharing at home because everyone is doing it. In time, the household becomes a community of learning and practice.

What the *General Directory for Catechesis* says about families can be applied to all households of faith throughout the life cycle—the new couple, families with children and teens, families with young adults, single adults, families in later life—and to all configurations of family relationships such as two-parent, single-parent, and multi-generational families.

> …The family is defined as a "domestic Church" (cf. LG 11; cf. *Apostolicam Actuositatem* 11; *Familiaris Consortio* [FC] 49), that is, in every Christian family the different aspects and functions of the life of the entire Church may be reflected: mission; catechesis; witness; prayer etc. Indeed in the same way as the Church, the family "is a place in which the Gospel is transmitted and from which it extends" (EN 71). The family as a *locus* of catechesis has a unique privilege: transmitting the Gospel by rooting it in the context of profound human values (cf. *Gaudium et Spes* 52, FC 37a)….It is, indeed, a Christian education more witnessed to than taught, more occasional than systematic, more ongoing and daily that structured into periods. (#255)

Lifelong faith formation provides individuals and families with the resources and tools they need to *extend* and *expand* their learning from a parish catechetical program and their experience of a Church event to their daily lives and home life. It provides event-specific home materials to help families and individuals celebrate traditions and rituals, continue their learning, pray together, serve others and work for justice, and enrich their relationships and family life.

WORKS CITED IN THIS CHAPTER

Congregation for the Clergy. *General Directory for Catechesis*. Washington, DC: USCC Publishing, 1997.

Department of Education, United States Catholic Conference. *Sowing the Seed: Notes and Comments on the General Directory for Catechesis*. Washington, DC: USCC Publishing, 2000.

Dykstra, Craig. *Growing in the Life of Faith: Education and Christian Practices*. Louisville, KY: Geneva Press, 1999.

Foster, Charles. *Educating Congregations*. Nashville: Abingdon, 1994.

Harris, Maria. *Fashion Me a People: Curriculum in the Church*. Louisville: Westminister/John Knox Press, 1989.

► Appendix

The Six Interrelated Tasks of Catechesis from the *General Directory for Catechesis* #85

Promoting knowledge of the faith

Who has encountered Christ desires to know him as much as possible, as well as to know the plan of the Father which he revealed. Knowledge of the faith (*fides quae*) is required by adherence to the faith (*fides qua*) (cf. DCG [1971] 36a). Even in the human order the love which one person has for another causes that person to wish to know the other all the more. Catechesis, must, therefore, lead to the "gradual grasping of the whole truth about the divine plan," (cf. DCG [1971] 24) by introducing the disciples of Jesus to a knowledge of Tradition and of Scripture, which is *"the sublime science of Christ"* (DV 25a). By deepening knowledge of the faith, catechesis nourishes not only the life of faith but equips it to explain itself to the world. The meaning of the Creed, which is a compendium of Scripture and of the faith of the Church, is the realization of this task.

Liturgical education

Christ is always present in his Church, especially in "liturgical celebrations" (*Sacrosanctum Concilium* [SC] 7). Communion with Jesus Christ leads to the celebration of his salvific presence in the sacraments, especially in the Eucharist. The Church ardently desires that all the Christian faithful be brought to that full, conscious and active participation which is required by the very nature of the liturgy (cf. SC 14) and the dignity of the baptismal priesthood. For this reason, catechesis, along with promoting a knowledge of the meaning of the liturgy and the sacraments, must also educate the disciples of Jesus Christ "for prayer, for thanksgiving, for repentance, for praying with confidence, for community spirit, for understanding correctly the meaning of the creeds..." (DCG [1971] 25b), as all of this is necessary for a true liturgical life.

Moral formation

Conversion to Jesus Christ implies walking in his footsteps. Catechesis must, therefore, transmit to the disciples the attitudes of the Master himself. The disciples thus undertake a journey of interior transformation, in which, by participating in the paschal mystery of the Lord, "they pass from the old man to the new man who has been made perfect in Christ" (AG 13). The Sermon on the Mount, in which Jesus takes up the Decalogue, and impresses upon it the spirit of the beatitudes,[5] is an indispensable point of reference for the moral formation which is most necessary today. Evangelization which "involves the proclamation and presentation of morality" (*Veritatis Splendor* 107), displays all the force of its appeal where it offers not only the proclaimed word but the lived word too. This moral testimony, which is prepared for by catechesis, must always demonstrate the social consequences of the demands of the Gospel (cf. CT 29f).

5. Cf. LG 62; CCC 1965-1986. The CCC 1697 specifies in particular the characteristics which catechesis must assume in moral formation.

Teaching to pray

Communion with Jesus Christ leads the disciples to assume the attitude of prayer and contemplation which the Master himself had. To learn to pray with Jesus is to pray with the same sentiments with which he turned to the Father: adoration, praise, thanksgiving, filial confidence, supplication and awe for his glory. All of these sentiments are reflected in the *Our Father*, the prayer which Jesus taught his disciples and which is the model of all Christian prayer. The *"handing on of the Our Father"* (RCIA 25 and 188-191) is a summary of the entire Gospel (cf. CCC 2761) and is therefore a true act of catechesis. When catechesis is permeated by a climate of prayer, the assimilation of the entire Christian life reaches its summit....

Other fundamental tasks of catechesis: initiation and education in community life and to mission (GDC #86)

Catechesis prepares the Christian to live in community and to participate actively in the life and mission of the Church....

Education for community life

a) Christian community life is not realized spontaneously. It is necessary to educate it carefully. In this apprenticeship, the teaching of Christ on community life, recounted in the Gospel of St. Matthew, calls for attitudes which it is for catechesis to inculcate: the spirit of simplicity and humility...; solicitude for the least among the brethren...; particular care for those who are alienated...; fraternal correction...; common prayer...; mutual forgiveness....Fraternal love embraces all these attitudes....

Missionary initiation

a) Catechesis is also open to the missionary dimension (cf. CT 24b and DCG [1971] 28). This seeks to equip the disciples of Jesus to be present as Christians in society through their professional, cultural and social lives....The evangelical attitudes which Jesus taught his disciples when he sent them on mission are precisely those which catechesis must nourish: to seek out the lost sheep, proclaim and heal at the same time, to be poor, without money or knapsack; to know how to accept rejection and persecution; to place one's trust in the Father and in the support of the Holy Spirit; to expect no other reward than the joy of working for the Kingdom (cf. Mt 10:5–42 and Lk 10:1–20).

▶ Foundational Resources for Faith Formation

Aron, Isa. *Becoming a Congregation of Learners: Learning as a Key to Revitalizing Congregational Life*. Woodstock, VT: Jewish Lights Publishing, 2001.

Aron, Isa, Sara Lee, and Seymour Rossel. *A Congregation of Learners: Transforming the Synagogue into a Learning Community*. New York: UAHC Press, 1995.

Bass, Dorothy (editor). *Practicing Our Faith*. San Francisco: Jossey-Bass, 1997.

Caldwell, Elizabeth. *Making a Home for Faith: Nurturing the Spiritual Life of Your Christian Children*. Cleveland: United Church Press, 2000.

Congregation for the Clergy. *General Directory for Catechesis*. Washington, DC: USCC, 1997.

Darcy-Berube, Francoise. *Religious Education at the Crossroads*. New York: Paulist Press, 1995.

Department of Education, United States Catholic Conference of Bishops. *Our Hearts Were Burning Within Us*. Washington, DC: USCC Publishing, 1999.

Dooley, Catherine. "Renewing the Parish." *Living Light,* Volume 40, Number 1 (Fall 2003).

————. "Liturgical Catechesis for Confirmation." *Traditions and Transitions*. Edited by Eleanor Bernstein, CSJ and Martin Connell. Chicago: Liturgy Training Publications, 1998.

————, "From the Visible to the Invisible: Mystagogy in the Catechism of the Catholic Church." *Living Light*, Spring 1995.

————. "Mystagogy: A Model for Sacramental Catechesis. The Candles Are Still Burning." Edited by Mary Grey, Andree Heaton, and Danny Sullivan. Collegeville, MN: Liturgical Press, 1995.

————. "Catechumenate for Children: Sharing the Gift of Faith." *Readings in the Christian Initiation of Children*. Edited by Victoria Tufano. Chicago: Liturgy Training Publications, 1994.

————. "Baptismal Catechesis for Children of Catechetical Age." *Issues in the Christian Initiation of Children*. Edited by Kathy Brown and Frank Sokol. Chicago: Liturgy Training Publications, 1989.

————. "The Lectionary as a Sourcebook for Catechesis in the Catechumenate." *Before and After Baptism*. Edited by James Wilde. Chicago: Liturgy Training Publications, 1988.

Dykstra, Craig. *Growing in the Life of Faith: Education and Christian Practices*. Louisville, KY: Geneva Press, 1998.

Groome, Thomas and Harold Daly Horell, editors. *Horizons and Hopes: The Future of Religious Education*. New York: Paulist Press, 2003.

Groome, Thomas and Michael J. Corso, editors. *Empowering Catechetical Leaders*. Washington, DC: National Catholic Education Association, 1999.

Foster, Charles. *Embracing Diversity*. Washington, DC: Alban Institute, 1997.

————. *Educating Congregations*. Nashville: Abingdon, 1994.

————. *Teaching in the Community of Faith*. Nashville: Abingdon Press, 1982.

————. "The Faith Community as a Guiding Image for Christian Education." *Contemporary Approaches to Christian Education.* Edited by Jack L. Seymour and Donald E. Miller. Nashville: Abingdon Press, 1982.

————. "Intergenerational Religious Education." *Changing Patterns of Religious Education.* Edited by Marvin Taylor. Nashville: Abingdon Press, 1984.

Foster, Charles and Theodore Brelsford. *We Are the Church Together: Cultural Diversity in Congregational Life.* Valley Forge, PA: Trinity Press International, 1996.

Harris, Maria. *Fashion Me a People: Curriculum in the Church.* Louisville, KY: Westminster/John Knox Press, 1989.

Huebsch, Bill. *Whole Community Catechesis in Plain English.* Mystic, CT: Twenty-Third Publications, 2002.

Mongoven, Anne Marie. *The Prophetic Spirit of Catechesis.* New York: Paulist Press, 2000.

Nelson, C. Ellis. *Where Faith Begins.* Richmond: John Knox Press, 1967.

Pope John Paul II. *Catechesis Tradendae.* Washington, DC: USCCB Publishing, 1979.

Regan, Jane. *Toward an Adult Church: A Vision of Faith Formation.* Chicago: Loyola Press, 2002.

Sawicki, Marianne. *The Gospel in History—Portrait of a Teaching Church: The Origins of Christian Education.* New York: Paulist Press, 1988.

Thompson, Margorie. *Family: The Forming Center.* Nashville: Upper Room Books, 1996.

Webber, Robert. *Ancient-Future Faith.* Grand Rapids, MI: Baker Books, 1999.

Westerhoff, John. *Will Our Children Have Faith?* (revised edition). New York: Morehouse Publishing, 2000.

Westerhoff, John. *Living the Faith Community: The Church that Makes a Difference.* San Francisco: Harper & Row, 1985.

————. *Learning through Liturgy.* New York: Seabury Press, 1978.

Westerhoff, John, editor. *A Colloquy on Christian Education.* Philadelphia: United Church Press, 1972.

Westerhoff, John and Gwen Kennedy. *Generation to Generation.* Philadelphia: United Church Press, 1974.

Westerhoff, John and William Willimon. *Liturgy and Learning through the Life Cycle* (revised edition). Akron, OH: OSL Publications, 1980, 1994.

White, James. *Intergenerational Religious Education.* Birmingham, AL: Religious Education Press, 1988.

Generations of Faith Orientation Workshop

Preparation This orientation workshop is designed to be used in conjunction with the Generations of Faith video, "Introducing Generations of Faith" (available by calling the Center for Ministry Development at 203-723-1622). The video is organized into three parts:

Part 1. Introducing Generations of Faith: Six Principles and Practices

Part 2. A Story of Holy Week: A Walk through a Preparation Program

Part 3. Parish Interviews with Parents, Pastors, Parish Staff, and Diocesan Staff

There are a variety of ways to use the video. Here are three examples.
- Use the video with parish leadership committees and parents to introduce the key principles of Generations of Faith and to show how other parishes are implementing the program.
- Use the video as part of an orientation program for your catechists and leaders who are working in preparation programs.
- Use the video as part of a workshop or training program for new members of your Generations of Faith core team.

Purpose To introduce parish leaders and leadership groups to the essential vision and features of the Generations of Faith approach to faith formation

Supplies and Equipment
- "Generations of Faith Vision and Practices" essay
- copies of the worksheet with reflection questions
- "Introducing Generations of Faith" video
- VCR and projector or TV
- newsprint, markers, and masking tape
- pens
- CD player and reflective music

Session Length: 45–60 minutes

Conducting the Session
1. Welcome the participants. If introductions are needed, take a few minutes to introduce yourself and participants introduce themselves to the group.
2. Read the opening prayer:

   Loving God, bless us with your Spirit, that we might clearly see the path and means for faith formation in our community. Help us to help our community to celebrate the gift of your son Jesus, and to lead one another into intimate communion with him. Amen.

3. Describe the shifts toward a new approach to faith formation using the essay "Generations of Faith: Vision and Practices."
4. Introduce the vision of Generations of Faith by reading aloud the following quote:

Generations of Faith provides an integrated and comprehensive approach to faith formation that equips the parish community to become a community of learning by creating lifelong faith formation that is centered in the events of Church life, that embraces all ages and generations, and that promotes faith growth at home, through parish preparation programs, and, most importantly, through participation in Church life.

5. Show Parts 1 and 2 of the video, which presents six of the seven practices that guide the development of a Generations of Faith parish community. (Intergenerational catechesis has now been singled out as a practice, but it is not included in the video program.)

   - events-centered
   - lifelong and cyclic
   - emergent content
   - prepare-engage-reflect/apply process of learning
   - alignment of learning
   - home faith formation

6. Introduce the seventh practice and review the practices, using the essay. Invite questions and observations from the group.

7. Distribute the worksheet and ask the participants to respond in writing to the questions.

8. Invite the participants to share their reflections. Record and discuss their responses. *Option:* Show Part 3 of the video, which includes interviews from Generations of Faith parishes. Conclude with reflections and insights from the participants.

9. Conclude in prayer, using the following quote from the *General Directory for Catechesis* and/or the Gospel reading:

…Hence, when catechesis transmits the mystery of Christ, the faith of the whole people of God echoes in its message through the course of history: the faith received by the Apostles from Christ himself and under the action of the Holy Spirit; that of the martyrs who have borne witness to it and still bear witness to it by their blood; that of the saints who have lived it and live it profoundly; that of the Fathers and doctors of the Church who have taught it brilliantly; that of the missionaries who proclaim it incessantly; that of theologians who help to understand it better; that of pastors who conserve it with zeal and love and who interpret it authentically. In truth, there is present in catechesis the faith of all those who believe and allow themselves to be guided by the Holy Spirit. (GDC #105)

A reading from the Gospel of Matthew 13:31–32:

Jesus put before them another parable: "The kingdom of heaven is like a mustard seed that someone took and sowed in his field; it is the smallest of all the seeds, but when it has grown it is the greatest of shrubs and becomes a tree, so that the birds of the air come and make nests in its branches."

Let us pray . . .

God of knowledge, wisdom, and learning, increase our determination to enrich the world with the gift of your Good News. May we celebrate your presence in our midst and be empowered to continue to plant and nurture the seeds of faith in one another and all those whom we are called to catechize. Amen.

Our Hopes and Dreams for Faith Formation

What are the benefits of the Generations of Faith approach? What do you hope the Generations of Faith approach to faith formation will do for the parish: for all its members, the families, the young, the old, etc.? What fruits do you hope it will bear?

What image, if any, comes to mind for you when you think of this approach? What Scripture passages, if any, surface for you?

What would it be like (or look like) if our parish implemented the Generations of Faith approach to faith formation? Concretely, what ideas do you have about what it will look like? What are the different ways that the Generations of Faith approach could be implemented in your community?

Generations of Faith Vision and Practice

Lifelong, Intergenerational, Events-centered Faith Formation

For over thirty years the Catholic Church has offered a comprehensive and compelling vision of faith formation and learning—lifelong, for all ages and generations, rooted in the life of the Church. Yet catechesis across the United States and Canada is still struggling under the burden of an outdated model of faith formation that is actually creating more problems than it is solving. Embracing the vision of faith formation in the *General Directory for Catechesis* requires moving away from the schooling paradigm to a community or "whole church" paradigm of faith formation.

- We will transform the focus on children-only (think of all the time, energy, resources we still commit to children only) by implementing lifelong faith formation for all ages and generations, including and especially adults.

- We will transform "start and stop" catechesis (think graduation at confirmation; think preparation for sacraments) by implementing lifelong and continuous faith formation—learning for a lifetime through involvement in the events of church life.

- We will transform age segregation (think grade levels or groups—youth group, older adults group) by implementing intergenerational faith formation—making connections among the generations in learning programs and parish involvement.

- We will transform the focus on the "textbook as the curriculum" by utilizing the events of Church life as the curriculum for all ages and generation—tapping into the educative and transformative power of the Church year, sacramental celebrations, community prayer, and works of justice and service, and providing catechesis that prepares everyone to learning by participating in the events of Church life.

- We will transform the attitude of blaming families for our current situation—the "family's faith is the problem"—by nurturing family faith at home as integral to faith formation.

- We will transform catechesis as a separate "program" by implementing a more collaborative and integrated approach that involves all of the parish's ministries in faith formation. Catechesis is interconnected with liturgy, sacraments, the Church year, justice and service, prayer.

The Church as Learning Community

This is a vision of the entire faith community as a learning community—a congregation of learners. This vision is echoed in the *General Directory for Catechesis*:

Catechesis is an essentially ecclesial act. The true subject of catechesis is the Church which, continuing the mission of Jesus the Master and, therefore animated by the Holy Spirit, is sent to be the teacher of the faith... (#78)

Catechesis is nothing other than the process of transmitting the Gospel, as the Christian community has received it, understands it, celebrates it, lives it, and communicates it in many ways. (#105)

In giving attention to the individual, it should not be overlooked that the recipient of catechesis is the whole Christian community and every person in it. (#168)

Catechetical pedagogy will be effective to the extent that the Christian community becomes a point of concrete reference for the faith journey of individuals. This happens when the community is proposed as a source, locus, and means of catechesis. Concretely, the community becomes a visible place of faith-witness. It provides for the formation of its members. ...It constitutes itself as the living and permanent environment for growth in faith. (#158)

To become more fully a learning community, parishes are implementing a new approach to faith formation. Generations of Faith provides an integrated and comprehensive approach to faith formation that equips the parish community to become a community of learning by creating lifelong faith formation that is centered in the events of church life, embraces all ages and generations, and promotes faith growth at home, through parish preparation programs, and, most importantly, through participation in Church life. This approach has seven defining features—key principles and practices—that guide the development of faith formation in a parish community.

Seven Key Practices

1. **Events-Centered Catechesis.** The lifelong curriculum and learning experiences are developed around the events of our shared life as Church: the Church year, sacraments and liturgy, prayer and spirituality, justice and service, community life, and proclamation of the Word. These events hold tremendous educative and transformative power. The key is to unlock their power through catechesis. Far too many of our parishioners are not prepared to participate in the events of church life and, therefore, do not learn through their participation.

2. **Lifelong and Systematic Catechesis.** Faith formation is cyclic, episodic, continuous and lifelong. It is formed around the natural rhythm and pattern of the faith community's life as experienced throughout the year. The events of church life form a spiral curriculum (think church year) that immerses people more deeply each year into the faith of the Church. The events of Church life are so theologically rich that it will take years to immerse people in their meaning and practice (think of the theological themes embedded in Lent). Our catechetical task is to continually deepen their understanding and practice.

3. **Emergent Catechetical Content.** The beliefs and practices for living as a Catholic today emerge from the life, events, and practices of the faith community. The beliefs and practices for living the Catholic faith are embedded in the events of church life. Our catechetical task is to uncover the theological and doctrinal message within the event. Consider the themes in Lent: baptism, salvation, sin and repentance, conversion, cross, Jesus Christ (messiah and suffering servant), justice, moral life, paschal mystery, and the three lenten practices (fasting, praying, almsgiving). A cyclic curriculum moves through these themes over multiple years—immersing people more deeply into the lenten experience. While every event is not as rich as Lent, the content that emerges from a multi-year, events-centered curriculum provides the foundations or essentials of the Catholic faith.

4. **Connected Catechesis.** Faith formation is a cyclic process of learning: preparing all ages and all generations for meaningful participation in church events, engaging all ages and generations in the events, and assisting people in reflecting on the significance and meaning of the event and applying the learning to their lives as Catholics. Events-centered catechesis seeks to help the learner develop:

   —*know-what*: understanding the meaning of the event and its Scriptural, doctrinal, and theological foundation

   —*know-why*: appreciating and valuing the meaning and significance of the event for their lives as Catholics

   —*know-how*: acquiring the ability to participate competently in the event and to live its meaning in their lives as Catholics.

   When people are prepared for an event they feel confident, comfortable, and competent to participate. This approach draws people into participating in the events of church life.

   Parishes are using a variety of learning models in their preparation programs. Some use age-group learning models, such as classes, workshops, retreats, faith sharing groups; while others use multi-age learning models such as family learning where the whole family comes together for learning and intergenerational learning where people of all ages from children through older adults learn together.

5. **Intergenerational Catechesis.** Faith formation provides events-centered, intergenerational catechetical programs for all ages and

generations in the parish community. The *General Directory for Catechesis* reminds us, "...it should not be overlooked that the recipient of catechesis is the whole Christian community and every person in it" (GDC #168) Intergenerational learning provides an opportunity to gather the whole parish to learn, pray, celebrate, and share. It has tremendous benefits for the parish and for individuals.

6. **Alignment of Catechesis for All Ages.** Faith formation provides alignment of learning through common events and themes that are experienced and explored by all ages and all generations in the faith community. The key in events-centered learning is that the whole parish is focused—everyone is preparing for the same event with the same theological focus. This attention to alignment and focus creates parish-wide synergy.

7. **Home Faith Formation.** Faith Formation integrates home and parish into a comprehensive model of faith formation. Empowering and equipping individuals and families to live their faith at home and in the world is constitutive of this approach to faith formation. Our catechetical task is to provide individuals and families with the resources and tools they need to extend and expand their learning from a preparation program and their experience of the event to their lives and home. We create event-specific home materials that help families and individuals celebrate traditions and rituals, continue their learning, pray together, serve others and work for justice, and enrich their relationships and family life. Attention to home resources and tools is as important as the parish preparation program.

A Parish Story

Imagine a parish that is embracing this vision of faith formation and preparing the entire faith community for Lent:

Lent is coming and the entire community of Holy Family Parish is preparing to immerse themselves in the lenten season through liturgy and prayer (Ash Wednesday, the Sunday liturgies, Holy Week, Stations of the Cross), justice and service (food and clothing collection, Operation Rice Bowl), and community life activities (Lenten meals)—in the parish and at home.

The Holy Family catechetical ministry has designed a variety of ways to prepare all of the generations for their participation in the lenten season. Their goal is to prepare everyone in the parish community for Lent focusing on the theme for the year: "The Three Practices of Lent: Fasting, Praying, and Almsgiving." Preparation programs guide people of all ages to understand the meaning of Lent and the three practices, to appreciate the significance of Lent and the three practices in our Catholic tradition, to participate actively in the lenten season, and to live the three practices at home and in the world. When people are prepared for an event they feel confident, comfortable, and competent to participate in the events of church life.

The lenten lectionary readings will be a primary resource for preparation. The music director has selected special lenten songs, one for each week of Lent, that express musically the lenten theme. These songs will be used in parish programs and at Sunday worship.

The week before Ash Wednesday, on a Wednesday night, Friday night, or Saturday morning, all ages—from families with children through older adults—arrive at the parish center for a light dinner or continental breakfast, followed by the feature activity—learning how to live the three practices of fasting, praying, and almsgiving. The program moves through several stages of activities:

- Everyone gathers together for a meal—a great time to build community.
- The program begins with prayer and song inspired by the lenten season and the three practices.
- An all-ages opening experience introduces everyone to the focus of preparation—the three practices of Lent.
- The in-depth learning component of the program helps everyone to explore the meaning of the event through age-appropriate learning groups. Families with children explore the lenten practices through three activity centers—praying, fasting, and

almsgiving/service. The adolescents explore the lenten practices and create contemporary ways to live the three practices today. A guest speaker presents an overview of the lenten lectionary and a contemporary interpretation of the lenten practices for adults.

- The entire group gathers again to share their learning from the in-depth sessions.
- One of the leaders reviews how to use the Lenten Home Kit which provides resources for families and individuals to experience Lent at home: a lenten calendar with daily activities and Scripture passages; a lenten journal for teens with daily readings, prayers, and activities; a daily lenten prayer guide for adults; placemats with weekly table prayers; suggested local service projects and Operation Rice Bowl; several learning activities on lenten themes; and a copy of the parish's lenten calendar.
- In family groupings and adult groupings, everyone develops a Lenten Pledge to live the three practices at home and in the world.
- The program closes in prayer and song.

Young adults—those at home, in college or in the military—receive, via e-mail, a special Lenten Journal with a daily lectionary reading, a reflection written by young adults, and a prayer. All of the adult faith sharing groups in the parish dedicate a session to the "Three Practices of Lent" by exploring the meaning of Lent and reflecting on the lenten lectionary readings. Each participant receives a booklet of daily lenten reflections to guide their journey through the season. All of the parish committees and councils that meet prior to or at the beginning of Lent open their meetings with a special prayer service on the Lenten theme. All of the adult participants receive a Lenten Home Kit and a copy of the parish's lenten calendar.

In addition to the Lenten Home Kit, the parish's web site, Holy Family On-Line, features the parish lenten calendar, prayers and reflections for all ages on the Lenten Scripture readings, and the entire Lenten Home Kit. A special bulletin insert for each week of Lent is distributed at all of the Masses.

Wherever you go in the Holy Family community people of all ages and generations are united in a common endeavor: to prepare for Lent, to experience Lent fully at home and in the parish, and to integrate their learning into their daily lives as Catholics.

Faith formation at Holy Family Parish is in the midst of a transformation. They are moving toward a curriculum that is centered on the formative events of the Church community and the participation of all ages and generations in the shared experiences of Church life. Holy Family Parish has embraced the Generations of Faith approach to faith formation.

Parish Examples

Parishes are utilizing a variety of ways to implement the vision of events-centered, lifelong, intergenerational faith formation. The key is creating a curriculum plan that reflects the character and culture of the parish—its size, cultures, languages, geography. Here are several examples of how parishes have taken this vision and implemented it around the particular character and culture of their parish.

Many parishes utilize the events-centered curriculum as the primary curriculum for all ages and generations. They have dramatically reduced their reliance on age-group catechesis and moved to intergenerational catechesis with preparation programs (usually monthly) that address the learning needs of children, adolescents, young adults, adults, and families in one learning model. Learning is both intergenerational and age-appropriate. Intergenerational learning models are usually held monthly or within close proximity to the event, require an extended timeframe, usually 2 1/2–3 hours, and are offered multiple times to attract a wide audience and make it easy to participate. For example parishes may offer programs on Wednesday from 6:00–9:00 PM, Friday from 6:00-9:00 PM and Saturday from 9:00–12:00 noon. Some even connect the preparation program to the Sunday liturgies, for example from 10:00 AM to 1:00 PM following the 9:00 AM Mass. Essential to events-centered preparation is the home kit of resources and tools for learning and living at home.

These "primary" parishes incorporate eight to

eleven events per year in their curriculum. For example. Here is a one-year plan for sacraments:

1. Feast of All Souls: Rite of Funerals (October Preparation)
2. Parish Celebration: Sacrament of the Anointing of the Sick (November Preparation)
3. Advent Season: Sacrament of Reconciliation (December Preparation)
4. Vocations Week/Call of the Disciples: Sacrament of Orders (January Preparation)
5. World Marriage Day: Sacrament of Marriage (February Preparation)
6. Lent: Sacrament of Baptism (March Preparation)
7. Holy Thursday: Sacrament of Eucharist (April Preparation)
8. Pentecost: Sacrament of Confirmation (May Preparation)

Many parishes utilize the events-centered curriculum as their lifelong curriculum for all ages and generations while maintaining their age-group catechesis, which might be lectionary based, textbook based, or program based. They blend age-group catechesis (often weekly) with events-centered catechesis on a monthly or seasonal basis, adjusting the number of sessions of age-group catechesis to incorporate events-centered preparation programs. Many parishes utilize intergenerational learning models in their events-centered preparation. Once again, essential to events-centered preparation is the home kit of resources and tools for learning and living at home.

There are wide variety of ways that parishes blend the two approaches (age-group catechesis and lifelong, events-centered catechesis). For example, one parish that has created a lifelong curriculum with eight events each year, integrates one or two preparation sessions for these events into their existing educational programs: weekly children's program, bi-weekly middle school program, bi-weekly high school program, weekly RCIA program, monthly adult education program, etc. Even meetings of parish organizations, committees, and councils all begin with a prayer service and Scripture reading on the theme of the event of the month.

A second parish that has created a lifelong curriculum with ten events each year, conducts a monthly, intergenerational, events-centered preparation program that they offer several times on the first week of the month. During the remaining weeks of the month they offer their age-specific catechetical program. Usually they "cancel" age group classes during the week of the actual event to highlight the importance of participating in the event.

A third parish that has blended age-group catechesis or events-centered catechesis uses a modular approach throughout the year. They utilize intergenerational learning during preparation weeks for the event. These preparation weeks take place one week before the event or the start of the season.

Here is an example of an annual plan of Church year feasts and seasons:

- September–October: 4–6 week unit of age-specific programming
- October–November: All Saints unit: preparation week, All Saints liturgy
- November: Thanksgiving unit: preparation week, service projects, Thanksgiving liturgy
- December: Advent-Christmas unit: preparation week, Advent-Christmas season (liturgies, prayer services, service projects, sacrament of Reconciliation, etc.)
- January–February: 4–6 week unit of age-specific programming
- February: Lent unit: preparation week, lenten season (liturgies, Stations of the Cross, service projects, simple meals, sacrament of Reconciliation, etc.)
- March: Holy Thursday unit: preparation week, Holy Thursday liturgy
- April-May: 4–6 week unit of age-specific programming
- May: Pentecost unit: preparation week, Pentecost liturgy

These are just several examples of the innovation which is taking place in catechesis today. We are at the beginning of an exciting new phase in the development of catechetical ministry—lifelong, events-centered, intergenerational. We are finally making the Church's vision of catechesis a reality.

CHAPTER 2

Fashioning a Lifelong Curriculum

▶ An Overview of the Planning Process

Developing Leadership Teams (Chapter 2)

Task: Developing leadership teams: core team, design team, and implementation team

Fashioning a Lifelong Curriculum (Chapter 2)

Task 1:   Determining your curriculum approach: primary or blended
Task 2:   Developing a multi-year curriculum plan

Implementing a Lifelong Curriculum (Chapter 3)

Task 1:   Developing a calendar and scheduling preparation programs
Task 2:   Determining a budget and participant fees
Task 3:   Developing promotional and registration strategies and materials

Developing Leadership for Lifelong Faith Formation (Chapter 4)

Task 1:   Inviting people into leadership
Task 2:   Preparing and training leaders
Task 3:   Supporting leaders

Designing a Learning Plan for an Event (Chapter 5)

Task 1:   Designing a Preparation Program
          Step 1: Identifying the catechetical-theological theme
          Step 2: Developing learning objectives
          Step 3: Designing preparation programs
          Step 4: Evaluating preparation programs

Task 2:   Designing Home Activities for an Event
          Step 1: Identifying target audiences
          Step 2: Designing or finding home activities
          Step 3: Design a format for each activity
          Step 4: Determining delivery methods
          Step 5: Developing a timeline and implementation plans

Task 3:   Designing Reflection Activities for an Event
          Step 1: Identifying target audiences
          Step 2: Designing reflection strategies and activities
          Step 3: Determining delivery methods

Evaluating the Curriculum

▶ Developing Leadership Teams

Fashioning and implementing a lifelong faith formation curriculum involves a variety of leadership teams and collaboration across all the parish's ministries. While the parish's catechetical leadership may take the lead, the involvement of other ministry leaders is essential. The faith formation plan draws upon the events of the entire parish community, making curriculum design a collaborative effort involving multiple ministries.

There are four different types of leadership roles involved in fashioning and implementing a lifelong curriculum.

1. The *core team* of parish staff and parish leaders guides the curriculum design process to fashion, implement, and evaluate the curriculum.
2. The *design team* creates the preparation programs, home activities, and reflection activities for each event.
3. The *implementation team* conducts preparation programs.
4. *Ministry partners* from other parish ministries and programs collaborate with the core team on specific projects that involve their particular ministry.

Core Team

The first task in planning is to develop a core team that will create the curriculum plan and guide its implementation. The team's major tasks include

- fashioning the lifelong curriculum
- developing the implementation procedures for the curriculum: scheduling, promoting, budgeting, etc.
- developing leadership—recruiting, providing training, and supporting leaders—for preparation programs and other important leadership roles
- coordinating the work of the design team and implementation team
- monitoring the progress of the curriculum
- evaluating the curriculum at the end of the year and planning for the next year.

The core team can be drawn from all ministry leaders (paid and volunteer) involved in faith formation within your parish community: pastor, DRE (Director of Religious Education), school principal, adult education coordinator, family ministry coordinator, youth ministry coordinator, liturgical ministry coordinator, RCIA coordinator, sacrament preparation coordinators, justice and service coordinators, small Christian community leaders, evangelization leaders, and key volunteer leaders, such as catechists and adult leaders in youth ministry.

Design Team

The design team has primary responsibility for creating the learning designs for Church events. The design team consists of members of the core team, especially parish staff and other faith formation leaders, who are invited to work on the design team because of their expertise with particular age groups (e.g., preschool children or teenagers) or particular tasks (e.g., creating home materials). The team's major tasks include:

- designing the preparation programs by selecting and/or creating the learning activities for an intergenerational, family-centered, and/or age group program;
- creating home kits and activities for a variety of ages and settings (e.g., participants in preparation programs, parishioners at Mass);
- designing reflection activities;

- preparing the learning materials.

Several months prior to a preparation program, the design team meets to begin design work around the event and theme that was selected by the core team when it created the curriculum. In parishes that offer monthly family or intergenerational preparation programs, the design team meets regularly. In other parishes the work of the design team is integrated into regular staff meetings or committee meetings.

Implementation Team

The implementation team has primary responsibility for conducting preparation programs. It includes catechists and a variety of other leaders essential for the successful implementation of a preparation program. Not all implementation team members teach or are even involved in the actual preparation program. There are a number of support roles—promotion, recordkeeping, creative arts, etc.—that are essential to the effectiveness of the preparation program. The work of the implementation team is coordinated by parish staff or core team members.

Implementation team roles vary depending on the learning model used in the preparation program and the number of preparation programs offered. To determine the exact jobs that are necessary, review the design of your preparation program to identify the leadership positions necessary to conduct the program (see Chapter 4: Developing Leaders, for tools). For example, a typical intergenerational learning program needs the following leaders:
- program facilitator
- learning-group facilitator, that is, a leader for age-specific learning groups (e.g., families with children, young adolescents, older adolescents, young adults, adults)
- facilitators/catechists for age-appropriate learning groups
- assistants to help with age-appropriate learning activities
- prayer leader for opening and closing prayer
- music leader and/or music team for prayer and activities
- set-up and clean-up staff
- food preparation and service staff
- creative arts staff for artwork, posters, signs, etc.
- promotion and correspondence staff
- hospitality and registration staff.

Ministry Partners

Ministry partners from other parish ministries and programs collaborate with the core team, design team, and/or implementation team on specific projects that involve their particular ministry. For example, a justice event might involve a number of leaders who are not regularly involved in a leadership role, but who are brought into the design and implementation process because of their justice and service expertise. Ministry partners serve as consultants in the design work and as resource people for the preparation programs.

Lifelong Faith Formation Coordinators

In most parishes one or two people take on the responsibility of coordinating the lifelong faith formation curriculum. Below is a list of the knowledge and skills needed by effective coordinators. This list will help you identify the essential competencies required for effective coordination of the lifelong faith formation curriculum in your parish.

Theological Competencies

▶ Understanding the theology, symbols, history, and tradition of the Church year;

▶ Understanding the theology, symbols, rituals, and history of the sacraments;

▶ Understanding the biblical and theological foundations and principles of Catholic social teaching;

▶ Familiarity with the key elements of the teachings of the *Catechism of the Catholic Church* on creed, sacraments, morality, justice, prayer and spirituality;

▶ Understanding the scriptural and theological content of the events and learning programs in the parish's curriculum plan (Church year feast or season, sacraments, justice and service event, prayer and spirituality event).

Catechetical Competencies

▶ Familiarity with the vision and practice of the Generations of Faith approach to faith formation and its grounding in the *General Directory for Catechesis;*

▶ Familiarity with a variety of learning models for faith formation (e.g., family-centered, intergenerational, etc.);

▶ Ability to facilitate intergenerational and family learning, as well age-specific learning;

▶ Ability to work with a variety of ages and generations—from childhood through older adulthood—and with families;

▶ Ability to use a variety of resources in faith formation—print, media, Internet, etc.;

▶ Ability to use the shared Christian praxis learning methodology in designing and conducting preparation programs;

▶ Ability to design an events-centered learning plan that includes preparation programs for all ages and generations, home materials, and reflection activities;

▶ Familiarity with learning styles, multiple intelligences, and experiential learning and their application to events-centered learning;

▶ Comfort in using the Internet as a resource for faith formation and training leaders.

Leadership Competencies

▶ Ability to convene a leadership group, representing a variety of ministries, to fashion a multi-year, lifelong, events-centered faith formation curriculum plan;

▶ Ability to facilitate the work of a team in developing an events-centered learning plan, including the design of preparation programs for all ages and generations, home materials, and reflection activities;

▶ Ability to work collaboratively in the implementation of a curriculum plan and individual learning plans;

▶ Ability to develop a leadership system for identifying, training, and supporting faith formation leaders (catechists, et al.);

▶ Ability to provide training for leaders, especially for catechists and facilitators.

▶ Fashioning a Lifelong Curriculum

The curriculum planning process is designed to guide your parish team in creating a multi-year plan using the Generations of Faith approach. This process assists you in developing a lifelong, events-centered, intergenerational faith formation curriculum in your parish; that is, translating the Generations of Faith vision into practice.

The word "curriculum" is derived from the Latin verb *currere*, which means "to run." In literal terms, a curriculum is a course to be run. The Generations of Faith approach sees all aspects of Church life as educative and educating and thus part of the curriculum. In *Fashion Me a People,* Maria Harris describes this fuller and more extensive understanding of curriculum when she writes,

> Printed resources that serve this wider curriculum are in the treasury of the Church, especially the comprehensive curricular materials designed over the last century in the United States. These, however, are not *the* curriculum. *The* curriculum is both more basic and more profound. It is *the entire course of the Church's life*, found in the fundamental forms of that life. It is the priestly, prophetic, and political work of *didache, leiturgia, koinonia, kerygma,* and *diakonia*. Where education is the fashioning and refashioning of these forms in interplay, curriculum is the subject matter and processes that make them to be what they are. Where education is the living and the fashioning, curriculum is the life, the substance that is fashioned. (63-64)

For too long we have limited our understanding of education and curriculum to a school model, and we have structured our parish faith formation using this model: classroom facilities, age-graded classes of students with a teacher, graded printed texts, weekly meetings of sixty to ninety minutes from September through May (the parish's "school year"), and so on. As Maria Harris further writes,

> …most curriculum today continue to be designed from five basic assumptions that must be challenged. These assumptions are: (1) The basic curriculum work—sometimes the only work—is that of teaching, or *didache*; (2) curriculum is equivalent to academic resources and printed materials; (3) curriculum is coextensive with the curriculum of schooling rather than the wider curriculum of education; (4) knowing and learning and understanding are measurable, quantitative realities—products rather than processes; (5) education comes to an end and is itself some thing that human beings designated as learners go to a place to get (as in "getting an education") rather than cultivated as lifelong involvement. (170)

It is important to restate what Harris writes: printed resources are not the curriculum. Curriculum—as the total life and experience of the Church—can never be limited to what is printed. Printed texts are at best a valuable curriculum resource.

Inspired by this understanding of curriculum, the Generations of Faith approach to faith formation fashions the curriculum around the events of Church life: Church year feasts and seasons, sacraments, justice, prayer and spirituality, and community life. The events-centered curriculum is both the subject matter and the process of learning. Church events are the life of the curriculum. Fashioning a curriculum involves selecting events from the life of the Church, exploring the theological richness of the event to identify a focusing faith theme, and patterning the curriculum plan, using the existing sequence (timing) of the events you have selected.

Task 1: Determine Your Curriculum Approach

There are three approaches to fashioning a lifelong, events-centered curriculum for the whole parish.

1. The *primary approach* to curriculum development utilizes the events of Church life as the primary curriculum for *everyone* in the parish. Age-group catechesis is refocused to address age-appropriate learning needs not included in the lifelong, events-centered curriculum.

2. The *blended approach* to curriculum development incorporates events-centered learning for the whole community with age-group catechesis in one integrated faith formation curriculum.

3. The *blended-toward-primary-approach* to curriculum development begins with four to six events in the first year (blended approach) and moves toward the primary approach over several years, gradually adding more events and reducing the reliance on age-group catechesis.

Before fashioning your events-centered curriculum, it is important to decide which approach you will adopt. Discuss your potential approaches with your team, weigh the strengths and weaknesses of each approach, and make your choice. Below are descriptions and examples of the approaches.

The Primary Approach

With this approach, an events-centered curriculum becomes the primary faith formation curriculum for all ages and generations, supported by focused age-specific catechesis. Parishes that adopt the primary approach fashion a curriculum plan that incorporates eight or more events per year over a six-year time frame. In the primary approach the curriculum must provide the foundations or essentials of the Catholic faith for all ages and generations.

Parishes using this approach usually adopt an intergenerational learning model for events-centered preparation. Intergenerational learning programs are usually held monthly or within close proximity to the event, require extended time frames (usually 2 1/2 –3 hours), and are offered multiple times to attract a wide audience and make it easy for everyone to participate. For example, some parishes may offer the same program on Wednesday from 6:00 PM–9:00 PM, Friday from 6:00 PM–9:00 PM, and Saturday from 9:00 AM-noon. Other parishes connect the preparation program to the Sunday liturgies, for example from 10:00 AM to 1:00 AM following the 9:00 AM Mass.

In the primary approach, age-group catechesis is refocused. Much of the catechesis being done in age-group settings is no longer necessary because topics or themes are addressed in the lifelong curriculum. There is still a need for catechesis with age groups that is focused on specific themes not addressed in the lifelong curriculum. Also, sacramental preparation programs need to continue as a separate program for those preparing to celebrate a sacrament.

RCIA preparation programs can be enhanced by incorporating the lifelong curriculum into the catechumenate. For example, each month catechumens can participate in the intergenerational learning program with other adults (during the month they would learn with other catechumens). The monthly learning program and its content, as well as participation in the Church event, become part of the catechumenal preparation. Catechumens have the opportunity to learn with the whole parish community and see firsthand that learning is for a lifetime. A lifelong curriculum can help to meet the challenge of engaging the newly baptized in mystagogy since it provides continuous learning for adults.

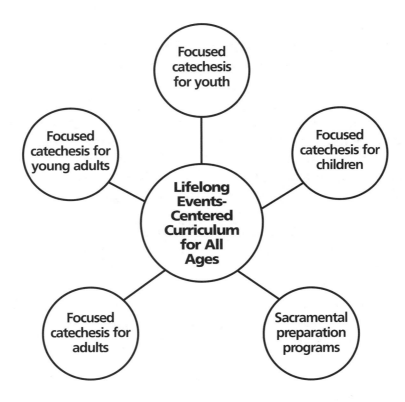

Adopting a primary approach does not affect the broader ministry with children, teens, and adults. It moves much of the catechesis for age groups into the lifelong curriculum for the whole parish community, but other ministry programming remains unaffected. For example, a parish youth ministry can focus its energy on the other important components of youth ministry, knowing that much of the catechesis for teens is being addressed in the lifelong curriculum. Monthly youth gatherings, retreats, social events, summer service projects, and other such programs can continue as usual. Adult Bible study groups can continue to meet and explore Scripture together. Children can continue to perform in the Christmas pageant and participate in Vacation Bible School. Age-group programming complements the primary, lifelong curriculum and enhances it by providing additional programs and ministry opportunities for specific age groups.

Examples of a Primary Curriculum Plan

Each parish fashions a primary curriculum around the life, character, culture, history, and people of its community. Whether your approach is primary or blended, there are two basic ways to organize a multi-year curriculum: a *single focus*, using one of the six core-content areas for each year of the six-year plan, or an *integrated focus*, which incorporates six core content areas each year: the Church year, sacraments, justice and service, prayer, morality, and Creed.

The following are two examples of a primary curriculum (one year of a six-year plan) for a parish that has adopted the primary approach to a lifelong, events-centered curriculum. Example 1 presents a primary curriculum with a single focus for the year—sacraments. Example 2 presents a primary curriculum with an integrated focus, incorporating events from the six content areas.

Curriculum Approach

　　Primary, with focused age-group catechesis

Learning Model

　　Intergenerational

Meeting Times for Preparation Programs

　　Wednesday (6:00 PM–9:00 PM), Friday (6:00 PM–9:00 PM), Saturday (9:00 AM–noon), and Sunday (10:00 AM–1:00 PM , after 9:00 AM Mass)

Focused Age-Group Catechesis through the Year

Children

▶ Sacramental preparation programs for First Eucharist and First Reconciliation (Format: family retreat day, at-home preparation, rehearsal meeting)

▶ Sexuality education (Format: four-week program for parents and children, offered twice, in fall and spring)

▶ Vacation Bible School

Youth

▶ Sacramental preparation program for Confirmation (Format: retreat weekend, six-week course, rehearsal meeting)

▶ Annual retreat programs for high-school youth

Adults

▶ Bible-study groups

▶ Monthly speaker series

Check online at www.generationsoffaith.org for stories and examples of parishes using the Primary Approach.

A Primary Curriculum Plan for All Ages

Example 1: Single-Focus Curriculum Plan: Sacraments

Events and Dates	Themes	Preparation Programs
Anointing the Sick • Parish Celebration (Oct)	• The Rite in Word and Symbol • Healing	2nd Week of September
Rite of Funerals • Feast of All Souls (Nov 2)	• The Rite in Word and Symbol • Life Everlasting	2nd Week of October
Sacrament of Reconciliation • Advent Celebration of Reconciliation (Dec)	• The Rite in Word and Symbol • Forgiveness	2nd Week of November
Sacrament of Marriage • Holy Family Sunday (Dec) • Wedding Feast of Cana (2nd Sunday of Ordinary Time—Year C) • World Marriage Day (2nd Sunday in Feb)	• The Rite in Word and Symbol • Fidelity	2nd Week of December
Sacrament of Eucharist • Sunday Mass	• The Rite in Word and Symbol • Four Movements of the Mass	2nd Week of January
Sacrament of Baptism • Lenten Season (especially the Gospel readings for the 3rd, 4th, and 5th Sundays of Lent—Cycle A) • Celebration of Baptism at the Easter Vigil (Mar)	• The Rite in Word and Symbol • Conversion	2nd Week of February
Sacrament of Eucharist • Holy Thursday (Mar) • Parish Celebration of First Eucharist (Apr)	• Eucharist as Meal, Sacrifice, and Real Presence of Christ	2nd Week of March
Sacrament of Holy Orders • World Day of Prayer for Vocations (4th Sunday of Easter—Good Shepherd)	• The Rite in Word and Symbol • Service	2nd Week of April
Sacrament of Confirmation • Pentecost • Parish Celebration of Confirmation	• The Rite in Word and Symbol • Mission	2nd Week of May
Sacrament of Eucharist • Sunday Lectionary in Ordinary Time	• Liturgy of the Word • Listening to God's Word	2nd Week of June

A Primary Curriculum Plan for All Ages

Example 2: Integrated Curriculum Plan: Sacraments

Events and Dates	Themes	Preparation Programs
Respect Life Sunday (Oct)	Morality: Respect for Human Dignity	2nd Week of September
Feast of All Saints (Nov 1)	Creed: Communion of Saints	2nd Week of October
Advent Season (Dec) Focus Event: Reconciliation Service	Sacrament: Parish Celebration of Reconciliation	2nd Week of November
Christmas Season	Creed: Incarnation	2nd Week of December
Poverty-Awareness Month (Catholic Campaign for Human Development) **Projects for Justice and Service**	Justice: Option for the Poor and Vulnerable	2nd Week of January
Lenten Season Focus Event: Ash Wednesday	Church Year: Three Practices of Lent—Praying, Fasting, Almsgiving	2nd Week of February
Easter Vigil (and Easter Season)	Sacrament: Baptism	2nd Week of March
Earth Day	Justice: Care for God's Creation	2nd Week of April
Feast of Corpus Christi	Sacrament: Eucharist and the Real Presence of Christ	2nd Week of May
Ordinary Time 2nd–9th Sundays—Year A	Morality: Moral Values—Living the Sermon on the Mount	2nd Week of June

The Blended Approach

Using this approach, parishes develop an events-centered curriculum as their lifelong curriculum for all ages and generations *and* continue offering age-group catechesis for children and youth. Parishes create *one* curriculum that blends age-group catechesis with events-centered catechesis that is provided on a monthly or seasonal basis.

A blended approach requires adjusting the number of sessions of age-group catechesis to incorporate events-centered preparation programs into the yearly calendar. It also requires adjusting the themes or topics addressed in age-specific catechesis to eliminate any overlap with events-centered catechesis. *In the blended approach there is one curriculum consisting of events-centered and age-group catechesis.* This curriculum provides the foundations or essentials of the Catholic faith for all ages and generations. Some of the content in the curriculum is addressed through events-centered catechesis for the whole community, while other content is addressed through age-group catechesis.

Parishes that adopt the blended approach fashion a lifelong curriculum that eventually incorporates eight to twelve events each year in a six-year curriculum plan. Many parishes using the blended approach often develop their curriculum over a number of years, growing from four events in the first year to eight or more events in the second, third, and fourth years.

There are a variety of ways to integrate events-centered catechesis for the whole community with age-group catechesis to create an integrated lifelong curriculum. Children's catechetical texts are increasingly developed as a spiraling curriculum of four to seven units each year. In a spiraling curriculum each unit is taught every year with increasing depth. This approach makes it easier to integrate an events-centered curriculum with a children's catechetical program. The advantage of a spiraling curriculum with units is that even if a parish eliminated one or more units in a given year to incorporate events-centered learning, those units would be taught again the following year.

Described in this section are three approaches for integrating an events-centered curriculum for the whole community with age-group catechesis: 1) *extending* a theme in age-group catechesis to the whole parish community, 2) *expanding* a theme in age-group catechesis to the whole parish community, and 3) *replacing* a theme in age-group catechesis with events-centered learning for everyone.

1. *Extending a theme.* Start with the units and learning sessions in children's catechesis and expand the topic or theme to the whole parish community. The events-centered curriculum can introduce or follow from a theme in the children's catechetical program. For example, a unit on Jesus Christ in the children's program can be extended to the whole parish by focusing on a Church-year feast or season, or on a Sunday (lectionary reading) that correlates well with the content in the children's program. Conduct an intergenerational learning program that involves all ages and generations in learning about Jesus and preparing to participate in the selected event.

2. *Expanding a theme.* Expand on topics in children's catechesis with a more thorough catechesis through events-centered learning for the whole parish community. For example, many of the children's catechetical programs which provide supplemental sessions on Church year feasts and seasons, incorporate one or more years of events-centered, intergenerational learning on the Church year to expand on the learning in the children's program. The same approach can apply to prayer and justice, which are included in a children's program, but could be addressed more thoroughly through events-centered, intergenerational learning.

3. *Replacing a theme.* Replace a theme in the children's program with events-centered learning on the same theme for the whole parish community. For example, throughout the year, the unit on sacraments for children can be replaced by multiple intergenerational sessions on sacraments for all members of the parish community. Or, an intergenerational session on one sacrament can replace a session in the children's catechetical program.

Examples of a Blended Curriculum

Each parish fashions a primary curriculum around the life, character, culture, history, and people of its community. Whether your approach is primary or blended, there are two basic ways to organize a multi-year curriculum: a *single focus* using one of the six core-content areas for each year of the six-year plan or an *integrated focus*, which incorporates the six core-content areas each year: Church year, sacraments, justice and service, prayer, morality, and Creed.

The following are several examples of curriculum plans that integrate children's catechesis with events-centered, intergenerational catechesis. Each example is a single-focus plan. For the purpose of each example, the children's program uses the four pillars of the

Catechism of the Catholic Church as the topics of the four units covered each year. Most children's textbooks incorporate four to seven units each year.

Example 1: Extending or Expanding a Theme—Church Year

The following chart demonstrates one way to blend Church year feasts and seasons with the existing curriculum and calendar of the children's program. An intergenerational learning program for Church year feasts or seasons can extend or expand the children's theme. For example the Advent season and intergenerational learning program can extend the focus on Jesus begun in Unit 1 with topics such as preparing for the Messiah and John the Baptist or images of the Messiah from the Hebrew Scriptures and Gospels. Lent can extend Unit 3 on Morality by focusing on conscience, sin, and reconciliation, etc. You can also expand to new themes in Church year events not covered in the children's programs.

Month	Catechism Theme	Church Year Event
September–October	Unit 1: Creed (6 sessions)	
Late October–November		**Feast of All Saints** Late October: Preparation Programs
November	Unit 2: Sacraments (3 sessions)	
Late November–December		**Advent Season** Late November: Preparation Programs
January	Unit 2: Sacraments (3 weeks)	
February	Unit 3: Morality	
Late February		**Lenten Season** Late February: Preparation Programs
March	Unit 3: Morality (continued)	
Late March		**Good Friday** Late March: Preparation Programs
April	Unit 4: Prayer	
May		**Pentecost** Mid-May: Preparation Programs

Example 2: Expanding on a Theme—Justice and Service

The following chart provides one example of how to develop events-centered, intergenerational catechesis that expands on the children's program with a more thorough approach. This example focuses on justice and service, utilizing events throughout the year. Each event would be greatly enriched by adding local justice and service projects that provide ways for people of all ages to be practically involved in the work of justice.

Month	Catechism Theme	Justice and Service Event
September	Unit 3: Morality—Part 1 (Taught in this sequence to complement the learning from Respect Life Sunday.)	
Late September–early October		**Respect Life Sunday** Preparation Programs: Dignity for the Human Person
October	Unit 3: Morality—Part 2	
November	Unit 1: Creed—Part 1	
November		**Thanksgiving and Service Projects** Preparation Programs: Option for the Poor and Vulnerable
December	Unit 1: Creed—Part 2	
January		**Poverty Awareness Month and Service Projects** (Catholic Campaign for Human Development) Preparation Programs: Rights and Responsibilities
January	Unit 2: Sacraments	
February		**Lent and Justice/Service/Almsgiving** Preparation Programs: Solidarity
March–April	Unit 4: Prayer	
April		**Earth Day** Preparation Programs: Care for God's Creation

Example 3: Replacing a Children's Theme—Sacraments

The following chart provides an example of how to replace a theme or unit in the children's program with an events-centered, intergenerational catechetical program. This example focuses on sacraments, but this template could be used to replace any theme with events-centered, intergenerational catechesis.

Month	Parish Event	Learning Program
September–October		Unit 1: Creed
Late October–November	Parish Celebration of Anointing of the Sick (November)	Preparation Programs: Sacrament of Anointing of the Sick (Late October)
Late November–December	Parish Celebration of the Sacrament of Reconciliation (Advent)	Preparation Programs: Sacrament of Reconciliation (Mid-November)
January	Vocations Week and Sunday Lectionary reading—Call of the Disciples: Sacrament of Orders	Preparation Programs: Sacrament of Orders (Mid-December or Early January)
January		Unit 2: Morality—Part 1
February	World Marriage Day: Sacrament of Marriage	Preparation Programs: Sacrament of Marriage (Late January or Early February)
February	Lent: Sacrament of Baptism Parish Celebration of Baptism (Easter Vigil and Easter Season)	Preparation Programs: Sacrament of Baptism (Late February)
March		Unit 2: Morality—Part 2
Late March	Holy Thursday: Sacrament of Eucharist	Preparation Programs: Sacrament of Eucharist (mid-March)
April		Unit 4: Prayer
May	Feast of Pentecost Parish Celebration of Confirmation	Preparation Programs: Sacrament of Confirmation (Mid-May)

Organizing a Blended Curriculum Plan

Parishes organize a blended curriculum in one of two ways: *monthly* or *annually*. A parish that adopts the *monthly* schedule fully implements a lifelong curriculum of eight to ten events each year with one event per month. Each month, one week is focused on events-centered learning programs (intergenerational, family-centered, and/or age-group) for that month's event. The remaining weeks of the month are focused on age-group catechetical programs. Many parishes cancel age-group programs when the event of the month is celebrated or conducted during the week (rather than on a Sunday). This highlights the importance of participation in the event as an integral element of faith formation.

> Week 1: Events-centered intergenerational learning programs scheduled multiple times during the week: evenings, Saturday, or Sunday.
>
> Weeks 2–4: Age-group catechesis for children, teens, adults.

A parish can use an *annual* approach by scheduling events-centered preparation programs in close proximity to the event (e.g., one week before the event). In the annual approach, events-centered learning programs are incorporated into the existing catechetical calendar, thereby eliminating age-group catechesis during the preparation week. Many parishes cancel age group programs when an event is celebrated or conducted during the week (rather than on a Sunday). All of the curriculum examples in the prior section are examples of an annual plan.

A Blended Curriculum Plan with a Monthly Schedule

Here is an example of one year of a six-year plan for a parish that has developed the blended approach with an event and intergenerational learning program each month.

Curriculum Approach

▶ Blended, with age-group catechesis

Learning Model for Events-Centered Catechesis

▶ Monthly intergenerational preparation programs

Meeting Times for Preparation Programs

▶ Tuesday and Wednesday: 5:30 PM–8:30 PM (chosen because they are the same days that children's catechetical program meets during the month)

▶ Saturday (9:00 am–noon), and Sunday (3:00 PM–6:00 PM before 6:00 PM Mass)

A sample curriculum plan follows on the next page.

A Blended Events-Centered Curriculum Plan
One-Year, Single Focus Curriculum Plan—Prayer

Events and Dates	Themes	Preparation Programs
Praying the Rosary (October) • Parish Rosary Month and Celebration	• Four Mysteries of the Rosary	1st Week of October
Age-Group Catechesis		
Praying with the Saints (November) • Feast of All Saints	Prayer Traditions of the Thirty Saints (30 days)	1st Week of November
Age-Group Catechesis		
Praying during Advent–Christmas • Advent and Christmas prayer traditions	• Advent Wreath • Praying the Lectionary	1st Week of December
Age-Group Catechesis		
Catholic Prayers and Devotions • Variety of events and prayer experiences during the year	• Eucharistic Adoration, Sign of the Cross, etc.	1st Week of January
Age-Group Catechesis		
Praying during Lent • Practice of prayer during Lent	• Forms of Prayer • Expressions of Prayer	1st Week of February
Age-Group Catechesis		
Praying during Holy Week • Parish celebration of the Stations of the Cross, morning and evening prayer during Holy Week, and liturgies of Holy Thursday and Good Friday	• Stations of the Cross • Liturgy of the Hours • Litanies	1st Week of March
Age-Group Catechesis		
Sacrament of Eucharist • Easter Season	• Centrality of Eucharist in communal prayer • Eucharistic prayers	1st Week of April
Age-Group Catechesis		
The Our Father • Praying at Sunday Mass, personal prayer	• Following God's will • Nourishment and healing	1st Week of May
Age-Group Catechesis		
Praying with Scripture • Sunday Lectionary in Ordinary Time	• Liturgy of the Word • Listening to God's Word	1st Week of June

The Blended-toward-Primary Approach

Many parishes chart a path toward a primary curriculum over several years, incorporating more events-centered learning each year. The blended-toward-primary approach to curriculum often begins with four to six events in the first year (blended approach) and moves toward the primary approach after three or four years, gradually adding more events-centered learning and reducing the reliance on age-group catechesis. For example:

- ▶ **Year 1:** Blended curriculum (4–6 events integrated with existing age-group catechesis)
- ▶ **Year 2:** Blended curriculum (6–8 events integrated with existing age-group catechesis)
- ▶ **Year 3:** Primary curriculum (8 or more events with targeted age-specific catechesis)

Summary and Planning for Task 1

There are a number of factors your parish needs to consider when determining your curriculum approach. Remember, the goal of all three approaches is to develop a lifelong, events-centered curriculum for the whole parish community. You need to select the approach that will work best for your parish. Here are several factors that parishes have used to determine where they will start:

1. *Parish vision.* The culture and character of the parish and the vision of faith formation are important factors in determining your curriculum approach. It is also important to consider the long-term vision for faith formation and which approach—primary or blended—best matches the parish's vision, now and in the future.

2. *Dedication to age-group catechesis.* Many parishes have a long tradition of age-group catechesis that is working effectively. They want to maintain a strong age-group catechesis while building a lifelong curriculum for everyone. On the other hand, many parishes have found that their age-group catechesis is not working effectively and they are seeking another approach to faith formation.

3. *Character of the parish.* Many parishes have found that adopting the primary approach consolidates, focuses, and simplifies their faith formation curriculum, while building a greater sense of community spirit.

4. *Staffing.* Many parishes have found that they do not have enough paid and volunteer leaders to support the blended approach. For these parishes, moving to the primary approach focuses their leadership and energy on events-centered, intergenerational learning.

Discuss the strengths of each approach—primary, blended, and blended-toward-primary—and select the approach that your parish will initiate in the coming year, as well as the approach that your parish will be working toward in future years.

Task 2: Develop a Multi-Year Curriculum Plan

A multi-year curriculum plan outlines the scope (content) and sequence (timing) of a lifelong curriculum. A six-year curriculum is recommended for several reasons. First, the six major content areas in an events-centered, lifelong curriculum (see p. 62) correspond well to the four pillars of the Catholic faith as presented in the *Catechism of the Catholic Church.*

Second, an events-centered curriculum needs to be systematic and substantial. The six-year curriculum affords the time to explore the Catholic faith with breadth and depth. And, an events-centered curriculum is a spiral curriculum, which means that the six themes are explored more deeply each time the six-year cycle begins again. There is a six-year rotation of the major content areas. The events of Church life are so theologically rich that a spiral approach over a number of years provides the opportunity to immerse people more deeply in the meaning and practice of the events.

Third, a six-year spiral is developmentally appropriate—people learn with more depth at each stage of their life cycle as they move through the curriculum. Children who begin the six-year cycle in grade one will be adolescents (grades 7–12) when the next curriculum rotation begins, young adults (18-24) for the next spiral, and so forth. At each stage of life they will explore the same events and content areas in age-appropriate ways with increasing depth and application of learning.

A Systematic and Substantive Curriculum

The events of Church life form a spiral curriculum that immerses people more deeply into the faith of the Church each year. The lifelong faith formation curriculum is formed around the natural rhythm and pattern of the faith community's life as experienced throughout the year. It provides common events and themes that are explored and experienced by all ages and all generations in the faith community.

This lifelong curriculum of Church events systematically and comprehensively presents the Gospel message and Catholic tradition through six major content areas: Church year feasts and seasons, sacraments, justice and service, morality, prayer and spirituality, and the Creed (see GDC #84–87, 97–115). The *General Directory for Catechesis* (#115) identifies the significance of these major aspects and dimensions of the Christian message for catechesis. The overview that follows presents key paragraphs from the *Directory* that demonstrate the centrality of the six content areas.

A Six Year, Spiraling Curriculum

The foundational events and themes for a systematic and comprehensive events-centered curriculum present the Gospel message and Catholic tradition. In fashioning a curriculum, parishes are not limited to these themes and events; rather, the Generations of Faith approach encourages parishes to utilize events which come from the life of the parish community, its history, its people, and its cultures. For a complete guide to events and themes see the *Scope of Church Events and Themes* on page 65.

Church Year Feasts and Seasons

The history of salvation, recounting the "marvels of God" (*mirabilia Dei*), what He has done, continues to do and will do in the future for us, is organized in reference to Jesus Christ, the "center of salvation history" (DCG [1971] 41). (GDC #115) (See also GDC #85, 97–98, 101, 102, 105, 108.)

Who has encountered Christ desires to know him as much as possible, as well as to know the plan of the Father which he revealed. Knowledge of the faith (*fides quae*) is required by adherence to the faith (*fides qua*) (cf. DCG [1971] 36a). Even in the human order the love which one person has for another causes that person to wish to know the other all the more. Catechesis, must, therefore, lead to the "gradual grasping of the whole truth about the divine plan" (cf. DCG [1971] 24), by introducing the disciples of Jesus to a knowledge of Tradition and of Scripture, which is *"the sublime science of Christ"* (DV 25a). (GDC #85)

Foundational Events	Potential Themes
Advent Season	Salvation history
Christmas Season	Incarnation
Lenten Season	Discipleship and conversion Praying, fasting, and almsgiving
Triduum	Paschal mystery, salvation, redemption
Easter Season	Resurrection
Ascension-Pentecost	Mission
Sundays in Ordinary Time	Reign of God, teachings and deeds of Jesus

Sacraments

The sacraments, which, like regenerating forces, spring from the paschal mystery of Jesus Christ, are also a whole. They form "an organic whole in which each particular sacrament has its own vital place" (CCC 1211). In this whole, the Holy Eucharist occupies a unique place to which all of the other sacraments are ordained. The Eucharist is to be presented as the "sacrament of sacraments" (*ibidem*). (GDC #115) (See also GDC #85, 108.)

Christ is always present in his Church, especially in "liturgical celebrations" (SC 7). Communion with Jesus Christ leads to the celebration of the salvific presence in the sacraments, especially in the Eucharist. The Church ardently desires that all the Christian faithful be brought to that full, conscious and active participation which is required by the very nature of the liturgy (cf. SC 14) and the dignity of the baptismal priesthood. For this reason, catechesis, along with promoting a knowledge of the meaning of the liturgy and the sacraments, must also educate the disciples of Jesus Christ "for prayer, for thanksgiving, for repentance, for praying with confidence, for community spirit, for understanding correctly the meaning of the creeds...," (DCG [1971] 25b) as all of this is necessary for a true liturgical life. (GDC #85)

Foundational Events	Potential Themes
Baptism	Initiation, conversion, mission: priest, prophet, king
Confirmation	Conformity to Christ, witness, discipleship
Eucharist	Meal, sacrifice, real presence of Christ
Reconciliation	Repentance, sin, conscience
Anointing of the Sick	Healing, suffering, hope, resurrection
Marriage	Covenant love, fidelity, vocation
Holy Orders	Vocation, service, mission

Justice and Service

Jesus, in announcing the Kingdom, proclaims the justice of God: he proclaims God's judgment and our responsibility....The call to conversion and belief in the Gospel of the Kingdom—a Kingdom of justice, love and peace, and in whose light we shall be judged—is fundamental for catechesis. (GDC #102) (See also GDC #86, 102–104, 108.)

Catechesis is also open to the missionary dimension (cf. CT 24b and DCG [1971] 28). This seeks to equip the disciples of Jesus to be present as Christians in society through their professional, cultural and social lives. ...The evangelical attitudes which Jesus taught his disciples when he sent them on mission are precisely those which catechesis must nourish: to seek out the lost sheep, proclaim and heal at the same time, to be poor, without money or knapsack; to know how to accept rejection and persecution; to place one's trust in the Father and in the support of the Holy Spirit; to expect no other reward than the joy of working for the Kingdom (cf. Mt 10:5–42 and Lk 10:1–20). (GDC #86a)

Justice Themes	Potential Events
Life and Dignity of the Human Person	Respect Life Sunday, saints' feast days, service and justice/advocacy projects (local and national), and Sunday lectionary readings
Call to Family, Community, and Participation	Holy Family Sunday, election day, service and justice/advocacy projects (local and national)
Dignity of Work and Rights of Workers	Labor Day, Feast of St. Joseph the Worker
Rights and Responsibilities of the Human Person	Thanksgiving, World Hunger Day, Migrant and Refugee Week, service and justice/advocacy projects (local and national), and Sunday lectionary readings
Option for the Poor and Vulnerable	Thanksgiving, Lent, Poverty Awareness Month, Feast of St. Vincent de Paul and other saints, service and justice/advocacy projects (local and national), and Sunday lectionary readings
Solidarity	Lent, Pentecost, Mission Sunday, sponsoring a development project (e.g., Catholic Relief Services)
Care for God's Creation	Earth Day, Feast of St. Francis, action projects (local, national, international)
Peace	Martin Luther King Jr. holiday, saints' feast days, national and international peace projects

Prayer and Spirituality

The Our Father gathers up the essence of the Gospel. It synthesizes and hierarchically structures the immense riches of prayer contained in Sacred Scripture and in all of the Church's life. (GDC #115) (See also GDC #85, 108.)

Communion with Jesus Christ leads the disciples to assume the attitude of prayer and contemplation which the Master himself had. To learn to pray with Jesus is to pray with the same sentiments with which he turned to the Father: adoration, praise, thanksgiving, filial confidence, supplication and awe for his glory. All of these sentiments are reflected in the *Our Father*, the prayer which Jesus taught his disciples and which is the model of all Christian prayer. The *"handing on of the Our Father"* (RCIA 25 and 188-191) is a summary of the entire Gospel (cf. CCC 2761) and is therefore a true act of catechesis. When catechesis is permeated by a climate of prayer, the assimilation of the entire Christian life reaches its summit.... (GDC #85)

Foundational Themes	Potential Events
Forms of prayer (blessing and adoration, petition, intercession, thanksgiving, praise)	Sunday Mass, Lent—practice of prayer, Holy Thursday, Good Friday, Stations of the Cross, World Day of Prayer, praying with the saints (feast days)
Expressions of prayer (vocal, meditation, and contemplation) Lectio Divina, Liturgy of the Hours	Praying in Advent and Christmas, Lent, Holy Week, and Easter seasons
The Lord's Prayer	Sunday Mass, 17th Sunday in Ordinary Time (Year C)
The Rosary	Marian feasts, praying the rosary through the year: joyful (Christmas), sorrowful (Holy Week), glorious (Easter), luminous (Ordinary Time)
Catholic prayers and devotions	Sign of the Cross, Stations of the Cross, Eucharistic adoration, devotion to the saints

Creed

The Apostles' Creed demonstrates how the Church has always desired to present the Christian mystery in a vital synthesis. This Creed is a synthesis of and a key to reading all of the Church's doctrine, which is hierarchically ordered around it.[6] (GDC #115) (See also GDC #85, 99–100, 108.)

Who has encountered Christ desires to know him as much as possible, as well as to know the plan of the Father which he revealed. Knowledge of the faith (*fides quae*) is required by adherence to the faith (*fides qua*) (cf. DCG [1971] 36a). Even in the human order the love which one person has for another causes that person to wish to know the other all the more. Catechesis, must, therefore, lead to the "gradual grasping of the whole truth about the divine plan (cf. DCG [1971] 24)," by introducing the disciples of Jesus to a knowledge of Tradition and of Scripture, which is *"the sublime science of Christ"* (DV 25a). By deepening the knowledge of the faith, catechesis nourishes not only the life of faith but equips it to explain itself to the world. The meaning of the creed, which is a compendium of Scripture and of the faith of the Church, is the realization of this task. (GDC #85)

6. St. Cyril of Jerusalem affirms with regard to the Creed: "This synthesis of faith was not made to accord with human opinions but rather what was of the greatest importance was gathered from all the Scriptures, to present the one teaching of the faith in its entirety. And just as a mustard seed contains a great number of branches in a tiny grain, so too the summary of faith encompassed in a few words the whole knowledge of the true religion contained in the Old and New Testaments."

Foundational Themes	Potential Events
We believe in one God…	Trinity Sunday, Easter Vigil, Easter Season, Rite of Baptism
We believe in one Lord, Jesus Christ… birth, mysteries of Christ's life, death, and resurrection	Christmas, Baptism of the Lord, Transfiguration, Triduum, Sunday lectionary readings
We believe in the Holy Spirit…	Easter season, Pentecost, Rite of Confirmation
We believe in one holy catholic and apostolic Church…	Easter season, Pentecost, Feast of Saints Peter and Paul
We acknowledge one baptism for the forgiveness of sins…	Rite of Baptism, Easter Vigil
We look for the resurrection of the dead, and the life of the world to come…	All Saints, All Souls

Morality

The double commandment of love of God and neighbor is—in the moral message—a hierarchy of values which Jesus himself established. "On these two commandments depend all the Law and the Prophets" (Mt 22:40). The love of God and neighbor, which sum up the Decalogue, are lived in the spirit of the Beatitudes and constitute the *magna carta* of the Christian life proclaimed by Jesus in the Sermon on the Mount.[7] (GDC #115) (See also GDC #85, 97, 104, 108.)

Conversion to Jesus Christ implies walking in his footsteps. Catechesis, must, therefore transmit to the disciples the attitudes of the Master himself. The disciples thus undertake a journey of interior transformation, in which, by participating in the paschal mystery of the Lord, "they pass from the old man to the new man who has been made perfect in Christ" (AG 13). The Sermon on the Mount, in which Jesus takes up the Decalogue, and impresses upon it the spirit of the beatitudes,[8] is an indispensable point of reference for the moral formation which is most necessary today….This moral testimony, which is prepared for by catechesis, must always demonstrate the social consequences of the demands of the Gospel (cf. CT 29f). (GDC #85)

7. St. Augustine presents the Sermon on the Mount as "the perfect charter of the Christian life and contains all the appropriate precepts necessary to guide it" (*De Sermone Domini in Monte* I, 1; *Patrologiae Cursus completus, Series Latina* 34, 1229-1231); cf. EN 8.

8. Cf. LG 62; CCC 1965-1986. The CCC 1697 specifies in particular the characteristics which catechesis must assume in moral formation.

Foundational Themes	Potential Events
Love of God, neighbor, and self (Commandments 1–4)	Sunday lectionary readings, e.g., Great Commandment (30th Sunday on Ordinary Time, Year A), Sermon on the Mount (4th–9th Sundays in Ordinary Time, Year A), Sermon on the Plain (6th–8th Sundays in Ordinary Time, Year C), Parable of the Good Samaritan
Respect for Human Dignity (Commandment 5)	Christ the King—Year A, Sunday lectionary readings, saints' feast days (see also justice themes and events on pg. 55)
Justice (Commandments 7 and 10)	Sunday lectionary readings, Sermon on the Plain (6th–8th Sundays in Ordinary Time, Year C), Parable of the Rich Man and Lazarus (see also justice themes and events on pg. 55)
Faithfulness (Commandments 6 and 9)	Sacrament of Marriage, World Marriage Day, Wedding Feast at Cana, Sunday lectionary readings
Honesty and Integrity (Commandments 8 and 10)	Sunday lectionary readings, saints' feast days
Care, Compassion, Forgiveness	Lectionary readings of Jesus' actions, Gospel stories such as prodigal son and woman caught in adultery, saints' feast days

Creating a Multi-Year Plan

Step 1. Develop a Church Events Profile

Review the list of events on the *Church Events Profile* on page 60. Add events that are particular to your parish community, local area, and/or diocese. Through this activity you will quickly see the tremendous potential that lies within your parish community for developing an events-centered faith formation curriculum.

Step 2. Determine an Organizing Principle

There are two basic ways to organize a multi-year curriculum: a *single focus* using one of the six core-content areas (e.g., sacraments) for each year of the six-year plan or an *integrated focus* which incorporates the six core content areas each year: Church year, sacraments, justice and service, prayer, morality, and Creed. Neither of these two approaches precludes a parish from focusing on a special annual theme that emerges from a significant parish or diocesan event, such as a milestone parish anniversary, dedication of a new Church, or a diocesan-wide event and theme.

Step 3. Select Events for Each Year

Using the completed *Church Events Profile* worksheet on page 60 and your focus (single or integrated) for each year, select events for each year of your curriculum. Carefully study the *Scope of Church Events and Themes* worksheet, which starts on page 63 to determine possibilities for finding events to teach core faith themes and for finding all of the content embedded in events. Use the *Lifelong Curriculum Plan of Events* worksheet to record your selections and create your multi-year plan.

For examples of curriculum plans review the examples included with the descriptions of the primary and blended approaches on pages 43-51.

Review the first draft of your curriculum plan to determine how well your plan addresses the six essential content areas of catechesis: Creed, sacraments, morality, justice and Catholic social teachings, prayer, and the Church year (and the lectionary). Use the description of the six core content areas and themes described in the prior section to review your curriculum. Look for content areas or themes that are missing or not fully addressed. Make sure that the theme is embedded in the event (*emergent catechetical content*). Make revisions as necessary.

WORKS CITED IN THIS CHAPTER

Harris, Maria. *Fashion Me a People: Curriculum in the Church*. Louisville: Westminister/John Knox Press, 1989.

Summary and Planning for Task 2

The goal is to develop for the whole parish community a six-year curriculum plan for lifelong, events-centered catechesis around the six major content areas that reflects the people, cultures, character, traditions, and history of your parish community.

1. Develop a Church Events Profile, adding events that are particular to your parish community, local area, and/or diocese. Use the *Church Events Profile* worksheet on page 61.

2. Determine an organizing principle for the multi-year plan: a single focus, using one of the six core content areas for each year of the six-year plan (e.g., sacraments) or an integrated focus, which incorporates the six core content areas each year—Church year, sacraments, justice and service, prayer, morality, and Creed.

3. Determine if during your first six-year plan, you have a special focus—a special annual theme that emerges from a significant parish or diocesan event (parish anniversary, dedication of a new Church, etc.).

4. Select events for each year of your plan, using the completed Church Events Profile and the Scope of Events and Themes. Use the Lifelong Curriculum Plan of Events worksheet to record your selections and create your multi-year plan. At this time, do not complete the column for preparation program dates. You will complete this when you work through the guide to implementing a curriculum in the next chapter.

5. Review the first draft of your curriculum plan to determine how well your plan addresses the six essential content areas of catechesis: Creed, sacraments, morality, justice and Catholic social teachings, prayer, and the Church year (and the lectionary). Look for content areas or themes that are missing or not fully addressed. Make sure that the theme is embedded in the event (emergent catechetical content). Make revisions as necessary.

Church Events Profile

Use this profile form to identify events particular to your parish community.

Major Church Year Feasts and Seasons

- ○ Advent Season
- ○ Our Lady of Guadalupe
- ○ Las Posadas
- ○ Christmas and Christmas Season
- ○ Feast of the Holy Family
- ○ Feast of the Epiphany
- ○ Feast of the Baptism of the Lord
- ○ Ash Wednesday
- ○ Lenten Season
- ○ Palm Sunday
- ○ Holy Thursday
- ○ Good Friday
- ○ Easter Vigil
- ○ Easter Sunday
- ○ Easter Season
- ○ Feast of the Ascension
- ○ Feast of Pentecost
- ○ Feast of the Trinity
- ○ Feast of Corpus Christi
- ○ Feast of All Saints
- ○ Feast of All Souls
- ○ Feast of Christ the King
- ○ Thanksgiving
- ○ Marian Feast: _____
- ○ Marian Feast: _____
- ○ Saint's Feast Day _____
  _____
  _____

Sacraments, Rituals, Prayer

- ○ Baptism
- ○ Confirmation
- ○ First Eucharist
- ○ Sunday Eucharist
- ○ RCIA
- ○ First Reconciliation
- ○ Reconciliation
- ○ Anointing of the Sick
- ○ Marriage
- ○ Holy Orders

- ○ Funerals
- ○ Devotions
  _____
  _____
  _____
  _____

Prayer Services and Traditions

_____
_____
_____
_____

Justice and Service Events

- ○ Respect Life Month (October)
- ○ Mission Sunday (October)
- ○ World Food Day (October)
- ○ Poverty Awareness Month (January)
- ○ Operation Rice Bowl (Lent)
- ○ Migrant & Refugee Week (February)
- ○ Earth Day (April)
- ○ Diocesan and National Service Projects
  _____
  _____
  _____

Parish and Community Service Projects

_____
_____
_____
_____

Community Life Events

- ○ Parish Anniversary
- ○ Parish Saint's Feast Day
- ○ Parish Community Events

(e.g., picnics, social events, seasonal and ethnic festivals)
_____
_____
_____

Lifelong Curriculum Plan of Events

Curriculum Plan Year #: _____

Curriculum Approach: ❑ Primary   ❑ Blended   ❑ Blended-toward-Primary

Focus for the Year: ❑ Integrated Focus   ❑ Single Focus: _____

Preparation Program Days and Times:

Day 1: _____   Day 2: _____   Day 3: _____   Day 4: _____

Day 5: _____   Day 6: _____   Day 7: _____   Day 8: _____

EVENT	DATE OF EVENT	THEME	PREPARATION PROGRAM DATES

Lifelong, Systematic Curriculum
Sample Six Year Plan

Church Year

Events and Dates	Themes	Preparation Programs
Feast of All Saints (November)	Communion of Saints	2nd Week of October
Advent Season (December)	Salvation History	2nd Week of November
Epiphany (January)	Manifestation	2nd Week of December
Baptism of the Lord (January)	Mission of the Christian	2nd Week of January
Lenten Season (February)	Praying, Fasting, Almsgiving	2nd Week of February
Triduum (March)	Paschal Mystery	2nd Week of March
Easter Season (April)	Resurrection	2nd Week of April
Ascension-Pentecost (May)	Mission of the Church	2nd Week of May
Corpus Christi (June)	Eucharist	2nd Week of June
Assumption (August)	Mary—Model of Faith	2nd Week of August
Triumph of the Cross (September)	Redemption	2nd Week of September

Prayer

Events and Dates	Themes	Preparation Programs
Praying the Rosary (October) • Parish Rosary Month and Celebration	• Four Mysteries of the Rosary	1st Week of October
Praying with the Saints (November) • Feast of All Saints	• Prayer traditions of the 30 saints (30 days)	1st Week of November
Praying during Advent-Christmas • Advent and Christmas prayer traditions	• Advent Wreath • Praying the lectionary	1st Week of December
Catholic Prayers and Devotions • Variety of events and prayer experiences during the year	• Eucharistic adoration, Sign of the Cross, etc.	1st Week of January
Praying during Lent • Practice of prayer during Lent	• Forms of Prayer • Expressions of Prayer	1st Week of February
Praying during Holy Week • Parish celebration of Stations of the Cross, and morning and evening prayer during Holy Week, liturgies of Holy Thursday and Good Friday	• Stations of the Cross • Liturgy of the Hours • Litanies	1st Week of March
Sacrament of Eucharist • Easter Season	• Centrality of Eucharist in communal prayer	1st Week of April
The Our Father • Praying at Sunday Mass, personal prayer	• Following God's will • Nourishment and healing	1st Week of May
Praying with Scripture • Sunday Lectionary in Ordinary Time	• Liturgy of the Word • Listening to God's Word	1st Week of June

Sacraments

Events and Dates	Themes	Preparation Programs
Anointing of the Sick • Parish Celebration (October)	• The Rite in Word & Symbol • Healing	2nd Week of September
Rite of Funerals • Feast of All Souls (November 2)	• The Rite in Word & Symbol • Life Everlasting	2nd Week of October
Sacrament of Reconciliation • Advent Celebration of Reconciliation (December)	• The Rite in Word & Symbol • Forgiveness	2nd Week of November
Sacrament of Marriage • Holy Family Sunday (December) • Wedding Feast of Cana (2nd Sunday in Ordinary Time-Year C) • World Marriage Day (February)	• The Rite in Word & Symbol • Fidelity	2nd Week of December
Sacrament of Eucharist • Sunday Mass	• The Rite in Word & Symbol • 4 Movements of the Mass	2nd Week of January
Sacrament of Baptism • Lenten season (especially the Gospel readings for the 3rd, 4th, and 5th Sundays of Lent-Cycle A) • Easter Vigil	• The Rite in Word & Symbol • Conversion	2nd Week of February
Sacrament of Eucharist • Holy Thursday (March) • Parish celebration of 1st Eucharist	• Eucharist as Meal, Sacrifice, and Real Presence of Christ	2nd Week of March
Sacrament of Orders • World Day of Prayer for Vocations (4th Sunday of Easter)	• The Rite in Word & Symbol • Service	2nd Week of April
Sacrament of Confirmation • Pentecost • Parish Celebration of Confirmation	• The Rite in Word & Symbol • Mission	2nd Week of May
Sacrament of Eucharist • Lectionary in Ordinary Time	• Liturgy of the Word • Listening to God's Word	2nd Week of June

Justice

Events and Dates	Themes	Preparation Programs
Respect Life Month (October)	• Dignity of the Human Person	2nd Week of September
All Saints: Justice Saints (November)	• Lives of Justice/ Solidarity	2nd Week of October
Thanksgiving (November)	• Option for the Poor	2nd Week of November
Christmas and World Day of Peace (January)	• Peace	2nd Week of December
Poverty Awareness Month (January)	• Rights and Responsibilities	2nd Week of January
Ash Wednesday & Lent (February)	• Solidarity with the Poor	2nd Week of February
Good Friday (March)	• Sacrificial Love	2nd Week of March
Earth Day (April)	• Care for God's Creation	2nd Week of April
Pentecost (May)	• Solidarity with the People of the World	2nd Week of May
Service/Mission Trips (June-Aug)	• Service to those in Need	2nd Week of June
Labor Day (September)	• Dignity of Work and Rights of Workers	2nd Week of August

Lifelong, Systematic Curriculum Sample Six-Year Plan

Creed		
Events and Dates	**Themes**	**Preparation Programs**
Christmas (December)	God sent his only son/ Incarnation	2nd Week of December
Ordinary Time (January–February)	Life of Christ: Baptism/ Mission	2nd Week of January
Lent: 3rd-4th-5th Sundays (Gospel of John) (March)	"One baptism for the forgiveness of sins"	2nd Week of February
Good Friday/ Easter Vigil (March)	Death and Resurrection/ Paschal Mystery	2nd Week of March
Easter Season/ Pentecost (April–May)	Holy Spirit	2nd Week of April
Trinity Sunday (May–June)	Trinity/ God the Father	2nd Week of May
Feast of Sts. Peter and Paul (June)	Church	2nd Week of June
Transfiguration/ 21st Sunday- Year A or 24th Sunday- Year B (Who do you say I am?) (August–September)	Jesus, Son of God	2nd Week of August
30th Sunday-Year A or 31st Sunday-Year B (October)	Love the Lord your God with all your heart, soul, mind, strength	2nd Week of September
All Saints and All Souls (November)	Resurrection of the Dead	2nd Week of October
Christ the King (November)	Jesus and Reign of God	2nd Week of November

Morality	
Foundational Themes	**Potential Events**
Love of God, neighbor and self (Commandments 1–4)	• Great Commandment (30th Sunday-Year A) • Sermon on the Mount (4th–9th Sundays-Year A) • Sermon on the Plain (6th–8th Sundays-Year C) • Parable of the Good Samaritan (15th Sunday-Year C)
Respect for human dignity (Commandment 5)	• Christ the King-A • Respect Life Sunday (October) • Gospel Stories: Samaritan Woman at the Well, Woman Caught in Adultery, Prodigal Son, Man Born Blind, etc.
Justice (Commandments 7 and 10)	• Sermon on the Plain (6th–8th Sundays-Year C) • Parable of the Rich Man and Lazarus (26th Sunday-Year C)
Faithfulness (Commandments 6 and 9)	• Sacrament of Marriage • World Marriage Day (February) • Wedding Feast at Cana (January, Year A) • Holy Family Sunday (December)
Honesty and Integrity (Commandments 8 and 10)	• Saints' Feast Days • All Saints • Lectionary Readings
Care, Compassion, Forgiveness	• Gospel stories (Lectionary) of Jesus' ministry of healing and forgiveness • Saints' feast days

Scope of Church Year Events and Themes

Use this guide to find catechetical-theological themes for events and to find events for themes or teachings you want to address in your curriculum (e.g., Creed, Morality, Prayer, and Justice).

CHURCH YEAR FEASTS AND SEASONS

Advent-Christmas Themes / **Catechism of the Catholic Church**

Conversion — #541-46, #1427-33, #1886-89, #1896, #2581-84, #2608-09
Faith — #142-84, #1814-16
Hope — #162, #673-74, #1817-21, #1843, #2090
Incarnation — #422-43, #456-69, #479, #478, #483, #522-34,
Jesus Christ (Son of God) — #422-83, #512-682
Justice — #1807, #1905-12, #1928-48, #2407-63
Manifestation — #528, #535
Mary—model of faith — #64, #144, #148-49, #165, #273, #484-511, #721-26, #963-75, #2030
Mission of Jesus — #430, #436, #438, #534, #536, #606, #608
Paschal mystery — #571-73, #599-618, #638-58
Prophetic tradition — #64, #201, #218, #522-23, #762, #2581-84, #2595
Reign of God — #541-50, #763-65, #768, #2816-21
Repentance and reconciliation — #1427-60
Salvation — #456-57, #541-50, #599-605
Salvation history — #51-73, #430-40

Baptism of the Lord Themes / **Catechism of the Catholic Church**

Baptism — #1213-45, #1262-74
Jesus Christ, Son of God — #422-83, #512-682
Mission of Jesus — #430, #436, #438, #534, #536, #606, #608

Lenten Themes / **Catechism of the Catholic Church**

Baptism — #1213-45, #1262-74
Conversion — #541-46, #1427-33, #1886-89, #1896, #2581-84, #2608-09
Cross — #616-18, #1741
Grace — #1996-2005
Jesus Christ (messiah) — #436-40, #528-29, #702, #711-16
Jesus Christ (suffering servant) — #608, #623
Justice — #1807, #1905-12, #1928-48, #2407-63
Moral life — #1699-1729, #1776-89, #1830-45, #1965-1964
Paschal mystery — #571-73, #599-618, #638-58
Practices of Lent — #1434, #2464, #2443-2449, #2558-2758 (prayer)

Scope of Church Year Events and Themes

Prophetic tradition
Reign of God
Salvation
Sin and repentance
Suffering

Holy Week Themes
Baptism
Bread and wine
Conversion
Cross
Eucharist
Jesus Christ (suffering servant)
Justice
Paschal mystery
Passion and death of Jesus
Resurrection
Salvation
Suffering and redemption

Pentecost Themes
Evangelization
Gifts and charisms
Holy Spirit
Mission of Jesus
Mission of Church
Ministries of the Church
Mystery of the Church
Prayer
Witness

Trinity Sunday Themes
God the Father
Jesus Christ, Son of God
Jesus Christ, Messiah
Holy Spirit
Trinity

Corpus Christi Themes
Sacrament of Eucharist

Catechism of the Catholic Church
#64, #201, #218, #522-23, #762, #2581-84, #2595
#541-50, #763-65, #768, #2816-21
#218, #430-31, #456-57, #541-50, #599-605, #620-22, #1019, #1811, #1816
#386-87, #1427-60, #1846-76
#571-73, #612-618, #623

Catechism of the Catholic Church
#535-37, #1213-45, #1262-74
#1329, #1333-36, #1375-76, #1406, #1413,
#541-46, #1427-33, #1886-89, #1896, #2581-84, #2608-09
#616-18, #1741
#1322-1414
#608, #623
#1807, #1905-12, #1928-48, #2407-63
#571-73, #599-618, #638-58
#571-630
#638-658
#218, #430-31, #456-57, #541-50, #599-605, #620-22, #1019, #1811, #1816
#571-73, #601, #605, #612-618, #623, #776,

Catechism of the Catholic Church
#849-52, #905, #2044-46
#787-95, #799-801, #1830-32
#243-46, #683-747, #1830-32
#430, #436, #438, #534, #536, #606, #608
#781-86, #949-53, #849-65,
#949-53
#748-870, #949-53
#2558-2758
#897-913

Catechism of the Catholic Church
#198-227
#422-83, #512-682
#436-40, #528-29, #702, #711-16
#683-741
#232-260

Catechism of the Catholic Church
#1322-1405

Scope of Church Year Events and Themes

Bread and wine
Paschal mystery
Sacrifice, meal, real presence
Church—Body of Christ

Catechism of the Catholic Church
#1329, #1333-36, #1375-76, #1406, #1413,
#571-73, #599-618, #638-58,
#1356-1381
#787-796

All Saints & All Souls Themes
The Beatitudes
Communion of Saints
Eschatology
Holiness
Reign of God
Witness
Resurrection of the body
Life everlasting

Catechism of the Catholic Church
#1716-24
#946-48, #956-57, #2683
#668-82, #988-1019, #1020-60
#2012-15, #2030, #2045
#541-50, #763-65, #768, #2816-21
#897-913
#988-1014
#1020-1050

Marian Feasts Themes
Immaculate Conception
Annunciation
Mary's Virginity
Mary—model of faith

Catechism of the Catholic Church
#487-493
#494-495
#496-507
#64, #144, #148-49, #165, #273, #484-511, #721-26, #963-75, #2030

THE CREED

Creed
We believe in one God...
the Father, the Almighty,
maker of heaven and earth,
of all that is seen and unseen.

Event Suggestions
• Easter Vigil and Easter Season
• Trinity Sunday
• Sacrament of Baptism
• Lectionary readings

Catechism of the Catholic Church
Part One, Section 2, Chapter 1, Article 1

We believe in one Lord, Jesus Christ...
For us men and for our salvation he came
down from heaven; by the power of the Holy Spirit
he was born of the Virgin Mary,
and became man.
For our sake he was crucified under Pontius Pilate;
he suffered, died, and was buried. On the third day
he rose again in fulfillment of the Scriptures;

• Advent: Coming of the Messiah
• Annunciation
• Immaculate Conception
• Christmas: Incarnation
• Baptism of the Lord: Son of God
• Transfiguration: Son of God
• Triduum: Paschal Mystery (Holy Thursday,
  Good Friday, Easter Vigil and Easter Sunday)

Catechism of the Catholic Church
Part One, Section 2, Chapter 2, Articles 2-7

Scope of Church Year Events and Themes

	Church Year Events	Catechism of the Catholic Church
He ascended into heaven and is seated at the right hand of the Father. He will come again in glory to judge the living and the dead. And his kingdom will have no end.	• Ascension • Pentecost • Christ the King: Judge and Kingdom • Trinity Sunday • Celebration of Baptism and Confirmation	Part One, Section 2, Chapter 3, Article 8
We believe in the Holy Spirit...	• Easter Vigil and Easter Season • Ascension and Pentecost • Trinity Sunday • Sacrament of Baptism • Sacrament of Confirmation • Lectionary readings on the Holy Spirit	
We believe in one, holy, catholic, and apostolic Church.	• Easter Season • Pentecost • Feast pf Saints Peter and Paul • Lectionary readings on Christian community, mission, ministry	Part One, Section 2, Chapter 3, Article 9, Paragraphs 1-3
We acknowledge one baptism for the forgiveness of sins.	• Sacrament of Baptism: Infant and Adult • Easter Vigil • Lent (3rd, 4th, 5th Sundays of Lent)	Part One, Section 2, Chapter 3, Article 10
We look for the resurrection of the dead, and the life of the world to come. Amen.	• All Saints • All Souls	Part One, Section 2, Chapter 3, Articles 11-12

SACRAMENTS AND CHURCH RITUALS

Sacrament	Event Suggestions	Themes	Catechism of the Catholic Church
Baptism	• Celebration of infant baptisms through the year • Celebration of Initiation at the Easter Vigil • Lent (Lectionary for the 3rd, 4th, 5th Sundays of Lent) • Baptism of the Lord Sunday	• Rite of Baptism: symbols, gestures, prayers, Scripture readings • Profession of faith • Initiation • Paschal mystery • Mission of Jesus: priest, prophet, and king • Conversion • Sin and repentance • Witness • Holy Spirit • Rite of Confirmation: symbols, gestures,	Sacrament of Baptism: #1213-1274 Paschal mystery: #571-73, #599-618, #638-58 Mission of Jesus: #430, #436, #438, #534, #536, #606, #608 Conversion: #541-46, #1427-33, #1886-89, #1896, #2581-84, #2608-09 Sin and repentance: #386-87, #1427-60, #1846-76 Witness: #897-913
Confirmation	• Celebration of Confirmation	• Rite of Confirmation: symbols, gestures,	Sacrament of Confirmation: #1285-1321

Scope of Church Year Events and Themes

Sacrament	Church Year Events	Themes	Catechism References
Confirmation	■ Celebration of Confirmation in the parish ■ Celebration of Initiation at the Easter Vigil ■ Pentecost	• Rite of Confirmation: symbols, gestures, prayers, Scripture readings • Holy Spirit • Gifts of the Holy Spirit • Conformity to Christ • Bearing witness to Christ • Gifts and charisms • Mission of Jesus: priest, prophet, and king • Mission and ministries of the Church • Mystery of the Church	Sacrament of Confirmation: #1285-1321 Gifts and charisms: #787-95, #799-801, #1830-32 Holy Spirit: #243-46, #683-747, #1987-95, #2670-72 Mission of Jesus: #430, #436, #438, #534, #536, #606, #608 Mission of Church: #781-86, #949-53, #849-65 Ministries of the Church: #949-53 Mystery of the Church: #748-870, #949-53 Witness: #897-913
Eucharist	■ Sunday Eucharist ■ Holy Thursday ■ Easter Season (Sunday with the Emmaus story or other Eucharistic themes) ■ Corpus Christi ■ Celebrations of First Eucharist	• Four Movements of the Mass • Liturgy of the Word and the lectionary • Liturgy of the Eucharist (sacrifice, meal, real presence of Christ) • Symbols: bread and wine • Paschal mystery • Body of Christ • Sabbath / Lord's Day	Sacrament of Eucharist: #1322-1405 Bread and wine: #1329, #1333-36, #1375-76, #1406, #1413 Paschal mystery: #571-73, #599-618, #638-58 Sacrifice, meal, real presence: #1356-1381 Sabbath / Lord's Day: #2168-2188 (The Third Commandment)
Reconciliation	■ Advent ■ Lent ■ Celebration of the Sacrament of Reconciliation (Advent, Lent) ■ Celebrations of First Reconciliation ■ Sunday with Prodigal Son story	• Rite of Penance: ritual, symbols, gestures, Scripture readings • Forgiveness • Repentance • Reconciliation • Sin • Conscience • Moral Life • Ten Commandments • Conversion	Sacrament of Reconciliation: #1422-1484 Conversion: #541-46, #1427-33, #1886-89, #1896, #2581-84, #2608-09 Moral life: #1699-1729, #1776-89, #1830-45, #1965-1964 Sin and repentance: #386-87, #1427-60, #1846-76
Anointing of the Sick	■ Lent ■ Celebration of Anointing the Sick as a parish community ■ Sundays with lectionary readings on healing	• Rite of Anointing of the Sick: ritual, symbols, gestures, Scripture readings • Healing • Suffering and the cross	Sacrament of the Anointing of the Sick: #1499-1525

Scope of Church Year Events and Themes

Marriage

- Celebration of the Sacrament of Matrimony
- World Marriage Day
- Holy Family Sunday
- Lectionary: Wedding Feast at Cana

• Rite of Marriage: ritual, symbols, gestures, Scripture readings
• Vocation
• Family as domestic Church
• Service

Sacrament of Marriage: #1601-1658
Love of Husband and Wife: #2360-2379
Family: #2201-2233

Holy Orders

- Celebration of Ordination or Anniversary of Ordination
- World Day of Prayer for Vocations (4th Sunday of Easter)
- Lectionary: Call of the Disciples
- Sundays with lectionary readings on service

• Rite of Ordination: ritual, symbols, gestures, Scripture readings
• Mission of Jesus: priest, prophet, and king
• Mission and ministries of the Church
• Service

Sacrament of Holy Orders: #1536-1589
Mission of Jesus: #430, #436, #438, #534, #536, #606, #608
Mission of Church: #781-86, #949-53, #849-65
Ministries of the Church: #949-53

Rite of Funerals

- Celebration of the Rite of Funerals
- All Souls Day
- Sundays with lectionary readings on dying and rising (Raising of Lazarus)

• Rite: ritual, symbols, gestures, Scripture readings
• Baptism
• Paschal mystery
• Eternal life

Christian Funerals: #1680-1690
Communion of Saints: #946-48, #956-57, #2683
Resurrection of the body: #988-1014
Life everlasting: #1020-1050

MORALITY

Moral Teachings

Love of God, neighbor and self
(Commandments 1-4)

Respect for human dignity
(Commandment 5)

Event Suggestions

- Great Commandment (30th Sunday in OT, Year A)
- Sermon on the Mount (4th-9th Sundays in OT, Year A)
- Sermon on the Plain (6th-8th Sundays of OT, Year C)
- Parable of the Good Samaritan
- Sacrament of Reconciliation

- Christ the King—Year A
- Sunday lectionary readings
- Saints feast days: saints that exemplify respect for human dignity
- See also justice events and themes

Catechism of the Catholic Church

The Law of the Gospel: #1965-1974, #2052-2055
Beatitudes: #1716-24
The Law of the Gospel: #1965-1974
Ten Commandments: Part Three, Chapter 1, Articles 1-3; and Chapter 2, Articles 4-10

#2052-2074
Ten Commandments: Part Three, Chapter 1, Articles 1-3; and Chapter 2, Articles 4-10
#1929-1938

Scope of Church Year Events and Themes

Theme	Church Year Events	Catechism References
Justice (Commandments 7, 10)	■ Sermon on the Plain (6th-8th Sundays of OT, Year C) ■ Parable of the Rich Man and Lazarus ■ See Justice events and themes.	Ten Commandments: Part Three, Chapter 1, Articles 1-3; and Chapter 2, Articles 4-10 #1807, #1905-12, #1928-48, #2407-63
Faithfulness (Commandments 6, 9)	■ Sacrament of Marriage ■ World Marriage Day ■ Wedding Feast at Cana ■ Sunday lectionary readings	Ten Commandments: Part Three, Chapter 1, Articles 1-3; and Chapter 2, Articles 4-10
Honesty and Integrity (Commandments 8 and 10)	■ Sunday lectionary readings ■ Saints feast days: saints that exemplify moral values ■ Justice and service events and projects	Ten Commandments: Part Three, Chapter 1, Articles 1-3; and Chapter 2, Articles 4-10
Care, Compassion, Forgiveness	■ Lectionary readings of Jesus' actions ■ Gospel stories such as prodigal son and woman caught in adultery ■ Saints feast days: saints that exemplify care and compassion ■ Sacrament of Reconciliation	Sacrament of Reconciliation: #1422-1484
Conscience	■ Lenten season ■ Sunday Lectionary readings such as the Sermon on the Mount, Sermon on the Plain, the teachings of Jesus, story of Zacchaeus ■ Sacrament of Reconciliation	Sources of morality: #1749-56 Moral conscience: #1776-1794 Sacrament of Reconciliation: #1422-1484 #1830-45 #1965-1964
Sin and Repentance	■ Advent and Lent seasons ■ Sacrament of Reconciliation ■ Sunday Lectionary readings with stories such as the woman caught in adultery, prodigal son, Zacchaeus, and woman at the well	Repentance: #1430-60 Sin: #1846-76

JUSTICE, PEACE, AND CATHOLIC SOCIAL TEACHINGS

Catholic Social Teachings	Event Suggestions	Catechism of the Catholic Church
Peace	■ World Day of Peace (January 1) ■ Martin Luther King Jr. (January) ■ Saints feast days who worked for peace ■ National and international peace projects	#2302-2317
Life and Dignity of the Human Person	■ Respect Life Sunday (October) ■ Saints feast days ■ Justice, advocacy, and service projects ■ Sunday lectionary readings	#1929-1938 #2259-2283
Call to Family, Community, and Participation	■ Holy Family Sunday ■ Local, state, and national elections ■ Justice, advocacy, and service projects	Family: #2201-2233 Citizens: #2238-2243
Dignity of Work and Rights of Workers	■ Labor Day ■ Feast of St. Joseph the Worker	
Solidarity	■ Lent ■ Pentecost ■ Mission Sunday (USSCB) ■ Sponsoring a development project (e.g. Catholic Relief Services)	#1939-1942
Human Rights and Responsibilities and Option for the Poor and Vulnerable	■ Advent ■ Lent (practice of almsgiving) ■ Thanksgiving (feeding the hungry) ■ Las Posadas (hospitality, shelter, housing) ■ Poverty Awareness Month (Catholic Campaign for Human Development, January) ■ Operation Rice Bowl (CRS, Lent) ■ World Hunger Day (October) ■ Mission Sunday (USSCB) ■ Migrant Refugee Week (USSCB) ■ Sunday lectionary readings	Common Good: #1905-1912 Responsibility: #1913-1917 Option for the Poor: #2443-2449
Care for God's Creation	■ Earth Day ■ Feast of St. Francis of Assisi	#295, #299, #2415-2418

Scope of Church Year Events and Themes

PRAYER AND SPIRITUALITY

Prayer Themes and Forms

Forms of prayer (blessing and adoration, petition, intercession, thanksgiving, praise)

Expressions of prayer (vocal, meditation, and contemplation)

Lectio Divina, Liturgy of the Hours

The Rosary

The Lord's Prayer

Catholic prayers and devotions

Event Suggestions

- Sunday Mass
- Lent—practice of prayer
- Holy Thursday
- Good Friday
- World Day of Prayer
- Praying with the saints: Feast of All Saints and saint feast days
- Praying in Advent and Christmas, Lent, Holy Week, and Easter seasons
- Praying with Scripture—the lectionary

- Sunday Mass
- 17th Sunday in OT (Year C)

- Marian feasts
- Praying the rosary through the year: joyful (Christmas), sorrowful (Holy Week), glorious (Easter),luminous (Ordinary Time)

- Sign of the cross
- Stations of the Cross
- Eucharistic adoration
- Devotion to the saints

Catechism of the Catholic Church

Part Four: Christian Prayer
Section 1: Prayer in the Christian Life
Section 2: The Lord's Prayer

Calendar of Saints' Days and Church Feasts
(General Roman Calendar)

Use this calendar to identify saints' days to include in your curriculum.

JANUARY
1	Solemnity of Mary, Mother of God
	Octave of Christmas
2	Basil the Great and
	Gregory Nazianzen
4	Elizabeth Ann Seton
5	John Neumann
6	Andre Bessette
7	Raymond of Penafort
13	Hilary of Poitiers
17	Anthony of Egypt
20	Fabian
	Sebastian
21	Agnes
22	Vincent
24	Francis de Sales
25	Conversion of Paul
26	Timothy and Titus
27	Angela Merici
28	Thomas Aquinas
31	John Bosco

FEBRUARY
2	Presentation of the Lord
3	Blase
	Ansgar
5	Agatha
6	Paul Miki and His Companions
8	Jerome Emiliani
10	Scholastica
11	Our Lady of Lourdes
14	Cyril and Methodius
17	Seven Founders of the
	Order of Servites
21	Peter Damian
22	Chair of Peter
23	Polycarp

MARCH
3	Katharine Drexel
4	Casimir
7	Perpetua and Felicity
8	John of God
9	Frances of Rome
17	Patrick
18	Cyril of Jerusalem
19	Joseph, Husband of Mary
23	Turibius de Mogrovejo
25	Annunciation of the Lord

APRIL
2	Francis of Paola
4	Isidore of Seville
5	Vincent Ferrer
7	John Baptist de la Salle
8	Julie Billiart
11	Stanislaus
13	Martin I
21	Anselm
23	George
24	Fidelis of Sigmaringen
25	Mark
28	Peter Chanel
29	Catherine of Siena
30	Pius V

MAY
1	Joseph the Worker
2	Athanasius
3	Philip and James
10	Damien
12	Nereus and Achilleus
	Pancras
14	Matthias
15	Isidore the Farmer
18	John I
20	Bernardine of Siena

Calendar of Saints' Days and Church Feasts

25 Bede the Venerable
   Gregory VII
   Mary Magdalene de Pazzi
26 Philip Neri
27 Augustine of Canterbury
30 Joan of Arc
31 Visitation of the Blessed
   Virgin Mary

JUNE

1 Justin
2 Marcellinus and Peter
3 Charles Lwanga and
   His Companions
5 Boniface
6 Norbert
9 Ephrem
11 Barnabas
13 Anthony of Padua
19 Romuald *← 14 Precious Body & Sacred Heart Blood*
21 Aloysius Gonzaga
22 Paulinus of Nola
   John Fisher and Thomas More
24 Birth of John the Baptist
27 Cyril of Alexandria
28 Irenaeus
29 Peter and Paul
30 First Martyrs of the
   Church of Rome

JULY

1 Junipero Serra
3 Thomas
4 Elizabeth of Portugal
5 Anthony Zaccaria
6 Maria Goretti
11 Benedict
13 Henry II
14 Kateri Tekakwitha
   Camillus of Lellis
15 Bonaventure
16 Our Lady of Mount Carmel
21 Lawrence of Brindisi

22 Mary Magdalene
23 Bridget of Sweden
25 James
26 Joachim and Ann
29 Martha
30 Peter Chrysologus
31 Ignatius of Loyola

AUGUST

1 Alphonsus Liguori
2 Eusebius of Vercelli
   Peter Julian Eymard
4 John Vianney
5 Dedication of St. Mary Major
6 Transfiguration
7 Sixtus II and his Companions
   Cajetan
8 Dominic
10 Lawrence
11 Clare of Assisi
13 Pontian and Hippolytus
14 Maximilian Maria Kolbe
15 Assumption of Mary
16 Stephen of Hungary
19 John Eudes
20 Bernard of Clairvaux
21 Pius X
22 Queenship of Mary
23 Rose of Lima
24 Bartholomew
25 Louis IX of France
   Joseph Calasanz
27 Monica
28 Augustine
29 Martyrdom of John the Baptist

SEPTEMBER

3 Gregory the Great
8 Birth of Mary
9 Peter Claver
13 John Chrysostom
14 Triumph of the Cross
15 Our Lady of Sorrows

Calendar of Saints' Days and Church FeastsS

16 Cornelius and Cyprian
17 Robert Bellarmine
19 Januarius
20 Andrew Kim Taegon, Paul Chong
   Hasang, and their Companions
21 Matthew
26 Cosmas and Damian
27 Vincent de Paul
28 Wenceslaus
   Lawrence Ruiz and His Companions
29 Michael, Gabriel, and Raphael,
   archangels
30 Jerome

OCTOBER
1 Thérèse of the Child Jesus
2 Guardian Angels
4 Francis of Assisi
6 Bruno
   Marie-Rose Durocher
7 Our Lady of the Rosary
9 Denis
   John Leonardi
14 Callistus I
15 Teresa of Avila
16 Hedwig
   Margaret Mary Alacoque
17 Ignatius of Antioch
18 Luke
19 Isaac Jogues, John de Brebeuf,
   and their Companions
   Paul of the Cross
23 John of Capistrano
24 Anthony Claret
28 Simon and Jude

NOVEMBER
1 All Saints
2 All Souls
3 Martin de Porres
4 Charles Borromeo

9 Dedication of Saint John Lateran
10 Leo the Great
11 Martin of Tours
12 Josaphat
13 Frances X. Cabrini
15 Albert the Great
16 Margaret of Scotland
   Gertrude
17 Elizabeth of Hungary
18 Dedication of the Churches
   of Peter and Paul
   Rose Philippine Duchesne
21 Presentation of Mary
22 Cecilia
23 Clement I
   Columban
   Miguel Agustin Pro
24 Andrew Dung-Lac and his
   Companions
30 Andrew

DECEMBER
3 Francis Xavier
4 John Damascene
6 Nicholas
7 Ambrose
8 Immaculate Conception
9 Juan Diego
11 Damasus I
12 Our Lady of Guadalupe
   Jane Frances de Chantal
13 Lucy
14 John of the Cross
21 Peter Canisius
23 John of Kanty
25 Christmas
26 Stephen
27 John the Evangelist
28 Holy Innocents
29 Thomas Becket
31 Sylvester I

Holy Family
Sun p Christma

Sunday Lectionary Readings for the Year

Use this guide to find lectionary readings for Sundays and feast days to include in your curriculum.

Year A	Year B	Year C
FIRST SUNDAY OF ADVENT		
Isaiah 2:1-5	Isaiah 63:16-17,19; & 64:2-7	Jeremiah 33:14-16
Romans 13:11-14a	1 Corinthians 1:3-9	1 Thessalonians 3:12—4:2
Matthew 24:37-44	Mark 13:33-37	Luke 21:25-28, 34-36
SECOND SUNDAY OF ADVENT		
Isaiah 11:1-10	Isaiah 40:1-5, 9-11	Baruch 5:1-9
Romans 15:4-9	2 Peter 3:8-14	Philippians 1:4-6, 8-11
Matthew 3:1-12	Mark 1:1-8	Luke 3:1-6
THIRD SUNDAY OF ADVENT		
Isaiah 35:1-6, 10	Isaiah 61:1-2, 10-11	Zephaniah 3:14-18
James 5:7-10	1 Thessalonians 5:16-24	Philippians 4:4-7
Matthew 11:2-11	John 1:6-8, 19-28	Luke 3:10-18
FOURTH SUNDAY OF ADVENT		
Isaiah 7:10-14	2 Samuel 7:1-5, 8-11, 16	Micah 5:1-4
Romans 1:1-7	Romans 16:25-27	Hebrews 10:5-10
Matthew 1:18-24	Luke 1:26-38	Luke 1:39-45
CHRISTMAS VIGIL MASS		
Isaiah 62:1-5	Acts 13:16-17, 22-25	Matthew 1:1-25
CHRISTMAS MIDNIGHT MASS		
Isaiah 9:1-7	Acts 13:16-17, 22-25	Luke 2:1-14
CHRISTMAS DAY		
Isaiah 52:7-10	Hebrews 1:1-6	John 1:1-18
HOLY FAMILY		
Sirach 3:2-6, 12-14	Genesis 15:1-6; 21:1-3	1 Samuel 1:20-22, 24-28
Colossians 3:12-21	Hebrews 11:8, 11-12, 17-19	1 John 3:1-2, 21-24
Matthew 2:13-15, 19-23	Luke 2:22-40 (22, 39-40)	Luke 2:41-52
JANUARY 1: MARY, MOTHER OF GOD: Numbers 6:22-27	Galatians 4:4-7	Luke 2:16-21
SECOND SUNDAY AFTER CHRISTMAS: Sirach 24:1-2, 8-12	Ephesians 1:3-6, 15-18	John 1:1-18 (1-5, 9-14)
EPIPHANY		
Isaiah 60:1-6	Ephesians 3:2-3a, 5-6	Matthew 2:1-12
BAPTISM OF THE LORD		
Isaiah 42:1-4, 6-7	Isaiah 55: 1-11	Isaiah 40: 1-5, 9-11
Acts 10:34-38	1 John 5:1-9	Titus 2:11-14; 3:4-7
Matthew 3:13-17	Mark 1:7-11	Luke 3:15-16, 21-22

Sunday Lectionary Readings for the Year

ASH WEDNESDAY

Joel 2:12-18	2 Corinthians 5:20—6:2	Matthew 6:1-6, 16-18

FIRST SUNDAY OF LENT

Genesis 2:7-9, 3:1-7	Genesis 9:8-15	Deuteronomy 26:4-10
Romans 5:12-19	1Peter 3:18-22	Romans 10:8-13
Matthew 4:1-11	Mark 1:12-15	Luke 4:1-13

SECOND SUNDAY OF LENT

Genesis 12:1-4	Genesis 22:1-2, 9:10-13, 15-18	Genesis 15:5-12, 17-18
2 Timothy 1:8-10	Romans 8:31-34	Philippians 3:14—4:1
Matthew 17:1-19	Mark 9:2-10	Luke 9:28-36

THIRD SUNDAY OF LENT

Exodus 17:3-7	Exodus 20:1-17	Exodus 3:1-8, 13-15
Romans 5:1-2, 5-8	1 Corinthians 1:22-25	1 Corinthians 10:1-6,10-12
John 4:5-42	John 2:13-25	Luke 13:1-9

FOURTH SUNDAY OF LENT

1Samuel 16:1, 6-7, 10-13	2 Chronicles 36:14-17,19-23	Joshua 5:9, 10-12
Ephesians 5:8-14	Ephesians 2:4-10	2 Corinthians 5:17-21
John 9:1-41	John 3:14-21	Luke 15:1-3. 11-32

FIFTH SUNDAY OF LENT

Ezekiel 37:12-14	Jeremiah 31:31-34	Isaiah 43:16-21
Romans 8:8-11	Hebrews 5:7-9	Philippians 3:8-14
John 11:1-45	John 12:20-33	John 8:1-11

PASSION SUNDAY (PALM SUNDAY): *Processional*

Processional	*Processional*	*Processional*
Matthew 21:1-11	Mark 11:1-10	Luke 19:28-40
Mass	*Mass*	*Mass*
Isaiah 50:4-7	Isaiah 50:4-7	Isaiah 50:4-7
Philippians 2:6-11	Philippians 2:6-11	Philippians 2:6-11
Matthew 26:14—27:66	Mark 14:1—15:47	Luke 22:14—23:56

HOLY THURSDAY

Exodus 12:1-8, 11-14	1 Corinthians 11:23-26	John 13:1-15

GOOD FRIDAY

Isaiah 52:12-53	Hebrews 4:14-16; 5:7-9	John 18:1—19:42

EASTER VIGIL

Genesis 1:1-2 and 2	Genesis 1:1-2 and 2	Genesis 1:1-2 and 2
Genesis 22:1-18	Genesis 22:1-18	Genesis 22:1-18
Exodus 14:15—15:1	Exodus 14:15—15:1	Exodus 14:15—15:1
Isaiah 54:5-14	Isaiah 54:5-14	Isaiah 54:5-14
Isaiah 55:1-11	Isaiah 55:1-11	Isaiah 55:1-11

Sunday Lectionary Readings for the Year

Baruch 3:9-15, 3:32—4:4	Baruch 3:9-15, 3:32—4:4	Baruch 3:9-15, 3:32—4:4
Ezekiel 36:16-28	Ezekiel 36:16-28	Ezekiel 36:16-28
Romans 6:3-11	Romans 6:3-11	Romans 6:3-11
Matthew 28:1-10	Mark 16:1-8	Luke 25:1-12

EASTER SUNDAY
Acts 10:34, 37-43

Colossians 3:1-4 or
1 Corinthians 5:6-8

John 20:1-9

SECOND SUNDAY OF EASTER

Acts 2:42-47	Acts 4:32-35	Acts 5:12-16
1 Peter 1:3-9	1 John 5:1-6	Revelation 1:9-11,12-13,17-19
John 20:19-31	John 20:19-31	John 20:19-31

THIRD SUNDAY OF EASTER

Acts 2:14a, 36-41	Acts 3:13-15, 17-19	Acts 5:27b-32, 40b-41
1 Peter 1:17-21	1 John 2:1-5a	Revelation 5:11-14
Luke 24:13-35	Luke 24:35-48	John 21:1-19 (21:1-14)

FOURTH SUNDAY OF EASTER

Acts 2:14a, 36-41	Acts 4:8-12	Acts 13:14, 43-52
1 Peter 2:20b-25	1 John 3:1-2	Revelation 7:9, 14b-17
John 10:1-10	John 10:11-18	John 10:27-30

FIFTH SUNDAY OF EASTER

Acts 6:1-7	Acts 9:26-31	Acts 14:21b-27
1 Peter 2:4-9	1 John 3:18-24	Revelation 21:1-5a
John 14:1-12	John 15:1-18	John 13:31-33a, 34-35

SIXTH SUNDAY OF EASTER

Acts 8:5-8, 14-17	Acts 10:25-26, 34-35, 44-48	Acts 15:1-2, 22-29
1 Peter 3:15-18	1 John 4:7-10	Revelation 21:10-14, 22-23
John 14:15-21	John 15:9-17	John 14:23-29

ASCENSION THURSDAY

Acts 1:1-11	Acts 1:1-11	Acts 1:1-11
Ephesians 1:17-23	Ephesians 4:1-13 (4:1-7,11-13)	Hebrews 9:24-28; 10:19-23
Matthew 28:16-20	Mark 16:15-20	Luke 24:46-53

SEVENTH SUNDAY OF EASTER

Acts 1:12-14	Acts 1:15-17, 20a, 20c-16	Acts 7:55-60
1 Peter 4:13-16	1 John 4:11-16	Revelation 22:12-14, 16-17, 20
John 17:1-11a	John 17:11b-19	John 17:20-26

PENTECOST SUNDAY

Acts 2:1-11	Acts 2:1-11	Acts 2:1-11
1 Corinthians 12:3b-7, 12-13	Galatians 5:16-25	Romans 8:8-17
John 20:19-23	John 15:26-27; 16:12-15	John 14:15-16, 23b-26

Sunday Lectionary Readings for the Year

TRINITY SUNDAY

Exodus 34:4b-6, 8-9	Deuteronomy 4:32-34, 39-40	Proverbs 8:22-31
2 Corinthians 13:11-13	Romans 8:14-17	Romans 5:1-5
John 3:16-18	Matthew 28:16-20	John 16:12-15

BODY AND BLOOD OF CHRIST

Deuteronomy 8:2-3, 14b-16a	Exodus 24:3-8	Genesis 14:18-20
1 Corinthians 10:16-17	Hebrews 9:11-15	1 Corinthians 11:23-26
John 6:51-58	Mark 14:12-16	Luke 9:11b-17

SECOND SUNDAY IN ORDINARY TIME

Isaiah 49:3, 5-6	1 Samuel 3:3b-10, 19	Isaiah 62:1-5
1 Corinthians 1:1-3	1 Corinthians 6:13-15, 17-20	1 Corinthians 12:4-11
John 1:29-34	John 1:35-41	John 2:1-11

THIRD SUNDAY IN ORDINARY TIME

Isaiah 8:23b—9:3	Jonah 3:1-5, 10	Nehemiah 8:2-4a, 5-6, 8-10
1 Corinthians 1:10-13, 17	1 Corinthians 7:29-31	1 Corinthians 12:12-30
Matthew 4:12-23 (4:12-17)	Mark 1:14-20	Luke 1:1-4; 4:14-21

FOURTH SUNDAY IN ORDINARY TIME

Zephaniah 2:3, 3:12-13	Deuteronomy 18:15-20	Jeremiah 1:4-5, 17-19
1 Corinthians 1:26-31	1 Corinthians 7:32-35	1 Corinthians 12:31—13:13
Matthew 5:1-12a	Mark 1:21-28	Luke 4:21-30

FIFTH SUNDAY IN ORDINARY TIME

Isaiah 58:7-10	Job 7:1-4, 6-7	Isaiah 6:1-2a, 3-8
1 Corinthians 2:1-5	1 Corinthians 9:16-19, 22-23	1 Corinthians 15:1-11
Matthew 5:13-16	Mark 1:29-39	Luke 5:1-11

SIXTH SUNDAY IN ORDINARY TIME

Sirach 15:15-20	Leviticus 13:1-2, 44-46	Jeremiah 17:5-8
1 Corinthians 2:6-10	1 Corinthians 10:31—11:1	1 Corinthians 15:12, 16-20
Matthew 5:17-37	Mark 1:40-45	Luke 6:17, 20-26

SEVENTH SUNDAY IN ORDINARY TIME

Leviticus 19:1-2, 17-18	Isaiah 43:18-19, 21-22, 24b-25	1 Samuel 26:2,7-9,12-13,22-23
1 Corinthians 3:16-23	2 Corinthians 1:18-22	1 Corinthians 15:45-49
Matthew 5:38-48	Mark 2:1-12	Luke 6:27-38

EIGHTH SUNDAY IN ORDINARY TIME

Isaiah 49:14-15	Hosea 2:16b, 17b, 21-22	Sirach 27:4-7
1 Corinthians 4:1-5	2 Corinthians 3:1b-6	1 Corinthians 15:54-58
Matthew 6:24-34	Mark 2:18-22	Luke 6:39-45

NINTH SUNDAY IN ORDINARY TIME

Deuteronomy 11:18, 26-28, 32	Deuteronomy 5:12-15	1 Kings 8:41-43
Romans 3:21-25a, 28	2 Corinthians 4:6-11	Galatians 1:1-2, 6-10
Matthew 7:21-27	Mark 2:23—3:6	Luke 7:1-10

Sunday Lectionary Readings for the Year

TENTH SUNDAY IN ORDINARY TIME

Hosea 6:3-6	Genesis 3:9-15	1 Kings 17:17-24
Romans 4:18-25	2 Corinthians 4:13—5:1	Galatians 1:11-19
Matthew 9:9-13	Mark 3:20-35	Luke 7:11-17

ELEVENTH SUNDAY IN ORDINARY TIME

Exodus 19:2-6a	Ezekiel 17:22-24	2 Samuel 12:7-10
Romans 5:6-11	2 Corinthians 5:6-10	Galatians 2:16, 19-21
Matthew 9:36—10:8	Mark 4:26-34	Luke 7:36—8:3 (7:36-50)

TWELFTH SUNDAY IN ORDINARY TIME

Jeremiah 20:10-13	Job 38:1, 8-11	Zechariah 12:10-11; 13:1
Romans 5:12-15	2 Corinthians 5:14-17	Galatians 5:1, 13-18
Matthew 10:37-42	Mark 5:21-43 (5:21-24, 35b-43)	Luke 9:51-62

THIRTEENTH SUNDAY IN ORDINARY TIME

2 Kings 4:8-11, 14-16a	Wisdom 1:13-15; 2:23-24	1 Kings 19:16b, 19-21
Romans 6:3-4, 8-11	2 Corinthians 8:7, 9, 13-15	Galatians 5:1, 13-18
Matthew 10:37-42	Mark 5:21-43 (5:21-24, 35b-43)	Luke 9:51-62

FOURTEENTH SUNDAY IN ORDINARY TIME

Zechariah 9:9-10	Ezekiel 2:2-5	Isaiah 66:10-14c
Romans 8:9, 11-13	2 Corinthians 12:7-10	Galatians 6:14-18
Matthew 11:25-30	Mark 6:1-6	Luke 10:1-12, 17-20 (10:1-9)

FIFTEENTH SUNDAY IN ORDINARY TIME

Isaiah 55:10-11	Amos 7:12-15	Deuteronomy 30:10-14
Romans 8:18-23	Ephesians 1:3-14 (1:3-10)	Colossians 1:15-20
Matthew 13:1-23 (13:1-9)	Mark 6:7-13	Luke 10:25-37

SIXTEENTH SUNDAY IN ORDINARY TIME

Wisdom 12:13, 16-19	Jeremiah 23:1-6	Genesis 18:1-10a
Romans 8:26-27	Ephesians 2:13-18	Colossians 1:24-28
Matthew 13:24-43 (13:24-30)	Mark 6:30-34	Luke 10:38-42

SEVENTEENTH SUNDAY IN ORDINARY TIME

1 Kings 3:5, 7-12	2 Kings 4:42-44	Genesis 18:20-32
Romans 8:28-30	Ephesians 4:1-6	Colossians 2:12-14
Matthew 13:44-52 (13:44-46)	John 6:1-15	Luke 11:1-13

EIGHTEENTH SUNDAY IN ORDINARY TIME

Isaiah 55:1-3	Exodus 16:2-4, 12-15	Ecclesiastes 1:2; 2:21-23
Romans 8:35, 37-39	Ephesians 4:17, 20-24	Colossians 3:1-5, 9-11
Matthew 14:13-21	John 6:24-35	Luke 12:13-21

NINETEENTH SUNDAY IN ORDINARY TIME

1 Kings 19:9a, 11-13a	1 Kings 19:4-8	Wisdom 18:6-9
Romans 9:1-5	Ephesians 4:30—5:2	Hebrews 11:1-2, 8-19
Matthew 14:22-23	John 6:41-51	Luke 12:32-48 (12:35-40)

Sunday Lectionary Readings for the Year

TWENTIETH SUNDAY IN ORDINARY TIME

Isaiah 56:1, 6-7	Proverbs 9:1-6	Jeremiah 38:4-6, 8-10
Romans 11:13-15, 29-32	Ephesians 5:15-20	Hebrews 12:1-4
Matthew 15:21-28	John 6:51-58	Luke 12:49-53

TWENTY-FIRST SUNDAY IN ORDINARY TIME

Isaiah 22:19-23	Joshua 24:1-2a, 15-17, 18b	Isaiah 66:18-21
Romans 11:33-36	Ephesians 5:21-32	Hebrews 12:5-7, 11-13
Matthew 16:13-20	John 6:60-69	Luke 13:22-30

TWENTY-SECOND SUNDAY IN ORDINARY TIME

Jeremiah 20:7-9	Deuteronomy 4:1-2, 6-8	Sirach 3:17-18, 20, 28-29
Romans 12:1-2	James 1:17-18, 21b-22, 27	Hebrews 12:18-19, 22-24a
Matthew 16:21-35	Mark 7:1-8, 14-15, 21-23	Luke 14:1-32 (15:1-10)

TWENTY-THIRD SUNDAY IN ORDINARY TIME

Ezekiel 33:7-9	Isaiah 35:4-7a	Wisdom 9:13-19
Romans 13:8-10	James 2:1-5	Philemon 9b-10, 12-17
Matthew 18:15-20	Mark 7:31-37	Luke 14:25-33

TWENTY-FOURTH SUNDAY IN ORDINARY TIME

Sirach 27:33—28:9	Isaiah 50:5-9a	Exodus 32:7-11, 13-14
Romans 14:7-9	James 2:14-18	1 Timothy 1:12-17
Matthew 18:21-35	Mark 8:27-35	Luke 15:1-32 (15:1-10)

TWENTY-FIFTH SUNDAY IN ORDINARY TIME

Isaiah 55:6-9	Wisdom 2:12, 17-20	Amos 8:4-7
Philippians 1:20c-24, 27a	James 3:15—4:3	1 Timothy 2:1-8
Matthew 20:1-16a	Mark 9:30-37	Luke 16:1-13 (16:10-13)

TWENTY-SIXTH SUNDAY IN ORDINARY TIME

Ezekiel 18:25-28	Numbers 11:25-29	Amos 6:1a, 4-7
Philippians 2:1-11 (2:1-5)	James 5:1-6	1 Timothy 6:11-16
Matthew 21:28-32	Mark 9:38-43, 45, 47-48	Luke 16:19-31

TWENTY-SEVENTH SUNDAY IN ORDINARY TIME

Isaiah 5:1-7	Genesis 2:18-24	Habakkuk 1:2-3; 2:2-4
Philippians 4:6-9	Hebrews 2:9-11	2 Timothy 1:6-8, 13-14
Matthew 21:33-43	Mark 10:2-16 (10:2-12)	Luke 17:5-10

TWENTY-EIGHTH SUNDAY IN ORDINARY TIME

Isaiah 25:6-10a	Wisdom 7:7-11	2 Kings 5:14-17
Philippians 4:12-14, 19-20	Hebrews 4:12-13	2 Timothy 2:8-13
Matthew 22:1-14 (22:1-10)	Mark 10:17-30 (10:17-27)	Luke 17:11-19

TWENTY-NINTH SUNDAY IN ORDINARY TIME

Isaiah 45:1, 4-6	Isaiah 53:10-11	Exodus 17:8-13
1 Thessalonians 1:1-5b	Hebrews 4:14-16	2 Timothy 3:14—4:2
Matthew 22:15-21	Mark 1-:35-45 (10:42-45)	Luke 18:1-8

Sunday Lectionary Readings for the Year

THIRTIETH SUNDAY IN ORDINARY TIME

Exodus 22:20-26	Jeremiah 31:7-9	Sirach 35:12-14, 16-18
1 Thessalonians 1:5c-10	Hebrews 5:1-6	2 Timothy 4:6-8, 16-18
Matthew 22:34-40	Mark 10:46-52	Luke 18:9-14

THIRTY-FIRST SUNDAY IN ORDINARY TIME

Malachi 1:14b—2:2b, 8-10	Deuteronomy 6:2-6	Wisdom 11:22—12:2
1 Thessalonians 2:7b-9, 13	Hebrews 7:23-28	2 Thessalonians 1:11—2:2
Matthew 23:1-12	Mark 12:28b-34	Luke 19:1-10

THIRTY-SECOND SUNDAY IN ORDINARY TIME

Wisdom 6:12-16	1 Kings 17:10-16	2 Maccabees 7:1-2, 9-14
1 Thessalonians 4:13-18	Hebrews 9:24-28	2 Thessalonians 2:16—3:5
Matthew 25:1-13	Mark 12:38-44 (12:41-44)	Luke 20:27-38 (20:27, 34-38)

THIRTY-THIRD SUNDAY IN ORDINARY TIME

Proverbs 21:10-13, 19-20, 30-31	Daniel 12:1-3	Malachi 3:19-20a
1 Thessalonians 5:1-6	Hebrews 10:11-14, 18	2 Thessalonians 3:7-12
Matthew 25:14-30	Mark 13:24-32	Luke 21:5-19

FEAST OF CHRIST THE KING

Ezekiel 34:11-12, 15-17	Daniel 7:13-14	2 Samuel 5:1-3
1 Corinthians 15:20-26, 28	Revelation 1:5-8	Colossians 1:12-20
Matthew 25:31-46	John 18:33b-37	Luke 23:35-43

CHAPTER 3

Implementing a Lifelong Intergenerational Curriculum

▶ **Implementation Task 1: Scheduling**

▶ **Implementation Task 2: Budget and Fees**

▶ **Implementation Task 3: Promotion and Registration**

There are four major tasks in implementing a lifelong intergenerational curriculum: scheduling, budgeting, promotion, and developing leadership. The process and tools for leadership development include inviting people into leadership, preparing and training leaders, and supporting them, and we will cover this material in Chapter 4.

Two calendars need to be created for implementing your program: an external calendar for promotion that includes the dates, days, and times of the events and preparation programs, and an internal calendar that includes dates for planning meetings and leadership training sessions. Use the *Implementing a Lifelong Curriculum* worksheet on page 95 to record your decisions for this task.

▶ Implementation Task 1: Scheduling

Step 1. Identify the number of times and the days of the week on which you will offer your preparation program.

How do you determine the number of times you will offer a preparation program for an event? The two questions below are designed to help you answer this. They are focused on the intergenerational learning model and can be adapted for a family-centered plus age-group learning model. If you are organizing preparation programs in age groups, you will probably use your existing age-group catechetical program times and add new programs for people who are not currently reached (e.g., adults).

• How many preparation programs will you offer for each event?
• When will you offer the preparation programs, and at what times?

These questions will be answered within the processes that follow.

1. Determine the timeframe for your program(s).

Intergenerational learning is most effective within a 2 1/2 - to 3-hour period. Thirty minutes of this period are allotted for a meal. (The minimum amount of time needed for intergenerational learning without a meal is two hours.) The following is an overview of the timing for a 3-hour program. These times expand and contract based on the length of individual activities. (For a complete description of the intergenerational learning model, see Chapter 5.)

Design & Timing
Registration and hospitality
Meal *(30 minutes)*
Part 1: Gathering
Part 2: AllAges Opening Experience
(Parts 1 and 2 should take 30 minutes total)
Part 3: In-depth learning experience (90 minutes)
(Format options: activity centers, age groups, whole group)
Part 4: Whole Group Sharing Experience
Part 5: Reflection sharing and home application
Part 6: Closing prayer service
(Parts 4, 5, and 6 should take 30 minutes total)

If you are working within a 2 1/2-hour timeframe, reduce dinner by 5 minutes, Parts 1 and 2 by 5 minutes, Part 3 by 15 minutes, and Parts 4-6 by 5 minutes.

2. Survey your meeting space.

The parish facility (Church, hall, meeting rooms) is a major influence on the choices that you will make as you design and structure the intergenerational learning program. Before you make choices about where you will hold large group gatherings, where you will serve the meal, and which in-depth learning format you will use, survey your facility. Remember that a parallel learning format requires break-out space, activity centers require one or more larger meeting rooms, and the learning-group format requires a large meeting room for table groups.

Begin by making a facility inventory that considers the capacity of your meeting rooms. Consider the following meeting spaces:
- worship space
- large meeting spaces, e.g., parish hall, church basement, gathering space in the church
- medium-sized meeting rooms (twenty-five to fifty people), e.g., classrooms, conference rooms
- small-sized meeting rooms (under twenty-five people).

Next, determine what spaces you will need for intergenerational learning and how you will use your space. Sometimes you have to be very creative in the ways you use your space.
- Registration and hospitality: entrance to large meeting room, foyer, or gathering space
- Shared meal: large meeting room with tables and chairs
- Part 1. Gathering: large meeting room or worship space (Use the same space as All Ages Learning Experience so as to reduce movement.)
- Part 2. All Ages Learning Experience: large meeting room or worship space (Depending on the type of learning activity, you may need movable chairs or tables.)
- Part 3. In-depth learning experience: needs vary, as indicated below:
  — *activity center format:* large meeting room or separate meeting rooms for activity centers for families with children, adolescents, and adults
  — age *group format:* large meeting room for families with children; meeting rooms for preschool, young adolescents, older adolescents, young adults, and adults
  — *whole group format:* large meeting room with tables and chairs
- Part 4. Sharing Learning Reflections and Home Application: large meeting room or worship space
- Part 5. Closing Prayer Service: large meeting room or worship space.

3. Determine the number of program offerings based on your estimate of how many are expected to participate.

There is no precise way to determine how many people will participate in preparation programs, but you will need to develop an estimate so that you can decide how many preparation programs you will offer for each event. The following is a suggested approach to making a determination. Adjust the numbers to suit your parish.
- First, start with your largest meeting space. This will be the gathering space for the meal, large group gatherings (Parts 1–2 and 4–6), and the largest break-out group if you use parallel learning (Part 3). Determine how many people you can seat at tables. Many parishes with limited space use the church for the opening and closing large group gatherings (Parts 1–2 and 3–4) and provide a boxed meal rather than sit-down meal.

- Next, determine your potential numbers. You can begin with the total number of individuals currently involved in age-group programs and estimate participation by groups not served by age-group programs (young adults, adults, parents). Or you can begin with the total number of households in the parish.

Example 1: Uses current participation in faith formation programs.

- Total number of children and teens in faith formation programs from grade one through high school confirmation: 500
- Parents of participating children and teens: 700 (some families have more than one child participating)
- If 20% of the 1000 young adults and adults in the parish participated: 200
- Projected number: 1400

Example 2: Uses a parish of 1000 total households:

- Total number of households: 1000 (3000 people @ 3 people per household)
- Participating households: 500 (1500 people)
- If 50% of all active households participated: 250 households or 750 people
- Projected number: 750

Finally, compare your projected numbers with the capacity of your largest meeting space. If your facility can accommodate 250 people at tables and chairs, you will need to conduct six preparation programs to accommodate 1400 people (example 1) and three preparation programs to accommodate 750 people (example 2).

✓ How many preparation programs will you offer for each event?

4. Determine the days of the week for program offerings.

There is no best day of the week for preparation programs. Many parishes continue to use days and times that were established for age-group catechesis (e.g., Wednesday night). Other parishes offer preparation programs before or after the weekend Masses. This works well for an intergenerational audience, as they only need to come out once during the week for Mass and learning. The key is to offer a variety of days and times to attract different audiences. For example, if older adults prefer not go out at night (especially in climates with cold winters), will you offer a daytime option on Saturday or Sunday for them? Will you offer times conducive to young adult and adult participation, and not just to families? Here are some timing options:

Weekday evenings: Monday–Friday (e.g., 5:30–8:30 PM or 6:00–9:00 PM)

Saturday morning (e.g., 9:00 AM–Noon) or Saturday evening (after the Vigil Mass, e.g., 4:30 PM Mass, 5:30–8:30 PM)

Sunday morning (after Mass, e.g., 9:00 AM Mass, 10:00 AM–1:00 PM), Sunday afternoon, or Sunday evening

✓ When will you offer the preparation programs and at what times?

Step 2: Develop a calendar for the year with dates for preparation programs and events.

If you are working with a primary curriculum, develop a calendar with the dates of the events and the times and dates of the preparation programs. Be sure to add this information to the *Lifelong Curriculum Plan of Events* which you began in Chapter 2.

- Will you designate a set week or weeks for preparation programs (e.g., 2nd week of month), offer preparation on multiple weeks during the month, or adjust the preparation program dates based on the date of the event?

If you developed a blended curriculum, develop a calendar that blends the schedule of age-specific programming with the dates of the events and the times and dates of the preparation programs. Use the *Blended Curriculum Calendar* worksheet to do so.

It is essential to develop one faith formation calendar that incorporates age-group catechesis and events-centered catechesis. In this way participants and their families know that participation in preparation programs is not optional; it is part of the faith formation program. As mentioned above, be sure to add this information to the *Lifelong Curriculum Plan of Events*.

- Will you schedule events and age-specific programs on a monthly or annual cycle?

  Monthly: one week for preparation programs and multiple weeks for age-specific programming

  Annual: blend of classes and preparation programs throughout the year

Step 3: Develop a planning timeline for designing preparation programs and for training leaders.

The following is an example of a timeline that combines designing an individual preparation program with training leaders to teach the preparation program. The actual dates for each section are determined by the date of the preparation program. Start with the preparation program date and then move back through each of the other elements.

- Six to eight weeks before the preparation program, the design team meets to create the learning plan for the event including:
  - ▶ preparation program
  - ▶ home materials/home kit
  - ▶ reflection activities.
- Four weeks before preparation program, the key leadership of the design team develops preparation materials for the facilitator/catechist and conducts a planning meeting. (For more information on this task see Chapter 4: Developing Leadership.)
  - ▶ Individual catechist learning (two weeks before meeting)
  - ▶ Catechist meeting to prepare for teaching (two weeks before program).

After the preparation program, the teaching team meets to evaluate the program and make recommendations for improvement.

▶ Implementation Task 2: Budget and Fees

Use the *Implementing a Lifelong Curriculum* worksheet on page 95 to record your decisions for this task.

Step 1: Determine a budget for preparation programs and home materials.

To develop a budget for implementing an annual curriculum plan, determine your income (e.g., parish budget allocation, registration fees, and/or fundraising projects) and expenses. The standard expense items that should be included are:

1. Fixed expenses for organizing and conducting the program

- *Participant handouts and materials:* While each preparation program is different, some type of participant handout and other activity materials (paper, markers, craft materials, etc.) will be needed. Parishes typically spend $0.50–$1.00 per person per program.
- *Facilitator/catechist materials:* Catechists will need resources (articles, booklets, etc.) so that they can prepare to teach a program, and since there is no published teachers' manual, these materials are very important. For parishes with eight to ten events per year, the cost of a binder with session plans and background articles could be $20 per facilitator/catechist.
- *Program materials:* Additional program materials may be necessary for teaching preparation programs. Many programs consider the use of a video/DVD as integral to the learning experience; other programs may require the purchase of books, symbols, candles, prayer resources, etc. It is recommended that parishes budget at least $100 per program for these types of teaching materials.
- *Publicity and promotion:* Most parishes produce a brochure or booklet describing their plan for the year with a calendar and registration form. Some parishes also produce posters, banners, or displays. Your budget should include costs for design work, printing, and mailing. Many parishes produce a full-color information brochure. When doing so, it is best to print large quantities to keep your per-unit cost low. Producing a brochure without any dates (but with an annual calendar insert) allows parishes to print large quantities and use them for multiple years.

2. Variable per-household expenses

- *Home Kits:* Home Kits cost from $1 to $6 per household. If you develop your own materials and print them in-house or locally, you can keep Home Kit costs relatively low. If you purchase Home Kit materials, costs will be higher. Many parishes include both types of resources (locally developed and commercially produced) in the kits. The cost of Home Kits can be subsidized with registration fees or donations from parish organizations. To determine the annual cost per household for Home Kits, multiply the average Home Kit cost for each event ($1–$6) by the number of events in the year.

3. Variable per-person expenses

- *Meals and refreshments:* The cost of food for an extended program ranges from $2–$5 per person, depending on the food served and whether it is morning refreshments, lunch, or an evening meal. These costs can be offset by charging a per-person meal fee, or by having parish organizations contribute funds or prepare refreshments.

Step 2: Determine registration and/or material fees for households and individuals.

When you have determined your budget for the preparation programs you can set your fees for the programs. (Many parishes call them material fees rather than registration fees.) The registration or material fee should not include meals (this is a per-person expense, not per-household) and should be determined by combining your fixed expenses and per-household expenses (Home Kit). It is best to charge for the meal at the time of the program, although some parishes provide the food free or involve parish organizations in donating meals.

There is a wide range of program fee structures. Some parishes charge only for the meal because program expenses are covered in the parish budget, while other parishes must include staff salary expenses in their fees. All fees should include the cost of the Home Kit, but not the meal. (The examples below include only the program expenses, not salary or other overhead costs.)

- Determine your per-household fee by using the following calculations:
  - ▶ Add all of the total fixed expenses for the year and divide by the projected (or minimum) number of participating households. This figure represents each household's share of the fixed expenses.
  - ▶ Add the figure above to the cost of Home Kits for the year.
  - ▶ The sum represents the minimum per-household fee for conducting the preparation programs and creating Home Kits for the year.
- Develop two types of fees:
  - ▶ Annual Fee (season ticket): Traditionally, there is an annual fee for childhood programs and, sometimes, for adolescent programs. Continue the practice of an annual fee, basing the amount on your budget calculations. If you are conducting family-centered or intergenerational preparation programs, then the fee is for the entire family or household.

    Example: The following examples are from parishes with six to eleven events per year. The more events in the curriculum each year, the higher the registration fee. Many parishes charge from $50–$100 per household regardless of its size. Other parishes develop a fee structure based on size of household, for example, $50–$60 for a one- or two-person household and $80–$100 for a three- or more person household. This two-tier fee structure recognizes the lower expenses for a one- and two-person household.

  - ▶ Individual Program Fee (single-game ticket): There should be a per-program fee for all participants (especially adults) who are not accustomed to paying an annual fee and who may participate in selected events-centered preparation programs each year. Over time their participation will usually become more regular and they may then opt for an annual fee.

    Example: This fee should be slightly higher on a per-program basis than that factored into the annual fee. In this way you provide participants with an incentive to register for the whole year. Parishes typically charge $5–$10 per household per event or program.

In parishes that utilize a blended curriculum, the costs for families with children and teens need to be included within the current religious education registration fee. The primary cost is for the Home Kit. If the cost of your average Home Kit is $2–$3 and you have included four events in your curriculum for the year, the total cost per household is $8–$12. You will need to add this amount to your registration fee for the family. The easiest solution is to add a surcharge per household for the cost of the Home Kit.

▶ Implementation Task 3: Promotion and Registration

Use the *Implementing a Lifelong Curriculum* worksheet on page 95 to record your decisions for this task.

> Check online in the Design Lab at www.generationsoffaith.org for examples of promotional strategies, brochures, announcements, registration forms, etc.

Step 1: Develop a plan and materials for promoting your lifelong faith formation curriculum to the parish community.

The following questions will guide you in determining the design for your promotional materials and efforts.

Who will you include in the promotion?

- parish community-at-large
- targeted participants (e.g., parents of children and teens in catechetical programs who need specific information and program calendars; adults who need a special invitation)
- leadership groups.

What will you use for promotion?

- informational brochure or flyer and calendar for the year
- invitation letter with brochure and calendar to targeted audiences
- presentation at the weekend Masses
- presentations after Mass with refreshments
- presentations to parish leadership committees and organizations
- a skit at the weekend Masses or in a separate presentation
- meetings with targeted audiences (e.g., parents of children and teens)
- announcements at the weekend Masses and in the bulletin
- information in the parish newsletter
- e-mail invitations and information on the parish web site
- announcement banner or sign outside the church
- display with announcement, photos, and calendar (A display is especially effective after each preparation program. Be sure to take lots of pictures.)
- posters
- buttons
- magnets
- phone reminders to targeted audiences
- postcard reminders

How will you design your printed materials?

- Create a logo or symbol for consistent use to communicate identity.
- Use visuals: pictures, artwork/clip art, and color
- Make materials catchy. For example, print or stamp a catchy line on an envelope

to build interest.

- Make materials attractive. Use proper design and layout procedures. Make sure typefaces, pictures, humor, illustrations, and descriptions attract your target audience(s).
- Make materials easy to read. Identify the most important information and make it stand out, using typography, layout, or graphics. Use simple language that creates interest and invites further reading.
- Make materials that are unlikely to be discarded. Create a calendar that is attractive, and chances are that households will display and refer to it.
- Make materials diverse. Printed materials should look different each time they are produced, even if all you do is change the paper stock or typeface.

What types of information will you include in printed material?

- What will you call your program? Some parishes call it "Faith Formation for the Whole Parish Community," while others use a shorter name to catch people's attention, for example, "Generations of Faith." Others create a name such as "Faith Festivals," "Faith Gatherings," "Adventures in Faith," "Growing in Faith Together," "Living in Faith Together," or "Journey in Faith." There is no need to give it a name. A symbol or logo is important, however, to create an identity for the program.

Where will the events-centered preparation take place?

- On which dates will the event-centered preparation take place?
- At what times will the program begin and end?
- What is the cost of materials and a meal?
- When is the deadline for registration?
- What materials should people bring?
- What is the name, address, and phone number of the Church?
- Who can people contact for more information?

How will you present and describe your approach and lifelong plan?

- Show how the vision, philosophy, and goals of the program are compatible with the Catholic faith, the Church's catechetical vision, the parish mission and values, and the needs of your parish community.
- Describe the benefits and advantages of the plan.
- Present the key features. For example, everyone is welcome—all ages and all generations; the whole family participates; everyone receives home resources; it builds community among parishioners of all ages; it's fun, interactive, and enriching.
- Keep the presentation and description simple. Eliminate jargon.
- Use graphics and pictures in printed materials or in a laptop presentation.
- Consider using a question and answer format ("frequently asked questions").

  For parish examples, go to the Design Lab on "Implementing a Curriculum" at www.generationsoffaith.org. See the CD-ROM for a sample promotional announcement and samples of frequently asked questions that you can customize for your parish.

Talking Points

You will have to customize your presentation/description for different audiences, e.g., the entire parish, parents, adults, and so on. Work with your team to develop a series of audience-specific talking points about your vision and parish plan. For example, here are key points to make when talking to parents:

Our parish faith formation program:

- gives you a way to build up the faith of your family and to grow in faith as parents and as children;
- is a better model of learning because parents learn alongside their children at the preparation program, and this makes it easier to bring the learning home;
- builds up the confidence and ability of parents to share faith and values with their children;
- provides assistance to help families share faith at home, and to nurture the faith and values of their children through in-home resources;
- provides an opportunity for families to spend time together every month, and gives them time to complete activities at home, rather than driving to classes each week;
- encourages everyone to participate in Church life—Sunday Mass, Church events, etc.—in which the whole community gathers, celebrates, and lives their faith. If we want our children and teens to become lifelong Catholics and members of the Church we have to start now by involving the whole family in the life of the Church.
- covers the same content over six years as the children's textbook series; sacramental preparation for Eucharist, reconciliation, and confirmation will be separate programs, in addition to monthly intergenerational sessions.

Video Presentation

Introducing Generations of Faith is a video that provides an excellent introduction to the program. It can be used in a variety of settings and meetings. For a free copy call 203-723-1622. See Chapter 1 for an orientation workshop that can be used to accompany the video.

Step 2: Develop a registration procedure and form.

Registration procedures should include options for registering for the entire year as well as for individual programs. If you are conducting family-centered or intergenerational preparation programs, then registration is for the entire family or household.

- Establish a timeline for registrations and, if space is limited in your preparation programs, indicate that registration is on a first come, first served basis. Be sure that people indicate the first, second, and third choices for a preparation program.
- Establish procedures for registering individuals and households (letters, phone calls, postcards, e-mail, web site, etc.).
- Develop a plan for confirming a registrant's choice for a preparation program and for communicating the details of the program.

A registration form should include the following information:

- household name, address, phone number, and e-mail address
- number of people registering, their names and the ages of children; or have boxes to check whether a registrant is a parent, teenager, young adult, adult, older adult, etc.
- first, second, and third choice for the day and time of the preparation program
- if someone in the family is preparing to receive a sacrament during the year,

Implementing a Lifelong Curriculum

Task 1: Scheduling

✔ **Identify the number of times and the days of the week on which you will offer your preparation program.**

What is your timeframe for the preparation program?_____

How many preparation programs will you offer for each event? _____

When and at what times will you offer the preparation programs and what times?

❑ Monday evening   Time: _____

❑ Tuesday evening   Time: _____

❑ Wednesday evening   Time: _____

❑ Thursday evening   Time: _____

❑ Friday evening   Time: _____

❑ Saturday morning   Time: _____

❑ Saturday evening   Time: _____

❑ Sunday morning   Time: _____

❑ Sunday afternoon   Time: _____

❑ Sunday evening   Time: _____

✔ **Develop a calendar for the year with dates for preparation programs and events.**

Be sure to add the following information to your lifelong curriculum plan of events.

For primary curriculum parishes: Will you develop a set week(s) for preparation programs (e.g., 2nd week of month) or offer preparation on multiple weeks during the month or adjust the dates depending on the date of the event?

❑ Set week of the month   Week: _____

❑ Multiple weeks during the month   Weeks: _____

❑ Variable dates depending on the dates of the event

For blended curriculum parishes: Will you schedule events and age-specific programs on a monthly or annual cycle?

❑ Monthly Cycle

❑ Annual Cycle

Use the Blended Calendar worksheet to record your dates for preparation programs and age-group catechesis.

Implementing a Lifelong Curriculum

✔ **Develop a planning timeline for designing preparation programs and training leaders.**

Suggested Timeline	When and how will you do this?
6-8 weeks before preparation program • Design a learning plan. • Design preparation programs, home kits, and reflection activities. • Prepare all materials.	
4 weeks before preparation program: catechist/facilitator training • Provide individualized learning resources on the theme of the event (2 weeks before meeting) • Meet with the facilitators/ catechists to prepare for teaching (2 weeks before Preparation Program)	
After the preparation program: evaluation meeting	

Task 2: Budget and Fees

✔ **Determine a budget for preparation programs and home materials.**

Fixed Expenses	Projections
1. Participant handouts and materials (Compute costs per program x number of programs)	$ _____
2. Facilitator/catechist materials	$ _____
3. Program materials (Compute costs per program x number of programs)	$ _____
4. Publicity/promotion	$ _____
Total of fixed expenses	$ _____

Variable/Per Program Expenses

Home Kits (Range: $1-2 for self-produced to $5-6 for purchased resources)
Determine your average home kit expenses and multiply times the number of events in the year.

Your budget for home kits: $ _____ per household

Implementing a Lifelong Curriculum

Variable/Per Person Expenses
Meals and refreshments are per person expenses and not included in determining your registration/materials fee.

✔ **Determine program fees for households.**

To determine your per household fee:
- Add all of the total fixed expenses for the year and divide by the projected (or minimum) number of participating households. This figure represents each household's share of the fixed expenses.
- Take the above figure and add the cost of home kits for the year.
- This figure now represents the minimum household fee for conducting the preparation programs and creating home kits for the year.

Determine your annual fee ("Season Ticket")
Option 1: household fee, regardless of size of household: $ _____
Option 2: household fee based on size of household $ _____
   1-2 person household $ _____
   3 or more per household $ _____

Determine your single program fee ("Game Ticket") $ _____

**Determine the additional fee added to children
and teen registration in a Blended Curriculum parish** $ _____

Task 3: Promotion and Registration
✔ **Develop a plan and materials for promoting your lifelong curriculum to the parish community.**

Who will you include in promotion?
❑ Parish community-at-large
❑ Targeted participants: _____
❑ Leadership groups: _____

How will you promote?
❑ Informational brochure or flyer and calendar for the year
❑ Invitation letters with brochure and calendar to targeted audiences
❑ Presentation at the weekend Masses
❑ Presentations after Mass with coffee and donuts
❑ Presentations to parish leadership committees and organizations
❑ Meetings with targeted audiences, e.g., parents of children and teens
❑ Announcements at the weekend Masses and in the bulletin
❑ Information in the parish newsletter

Implementing a Lifelong Curriculum

❏ E-mail invitations and information on the parish web site.

❏ Announcement banner or sign outside the church

❏ Display with announcement, photos, calendar (A display is especially effective after each preparation program. Be sure to take lots of pictures.)

❏ Posters

❏ Buttons

❏ Magnet

❏ Phone call reminders to targeted audiences

❏ Post card reminders

What information should you include in a letter or printed material?

❏ Will you name your faith formation initiative? What will you call it?

❏ Where will the preparation programs take place?

❏ When (dates) will the preparation programs take place?

❏ When will the program begin and end?

❏ What is the cost (materials fee and meal fee)?

❏ When is the deadline for registration?

❏ What do people need to bring?

❏ What is the name of the church, address, and phone number?

❏ Who can people contact for more information?

Develop a registration procedure and form.

❏ Develop a timeline for registrations and, if space is limited in your preparation programs, indicate that it is first come, first served. Be sure that people indicate the first, second, and even third choices for a preparation program.

❏ Develop procedures for registering individuals and households (letters, phone calls, post cards, e-mail and web site, etc.).

❏ Develop a plan for confirming participation for those who register—confirming their choice for a preparation program and the details for the program.

A registration form can include the following information:

❏ Household name, address, phone, e-mail

❏ People registering: number of people, name with ages of children or boxes to check if you are a parent, teenager, young adult, adult, older adult, etc.

❏ Program selection: first choice, second choice, third choice for the day and time to participate in a preparation program

❏ Sacrament information if someone in the family is preparing for a sacrament this year: Baptism / RCIA, First Reconciliation, First Eucharist, Confirmation

Blended Curriculum Calendar

Dates List dates or months for: • Age-Group Session • Preparation Program • Church Event	Type of Learning Program or Name of Church Event Indicate if this is a • Age-Group Session • Preparation Program • Church Event	Theme of Event or Theme/ Topic of Age-Group Program

Sample Implementation Calendar

*Here is a sample of a parish calendar that includes a series of tasks beginning with the comple-
tion of planning and concluding with conducting the first intergenerational learning program.
The following list is only an example. Your may need to add other specific tasks to the list.*

▼

1. Presenting the lifelong faith formation plan to the religious education board and parish
council.

▼

2. Designing the flyer, question-and-answer brochure, web materials, registration forms, and
other promotional materials or strategies.

▼

3. Promoting the lifelong faith formation plan throughout the parish: mailings with flyer and
brochure, bulletin inserts, presentation at Sunday Mass, etc.

▼

4. Inviting people into leadership roles using a variety of recruitment strategies.

▼

5. Conducting a parish-wide introductory presentation after all of the weekend Masses with
time for registration.

▼

6. Reminding all parishioners to register through announcements at the weekend Masses and
targeted mailings.

▼

7. Meeting as a Design Team to create the learning plan for the first intergenerational learning
program (2 months before the date of the learning program).

▼

8. Meeting as a Design Team to finalize the learning plan and create the home kit.

▼

9. Ordering and assembling all of the materials for the learning program and home kits.

▼

10. Preparing and distributing the facilitator/catechist preparation materials (2 weeks before
the rehearsal meeting).

▼

11. Conducting a rehearsal meeting for facilitators/catechists and the Design Team to prepare
for teaching the intergenerational learning program.

▼

12. Conducting the intergenerational learning programs to prepare for the event.

▼

13. Involving the whole community in preparing for the event through preparation materials
and activities incorporated into existing meetings and programs (the practice of alignment).

▼

14. Reminding the whole community to participate actively in the event.

▼

15. Participating in the church event. Living the event at home using the home kit.

Sample Participant Evaluation Form

The questions on this form can be used to create a mid-year or end-of-year evaluation. It can be distributed before the conclusion of a preparation program. It is best if participants complete the form at the program. Customize this form by selecting or adding questions that relate to the specifics of your program design. Make sure your form has room to write suggestions or comments.

Please provide the following information:

People participating in the learning program (check all that apply):

❑ Parents and children   number of children: _____ ages: _____

❑ Teens

❑ Young Adults

❑ Adults

How many learning programs have you attended this year: _____

Name of individual or family (Optional): _____

Write an introduction paragraph explaining the purpose of the evaluation. Include information such as:

Please assess this year's program by rating each item from 1-4, with 1 being poor and 4 being excellent. After your rating please offer your comments on each item.

1. Overall rating of learning programs.   1 2 3 4
    Suggestions/Comments:

2. Opening Prayer Services   1 2 3 4
    Suggestions/Comments:

3. Learning session for families with children   1 2 3 4
    Suggestions/Comments:

4. Learning session for teens   1 2 3 4
    Suggestions/Comments:

5. Learning session for adults   1 2 3 4
    Suggestions/Comments:

6. The effectiveness of the program presenters and facilitators.   1 2 3 4
    Suggestions/Comments

7. Environment (Decorations, room set-up, meeting rooms)   1 2 3 4
    Suggestions/Comments:

8. Meals and refreshments   1 2 3 4
    Suggestions/Comments

9. Promotion and communication   1 2 3 4
    Suggestions/Comments:

10. Program times and days (length and timing)   1 2 3 4
    Suggestions/Comments:

Sample Participant Evaluation Form

11. Please rate the quality of each our learning programs

October	1	2	3	4
November	1	2	3	4
December	1	2	3	4
January	1	2	3	4
February	1	2	3	4
March	1	2	3	4
April	1	2	3	4
May	1	2	3	4
June	1	2	3	4

12. Please rate the value of the learning program for the faith development
of your children.   1   2   3   4

     Comments

13. The value of the learning program for faith development of parents.   1   2   3   4

     Comments

14. Home Kits   1   2   3   4

     Suggestions/Comments:

15. Did you use the at-home materials that were distributed at the learning program
     (Circle one.)

     1. We did not use the home materials.

     2. We used several activities during the year.

     3. We used 1 or 2 activities each month.

     4. We used most of the activities each month.

16. If you did use the at-home materials, please comment on the value of the materials.

     1. For children…

     2. For teens…

     3. For adults and parents…

     4. For the whole household…

17. List at least three things you have learned this year. (Feel free to share more if you can!)

18. Give us at least one way we can improve our parish faith formation.

Team and Staff Year End Assessment Process

In assessing each component consider feedback from the parish staff and core team, faith forma-
tion leaders involved in preparation, participants in preparation programs, parish at large, etc.

1. LEARNING PLAN: PREPARATION PROGRAMS

▲ Assess the effectiveness of your learning models (age group settings, family settings, intergenerational settings) in preparing people for the event.

▲ Assess the effectiveness of your scheduling, facilities, and other logistics in promoting learning.

▲ Assess who you are and are not reaching or involving in preparation programs.

▲ Assess the quality of the learning experiences: appropriate and meaningful content and activities, engagement of learners in the program, performance of catechists/ program leaders, resources and learning materials, etc.

▲ Assess the overall effectiveness of your learning plan for the whole parish community and the variety of strategies used—gathered learning, individualized, at home, etc.

Strengths / Positive Impact	Areas for Improvement

2. LEARNING PLAN: HOME ACTIVITIES

▲ Assess the effectiveness of your home materials for each event in helping people learn and live their faith at home.

▲ Assess how well your home materials incorporated activities for learning, praying, celebrating rituals, service, and enriching family relationships.

▲ Assess the quality of the home materials: appropriate and meaningful content and activities, family-friendly or user-friendly format, easy to use.

▲ Assess how well your delivery system worked in getting the activities into the home.

▲ Assess who you are and are not reaching through home activities.

Strengths / Positive Impact	Areas for Improvement

3. LEARNING PLAN: REFLECTION AND APPLICATION

▲ Assess the effectiveness of your reflection and application strategies/activities (format, content, design) for each event in helping individuals and families in reflecting upon their experience and learning, and apply their learning to their daily lives as Catholics.

▲ Assess the approach you used for reflection: at home, in programs, at the event.

▲ Assess how well your delivery system worked in getting the reflection strategies/activities to people.

Strengths / Positive Impact	Areas for Improvement

Team and Staff Year End Assessment Process

4. TRAINING OF CATECHETICAL LEADERS
- ▲ Assess how well leaders were prepared for teaching—training opportunities, teaching materials and resources, background readings, etc.

Strengths / Positive Impact	Areas for Improvement

5. LEADERSHIP AND ORGANIZATION
- ▲ Assess the effectiveness of your leadership teams in planning and implementing life-long faith formation in your parish:

  1. The Core Team of parish staff and parish leaders who guide the curriculum design process—fashioning a curriculum, implementing a curriculum, and evaluating the curriculum.

  2. The Design Team who creates the preparation programs, home activities, and reflection activities for each event.

  3. The Implementation Team who administer the program and conduct preparation programs.

  4. Ministry Partners from other parish ministries and programs who collaborate with the core team on specific projects that involve their particular ministry.

- ▲ Assess the effectiveness of your leadership structure to implement a more collaborative approach to faith formation. Assess how effective you have been in engaging leaders from other parish ministries and programs in events that involve their ministries.

- ▲ Assess the effectiveness and regularity of your planning time for the overall planning and designing of preparation programs, home activities, and reflection strategies.

- ▲ Assess the effectiveness of your organizational procedures: registration process, fees and budget, scheduling, facilities, promotion and marketing, etc.

Strengths / Positive Impact	Areas for Improvement

6. OVERALL ASSESSMENT
- ▲ What is your overall assessment of the significant strengths or positive impact of your curriculum plan and learning plans?

- ▲ How do you want to improve your performance in the coming year? What would you identify as your most critical areas for improvement in the coming year?

CHAPTER 4

Developing Leadership

▶ An Empowerment Mindset

Churches that are effective in developing leaders first embrace a set of principles that constitute an empowerment mindset to guide their efforts. These principles are rooted in the Christian tradition. In 1 Corinthians 12:4–31, mirrored in Romans 12 and Ephesians 4, St. Paul offers a vision of *Church* (body of Christ), of *ministry* (Spirit-led service to the Church and world), of *gifts* (given by the Holy Spirit for building up the body of Christ), and *mutuality* or *partnership* (complementary gifts given by the Holy Spirit for the common good).

These principles are echoed in Church teachings:

> The Second Vatican Council has reminded us of the mystery of this power and of the fact that the mission of Christ—Priest, Prophet-Teacher, King—continues in the Church. Everyone, the whole people of God, shares in this threefold mission. (John Paul II)

> Through the sacraments of baptism, confirmation, and Eucharist, every Christian is called to participate actively and co-responsibly in the Church's mission of salvation in the world. Moreover, in those same sacraments, the Holy Spirit pours out gifts which make it possible for every Christian man and woman to assume different ministries and forms of service that complement one another and are for the good of all. (*Christifideles Laici*, no. 20)

> Everyone has a responsibility to answer the call to mission and to develop the gifts she or he has been given by sharing them in the family, the workplace, the civic community, and the parish or diocese. A parallel responsibility exists within the Church's leadership to acknowledge and foster the ministries, the offices, and the roles of lay faithful that find their foundation in the sacraments of baptism and confirmation, indeed, for a good many of them in the sacrament of matrimony. (*Christifideles Laici*, no. 23)

Inspired by these images from St. Paul and Church teachings, several important values of an empowering mindset emerge.

1. The Church is the Body of Christ, and through our baptism, we are members of the Body of Christ.

Paul reminds us that each person in the faith community is called to ministry and is blessed with gifts for ministry by the power of the Holy Spirit. In baptism we celebrate the call of each person to ministry within the Church community and the ministry of the Church to the world. We believe that each individual brings wonderful gifts to the work of the Church.

Baptism is empowerment. Through baptism, all Christians share in the mission of Christ and the Spirit. The gifts of the Spirit received at baptism empower us to fulfill the mission of Jesus Christ. All ministry serves this mission. The baptized serve this mission and share in Christ's priestly, prophetic, and royal office.

The presence of the Spirit of the risen Lord is the source of power in the ministry of the Church. The Church and all its members emerge from and draw nourishment from the breaking of the bread, the reality of the Resurrection and Pentecost, and the sending forth of the disciples to spread the Good News. It is from this perspective that all followers of Jesus share in his ministry.

2. Individuals and the entire community are blessed with gifts for ministry.

Christian ministry is gift-based. Special charisms of the Holy Spirit, which flow from the sacrament of initiation, equip Christians for their special tasks within the Church. In the early Church, as needs were recognized in the community, those who were discerned to be appropriately gifted by the Spirit were called forth to serve.

Every aspect of our humanity is intended to serve God's intent for the world. Each person is uniquely gifted for ministry, and these gifts consist of more than one's talents. Other aspects of our giftedness include our interests, motivations, values, passions, hopes, dreams, and life journeys. Gifts discernment must focus on the whole person and the entire context of his or her life: families, friendships, workplaces and schools, neighborhoods, the greater community, and the faith community itself.

3. There is an abundance of gifts available for ministry.

An abundance mentality means that there is a diversity of gifts already present in the faith community. The Spirit has blessed the community with gifts, and there is no shortage of gifts! The primary task of ministry leaders is to facilitate the discovery and the utilization of these gifts on behalf of God's kingdom. Some of the gifts will be utilized within parish-based ministries, while others will be exercised in the world.

4. Ministry leaders are called to empower and equip individuals, teams, and, in the end, the entire community to utilize their gifts for the mission of the Church.

Ministry leaders are servants to the needs of the community and stewards of the community's resources. They play an essential role in the Church by helping identify the gifts of the community, developing these gifts for ministry, utilizing these gifts on behalf of God's kingdom and the mission of the Church, and supporting the gifts of all Church members. Ministry leaders must be secure enough to equip others for ministry, give them responsibility, and support them as they do their ministry.

What does an empowerment mindset mean in practice? Several key practices emerge from the values that guide a parish's approach to volunteer leadership:

- Every volunteer leadership experience in the Church should encourage a healthy relationship with Jesus Christ. We recognize that leaders have an opportunity to grow in their faith through involvement in ministry. We are concerned about the spiritual growth of leaders and their knowledge and skills for the practice of ministry.
- Volunteer leadership honors the abilities, interests, and passions of the volunteer leader. We take the time to thoroughly interview leaders and see that they are placed appropriately. We provide a diversity of choices and positions to appeal to different time schedules and gifts. We recognize that it is better to leave a volunteer position unfilled than to put the wrong person in the position.
- Volunteer leaders are respected as full partners in ministry. We give volunteer leaders responsibility and work with them as team members who share in the decision making, as well as in the work.
- Volunteer leaders receive specialized training, resources, and support so that they can adequately perform their ministry, especially when the knowledge or skills involved are new to them. We ensure that volunteer leaders feel capable and confident that they can perform their ministry. We tailor the training and resources to the needs of the leader and his or her responsibilities.

- Volunteer leaders are appreciated and recognized for the value of their contributions to their ministry and to the Church. We take the time, formally and informally, to express gratitude for the work of the volunteer leaders. We create specific ways, such as dinners, gatherings, rituals, and thank-you notes, to demonstrate appreciation and recognize the contributions of leaders.

▶ Leadership Development System

There are three components in developing a leadership system:

1. inviting people into leadership,
2. preparing and training leaders for their ministry, and
3. supporting and nurturing leaders.

On the pages that follow, we will study the steps necessary to successful implementation of each of the three stages.

Component 1. Inviting People into Leadership

Step 1. Identify the leaders you need.

Once you have finalized your preparation programs (age-group, family, and/or intergenerational learning programs), it is time to identify and then invite the leaders needed to implement the programs. Using the *Leadership Tasks Listing* worksheet on page 120, identify and assign all the tasks involved in a particular program. Be specific. Once you have listed the necessary tasks, group them to a number of leadership positions. An individual leader may choose to take on more than one position, but it is easier to recruit several leaders for smaller jobs than to find one person to take on a large job.

The following list gives an example of a list of leadership positions for a typical intergenerational learning program:

- program facilitator
- learning group facilitator: leader for age-appropriate learning groups (e.g., families with children, young adolescents, older adolescents, young adults, adults)
- facilitators/catechists for age-appropriate learning groups
- assistants to help with age-appropriate learning activities
- prayer leader for opening and closing prayer
- music leader and/or music team for prayer and activities
- set-up and clean-up staff
- food preparation and service staff
- creative arts staff for artwork, posters, signs, etc.
- promotion and correspondence staff
- hospitality and registration staff.

Step 2. Develop job descriptions for each leadership position.

Before searching for leaders, anticipate the important questions that leaders will ask: How much time will this really take? What if I need help? What else will be expected? Is training available? Are there extra meetings?

Using your *Leadership Tasks Listing* worksheet from Step 1 (above), create short but complete job descriptions for each leadership position. These descriptions will serve as the basis for recruiting, training, supporting, and evaluating your leaders. Use the *Leadership Role Description* worksheet on page 121 to answer questions potential leaders may ask about specifc positions. The worksheet focuses on the following key elements:

- *Program and position.* Identify the program in which the leader will be involved, and include the title for this leadership role, if there is one.
- *Responsibilities.* List the tasks to be performed by the leader, and describe what you hope will be accomplished. Use clear, simple language. (Use the information from the *Leadership Tasks Listing* worksheet.)
- *Qualifications.* Identify the qualifications or abilities needed by the person who will fill this leadership role. Identify minimal abilities simply and directly. Try not to overwhelm people, yet be honest about the abilities that are needed.
- *Length of commitment.* Some positions are responsible for one-time events, while others are seasonal or ongoing. Be very clear in specifying the length of the commitment. Include the amount of time the leader will be directly involved in the program as well as in preparation and meetings.
- *Training provided.* Identify the training or preparation that will be provided.
- *Benefits.* People need to know that their time and effort will make a difference and be worthwhile. Identify the benefits of this position for the leader. It is very important to describe how the leader will grow and benefit from his or her involvement in a leadership role.

For examples see the *Sample Job Descriptions* on pages 123-125.

Step 3. Search for people with leadership potential.

Recruitment of leaders is best understood as an invitation to an opportunity. It is an educational process as well. There are a variety of ways to present leadership needs to the community: through the parish newsletter and/or bulletin; brochures; displays and posters; presentations to groups; and by using a time-and-talent survey. Avoid "pleading" or "begging" for volunteer leaders. This strategy does not attract the best people to leadership; instead, you may be "stuck" with a leader who is well-intentioned but unqualified for a position. Develop an approach that spells out exactly what a position requires. This process will usually encourage self-selection by qualified people.

Because most parishes have both immediate and long-range leadership needs, it is important to see the recruitment effort as a continuous process. Also, since many programs do not begin at the same time, there will be a need for leaders throughout the year. Potential leaders are always surfacing, so keep an ongoing list of potential leaders.

Here are several suggestions for developing a successful recruitment strategy:

- Do specific rather than general recruiting, whenever possible. Job descriptions, as well as a brochure with job descriptions and a leadership interest finder, will assist you in this task.
- Choose appropriate audiences whose interests and priorities match your needs. Look to renewal programs, adult education programs, newly baptized adults, etc.
- Determine who has the necessary skills for a position and actively seek them out. If you wait for volunteers to find you, the results will usually be disappointing.
- Be as specific and honest as possible in your appeal. Accurate job descriptions should help you to do this. Clearly state what the job involves and how much time it requires. In many ways you are "selling" the position by trying to link the person's interests, gifts, and skills to the task.

- Be sure to utilize existing information. Check out the parish census, time-and-talent survey, prospective leaders recommended by the parish staff, current leaders, and names of prospects from other ministries.
- Recruit by inviting people to respond to an opportunity to serve. Do not tell them that they ought to be concerned and involved. Offer them the opportunity to serve, to grow, and to make a difference in the lives of people.
- Be enthusiastic! If you and your team are not committed to or excited about your ministry, no one else will be, either. And most certainly, lack of enthusiasm will not attract or inspire leaders to want to serve.

✓ Recruitment Strategy: Personal Recommendations and Contact

Ask the parish staff and current leaders to recommend potential leaders. Write a letter to each person indicating that he or she has been recommended as a potential leader and inviting him or her to consider a leadership position. Enclose a brochure describing the leadership positions and the programs. Within two weeks, follow up with a phone call to discuss the invitation and, if the person is open to involvement, schedule a one-on-one meeting. You may want to encourage the person who recommended the individual to write the initial letter to enhance the likelihood that the invitation will be given serious consideration. Then you can follow up with a phone call and a meeting.

✓ Recruitment Strategy: Parish Newsletter or Bulletin

Many parishes have a parish-wide monthly or quarterly newsletter that offers a vehicle to promote and describe leadership needs to potential leaders. Try to include a regular column about your program in the bulletin. When you are looking for new leaders, regularly submit "want ads," giving plenty of information about open positions and telling prospective leaders whom to contact for further details. Be sure to include an interest finder in the bulletin or newsletter to collect information about potential leaders (see the *Leader Profile and Interest Finder* worksheet on pages 126-7).

✓ Recruitment Strategy: Brochures

An attractive and professional way of communicating opportunities for leadership is through a brochure that describes open leadership positions and the responsibilities of each one. In a short paragraph, you might list each leadership position, describing the required tasks, abilities, and time commitment. Be sure to include an application in the brochure, asking prospects to list their abilities, background information, and the positions that interest them. (See the *Leader Profile and Interest Finder* worksheet on pages 126-7.) You can distribute these brochures at Sunday liturgy.

Ask those who are interested in serving or who want more information to drop the application form in a special box as they leave the Church. You can then follow up on each application with a phone call and a personal visit. The brochure can also be used by the recruiter or recruiting team to match the individual's gifts with a leadership position when prospective leaders are contacted. Used in this way, the brochure communicates the value you place on leaders and also provides the recruiter with a concrete visual to augment his or her presentation.

✓ Recruitment Strategy: Displays or Posters

Use posters to announce leadership opportunities, or set up a display somewhere prominent in the church or parish hall. In addition to the poster and/or display, you may want to develop a multimedia presentation that includes slides, music, conversation, interviews, commentary, and photos on your parish program or ministry. Information on leadership opportunities can also be included. You can take this presentation to parish organizations and small group meetings. It can also serve as an excellent orientation for prospective leaders. (This is a great strategy after a parish has completed several learning programs. Take photos of the learning program and leaders in action. A photo display of leadership opportunities in the gathering space of the church at the weekend Masses will attract people's attention.)

✓ Recruitment Strategy: Presentations

Schedule presentations at parish meetings to discuss opportunities for service. You might also want to organize small group meetings for prospective leaders convened by your current key leaders at their homes. You can also convene a parish-wide meeting to present opportunities for service. This last option is the most difficult to organize effectively, but with good promotion it can work well.

Step 4. Develop a database of potential leaders.

Organize the information from your searching and surveying into a permanent, up-to-date database of potential leaders. You may even want to recruit several leaders whose leadership positions involve keeping accurate records for your volunteer leadership system.

Step 5. Secure needed leaders.

The next task is to match leadership positions with the talents of individuals. First, examine the list of positions that need to be filled. Then carefully study each person's interests, abilities, limitations, and potential to match people with leadership positions they can ably fill. Some names will appear in several places, while others will appear only once. Having matched each person with a leadership position(s) in which his or her skills and interests can enrich and expand the ministry, choose one or more prospects for each position, ranking them if desired.

Step 6. Meet with each prospective leader.

All members of the core team should meet personally with each prospective program leader. Review the variety of leadership positions and the interests of the prospective leader. Be sure to have a listing of all the leadership positions that are available. Determine which jobs are right for the prospective leader and guide the leader in selecting a leadership position. Share information about the leadership positions with the prospective leader: responsibilities, time commitment, required training, meetings, and other details about the job. Only after someone has been interviewed should he or she be confirmed as a leader.

Here is a suggested outline for a meeting:

1. *Introduction:* Be honest and challenging.
2. *Appeal to motives:* Draw out the best in the person.
3. *Factual information:* Describe the tasks, time commitment, and so on. Supply this information in writing, using a job description. Solicit the person's view of the task.
4. *Support:* Explain the type of training, resources, support, and guidance the volunteer leader can expect.
5. *Question:* Will he or she accept the challenge? Express trust and confidence in the person's decision, whatever it may be.

Here are sample questions for exploring a leadership job with a prospective leader:

What experiences have you had in working with ____ or being involved in ____?

What interests you most about working with ____ or being involved in ____?

What particular skills do you bring to working with ____ or being involved in ____?

What reservations do you have about working with ____ or being involved in ____?

What are the greatest things you can give to ____ or be involved in ____?

Component 2. Preparing and Training Leaders for their Ministry

Volunteer leaders need to receive specialized training and resources so that they can effectively perform their ministry. Preparing and training leaders is guided by several key principles about adult learning:

1. Training needs to be *applicable* to the job. There is no such thing as a one-size-fits-all approach to training leaders. Customize the training around the particular job and its required knowledge and skills. The scope and the depth of training are related to the requirements of the volunteer leadership position. This approach focuses the leader on what he or she needs to learn.

2. Training needs to be *experiential* (hands-on), so that leaders develop both the knowledge and the practical skills for their ministry.

3. Training needs to be *on-the-job*. The best context for training is the actual work the leader is doing. Learning and performing/leading are intertwined. In this sense training is invisible. It is embedded in the work processes of a project, such as planning meetings, individual preparation, teaching sessions, and evaluation meetings. Training is woven into every aspect of the project.

4. Training needs to be *timely* so that there is immediacy of application. This provides a way for the leader to see progress, immediate results, and some rewards for the time they put into training.

5. Training needs to use *a variety of learning approaches*—independent learning, apprenticeship learning, group and institutional learning.

Step 1. Provide an orientation workshop for all leaders.

To help leaders become familiar with the Generations of Faith vision, practices, and your parish plan for the year, provide an orientation workshop for all leaders. Here are several key activities and topics that you can include in the workshop:

1. Provide a community building activity so that leaders in all areas of faith formation get an opportunity to meet each other.

2. Identify the various leadership roles and the people who will be leading different aspects of the program. Ask people to stand as you identify them.

3. Introduce the Generations of Faith vision and practices through a presentation and/or video.

4. Present the parish faith formation plan and the calendar for the year.

5. Organize leaders in groups based on the type of leadership position (e.g., facilitators, catechists, hospitality leaders, logistics staff) to meet each other and discuss their work.

You can use the *Introducing Generations of Faith* video (available free from the Center for Ministry Development at 203-723-1622), along with the Generations of Faith Orientation Workshop in Chapter 1 as resources for your orientation workshop.

Step 2. Develop a training plan.

It is essential that training be focused on the particular knowledge and skills required for the leadership position. Begin by determining whether the position requires formal training. Oftentimes a meeting, phone call, or printed material will provide this information. For example, the set-up and clean-up crew for an intergenerational learning program may need only floor plans with room arrangements and the times for set-up and clean-up. On the other hand, facilitators/catechists will need formal training for each new intergenerational learning program. Review all of the leadership positions and determine what types of training and resources are necessary.

For a leadership position requiring formal training, use the job description to determine the training topics and content. Then develop a training plan for each training topic, using one or more of the following learning approaches:

- *Independent learning* provides maximum flexibility for the learner—when to learn, how to learn, where to learn, etc. Learning formats include guided reading, online learning, video-assisted and video-based learning, and audio learning.

- *Apprenticeship learning* provides an experiential, hands-on mentoring relationship between a veteran leader and a developing leader. Through on-the-job training and one-on-one instruction, the apprentice can practice new skills and become comfortable with program demands before taking full responsibility.

- *Group learning* provides a format in which the common learning needs of a group of leaders can be addressed through one learning experience. Group learning formats include courses, workshops, action projects, clinics, conferences, demonstrations, exhibits, trips, and tours. Online-learning and video-learning programs can also be used in a group setting.

- *Institutional learning* takes advantage of existing training programs to address the learning needs of leaders, whether individually or as a group. Institutional learning includes courses, workshops, seminars, and conferences sponsored by the diocese, community agencies, other congregations, and local colleges and universities.

The following is an example of a training plan for facilitators/catechists who are to conduct an intergenerational learning program. Notice how this plan utilizes the various learning principles listed and explained above.

Part 1. Independent Learning Packet

Distribute four weeks prior to the intergenerational learning program.

Using the examples below, create an independent learning packet for facilitators/catechists that provides the foundational knowledge they need to teach the learning program:

- an online learning session from the Training Center at www.generationsoffaith.org
- short, guided readings, such as *Catholic Update* or excerpts from books and teaching manuals
- audio learning programs (cassette or CD), such as presentations from a conference on books on tape or CD
- video learning programs, such as *Echoes of Faith* or *Catholic Update* videos.

Part 2. Group Learning: Facilitator/Catechist Meeting

Held two weeks prior to the intergenerational learning program.

The facilitator/catechist meeting provides an opportunity to help leaders prepare for and rehearse the learning program. It is also a time to provide leaders with training that develops their skills for teaching the learning activities. A typical 2 to 2 1/2-hour meeting has the following agenda:

1. Distribution of the entire learning program to each facilitator/catechist.
2. Walk-through of each part of the learning program and the learning activities for families with children, teens, and adults.
3. Demonstration of teaching methods to be used by leaders during the learning program.
4. Meet in teaching teams to prepare for teaching a specific group (e.g., families with children, teens, adults).

Part 3. Group Learning: Evaluation Meeting

Held at the conclusion of the intergenerational learning program.

When the learning program concludes, gather the leaders to evaluate the program. The meeting has two purposes:

1. to identify the strengths of the program (content, methods, flow, etc.) and the areas for improvement;
2. to guide the catechists in identifying their teaching strengths and areas they need to develop further. The learning needs that are identified in the evaluation meeting can then become the focus of new training plans.

Here are three examples of independent learning plans and resources.

Independent Learning Plan: Baptism

1. Online learning session: "Baptism" (45-60 minute online program)
2. Guided reading:
   - *Infant Baptism*. Thomas Richstatter (*Catholic Update*)
   - *The Sacraments of Initiation: Sacraments of Invitation*. Thomas Richstatter (*Catholic Update*)
3. Video-based learning options:
   - *Echoes of Faith: Liturgy and Sacraments—3. Sacraments of Initiation* (RCL)
   - *Catholic Update Video: Adult Baptism* (St. Anthony Messenger Press)
   - *Catholic Update Video: Infant Baptism* (St. Anthony Messenger Press)
   - *The Sacrament of Baptism*. Kathleen Chesto (Twenty-Third Publications)
4. *Interview:* Develop a set of questions based on your study of baptism and interview the pastor or RCIA leaders in person or via e-mail or phone.

Independent Learning Plan: Eucharist

1. Online learning session: "Eucharist" (45-60 minute online program)
2. Guided reading:
   - *A Walk through the Mass*. Thomas Richstatter (*Catholic Update,*)
   - *Eucharist: Understanding Christ's Body*. William Shannon (*Catholic Update*)
3. Video-based learning options:
   - *Echoes of Faith: Liturgy and Sacraments—1. What is Liturgy* (RCL)
   - *Echoes of Faith: Liturgy and Sacraments—2. Liturgy and Christian Identity* (RCL)
   - *Catholic Update Video: A Walk through the Mass* (St. Anthony Messenger Press)
   - *The Sacrament of Eucharist*. Kathleen Chesto (Twenty-Third Publications)
   - *Why We Go to Mass*. Rev. J-Glenn Murray, S.J. (Loyola Press)
4. *Interview:* Develop a set of questions based on your study of the Eucharist and interview the pastor, liturgist, and/or parish staff in person or via e-mail or phone.

Independent Learning Plan: Reconciliation

1. Online learning session: "Reconciliation" (45-60 minute online program)
2. Guided reading:
   - *How to Celebrate the Sacrament of Reconciliation Today*. Thomas Richstatter (*Catholic Update*)
   - *The Gift of Reconciliation: Ten Tips for Better Confessions*. Thomas Richstatter (*Catholic Update*)
3. Video-based learning options:
   - *Echoes of Faith: Liturgy and Sacraments—4. Sacraments of Healing* (RCL)
   - *Catholic Update Video: The Church Celebrates the Reconciling God* (St. Anthony Messenger Press)
   - *Catholic Update Video: The God Who Reconciles* (St. Anthony Messenger Press)

   Check the online Design Lab at www.generationsoffaith.org for additional examples of independent learning plans and additional training resources.

To develop your own training plan and approach use *A Training Plan for All Leaders* and *A Training Plan for Facilitators/Catechists* worksheets found on pages 128-131.

Component 3. Supporting and Nurturing Leaders

To keep leaders motivated and active, you need to develop an effective plan for supporting them. Supervision and support may be the two most overlooked elements in leadership development, and a plan that includes both is essential for the successful operation of a leadership system. The time invested in supporting leaders reaps immense benefits.

Step 1. Authorize leaders to begin service.

Leaders need a formal way to begin their ministry. You can mark the beginning of their service through a formal worship service. For example, Catechetical Sunday has become a formal time to authorize the ministry of the catechists. This formal commissioning serves to authorize leaders for their ministry and recognize them in a public way.

Step 2. Provide the needed information and resources.

Provide leaders with the resources, information, and tools they need to accomplish their task. Many parishes provide a library or learning resource center for leaders with print, audio, and video resources for their ministry, as well as for their spiritual growth. See the Resources for Leadership Development on page 117 for some suggestions.

Step 3. Evaluate the effectiveness of leaders.

Gather information about the performance of leaders through observation, consultation, group discussion, evaluation instruments, or other means. Weigh the leader's actual performance against the goals of the program and the criteria in the job description. Regular meetings throughout the year provide opportunities to review with volunteer leaders the effectiveness of their planning and implementation of their ministries.

Step 4. Deal with problems.

Despite your best efforts, some volunteer leaders will not work out. You may have tried to provide clear job descriptions, conduct thorough interviews, and offer quality training and helpful support systems, constructive feedback, and personal assistance, but to no avail.

When a leader does not work out, deal with the problem honestly and openly. Do not resort to any tricks or maneuvers, or let the problem go unattended. Many coordinators erroneously believe that the problem will go away all by itself—but it never does. You need to realize that the problem will affect your entire ministry. The negative feelings or climate generated when a volunteer leader is not performing well or is unhappy, angry, or frustrated spread throughout the entire ministry, affecting your volunteer leaders and the participants themselves. It is up to the coordinator to face the volunteer and take definite action.

Here are some helpful suggestions for addressing a problem with a volunteer leader:

- Gather accurate information about the leader's performance: conduct evaluations, observe performance, consult other veteran and trusted volunteer leaders.

- Deal with the problem immediately, and you might still be able to improve the leader's performance. If not, you will want the person to leave the ministry quickly.

- Consult with the pastor to discuss the situation and the course of action to be taken.

- Reflect on the situation carefully and then act: If the leader is mismatched with a job, consider alternative ministry assignments in the parish community. However, do not recommend a leader for another ministry if he or she is not suitable. Don't give someone else your problem!

- Meet one-on-one with the leader, presenting the relevant information and your assessment of the situation. Let the leader respond, allowing him or her a graceful way of resigning. If he or she does not see the situation as you do, repeat your analysis and then take action. In your meeting be honest and caring. Make sure the leader understands that his or her ministry is not working out and the reasons why. Try to identify his or her positive attributes. Keep the discussion focused on his or her work performance—not the leader's personal life.

Step 5. Express and celebrate the Church's support of volunteer leaders.

It is essential to regularly express gratitude, appreciation, and support for all leaders. Too often we take our leaders for granted, and then wonder why they do not return. Supporting leaders is a year-round task. We celebrate this support in formal ways at Mass, special recognition ceremonies, parties, and/or dinners, as well as through informal ways, such as thank-you notes. We recognize those who have given five, ten, fifteen, and twenty years of service. We express appreciation to each leader at the conclusion of his or her service.

There are many ways, both formal and informal, to express and celebrate the Church's support of volunteer leaders:

- Verbally acknowledge leaders' hard work and accomplishments before the entire parish.

- Print a list of leaders in the parish bulletin and newsletter.

- Send birthday and special-occasion cards to leaders.

- Hold a recognition dinner and invite spouses and family members to attend. Award leaders with certificates, honors, mementos.

- Provide child care for leaders who will need it during their times of service.

- Send personal notes of appreciation.

- When a leader handles a difficult situation well, praise him or her. Ask the leader to share with other leaders how they dealt with the matter.

- Provide an annual retreat for leaders.

- Pray with leaders frequently.
- Publish an occasional article about the work of leaders in the local or diocesan newspapers.
- Celebrate together at social events and parties.
- Pay all fees for leaders to attend workshops, seminars, courses, etc.
- Develop monthly and annual recognition mechanisms, such as naming a Leader of the Month.
- Plan an annual family picnic for all ministry leaders.

▶ Resources for Leadership Development

Print Resources for Developing Leaders

Malloy, Sue. *The Equipping Church: Serving Together to Transform Lives*. Grand Rapids, MI: Zondervan, 2001.

Malloy, Sue and Brad Smith. *The Equipping Church Guidebook*. Grand Rapids, MI: Zondervan, 2001.

Ratcliff, Donald and Blake J. Neff. *The Complete Guide to Religious Education Volunteers*. Birmingham, AL: Religious Education Press, 1993.

Senter, Mark. *Recruiting Volunteers in the Church*. Wheaton, IL: Victor Books, 1990.

Trumbaurer, Jean Morris. *Created and Called: Discovering Our Gifts for Abundant Living*. Minneapolis: Augsburg Fortress, 1998.

———. *Sharing the Ministry: A Practical Guide for Transforming Volunteers into Ministers*. Minneapolis: Augsburg Fortress, 1998.

Wilson, Marlene (author and general editor). *Volunteer Leadership Series*. Loveland, CO: Group Publishing, 2004. (6 book, boxed set)

———. *You Can Make A Difference? Helping Others and Yourself through Volunteering*. Boulder, CO: Volunteer Management Associations, 1990.

———. *How to Mobilize Church Volunteers*. Minneapolis, MN: Augsburg, 1983.

Online Training for Facilitators/Catechists

The Generations of Faith Online Training Center has 45-60 minute online training programs to prepare leaders with the knowledge needed to teach events-centered learning programs. Go to www.generationsoffaith.org for a free tour of one training program. (The Online Training Center is a benefit of subscribing to Generations of Faith Online.)

Video Training for Facilitators/Catechists

Catholic Update Videos. Cincinnati: St. Anthony Messenger Press.

The Liturgical Year and Sunday
Lent and Easter
Understanding the Sacraments
Adult Baptism
Infant Baptism

Sacrament of Confirmation
The Church Celebrates the Reconciling God
The God Who Reconciles
A Walk through the Mass
Eucharist: Celebrating Christ Present

Echoes of Faith (video-assisted resource). National Conference of Catechetical Leadership. Allen, TX: Resources for Christian Living, 1998.
Echoes of Faith: Theology Set (5 videos: Prayer and Spirituality, Liturgy and Sacraments, Catholic Morality, Introduction to the Scriptures, I Believe/We Believe)
Echoes of Faith: Catechetical Set (3 videos)
Echoes of Faith: Methodology Set (5 videos, Grades 1-8)

Leadership System Checklist

The checklist includes all of the major tasks of a leadership development system. Review the work you have completed and work that still needs to be done.

PART 1. INVITING PEOPLE INTO LEADERSHIP

_____ We list all the tasks and positions for which leaders will needed.   Yes / No

_____ We write a job description for each leadership position.   Yes / No

_____ We use a variety of targeted strategies for recruiting leaders.   Yes / No

_____ We use a variety of community-wide strategies for recruiting leaders.   Yes / No

_____ We survey the parish community to discover leadership abilities and interests
     (e.g., time and talent survey)   Yes / No

_____ We search throughout the year for persons with leadership potential.   Yes / No

_____ We maintain an up-to-date database of potential leaders.   Yes / No

_____ We select each prospective leader based on a thorough knowledge of
     both the job and the person.   Yes / No

_____ We interview each person and explain the responsibilities involved.   Yes / No

_____ With each leader, we establish a clear agreement regarding the responsibilities
     and terms of his or her service.   Yes / No

PART 2. PREPARING AND TRAINING LEADERS

_____ We customize the training to each leader and leadership position.   Yes / No

_____ We use a variety of learning approaches including independent learning,
     apprenticeship, group learning, and institutional learning.   Yes / No

_____ We provide an orientation program for all leaders.   Yes / No

_____ We develop a training plan to prepare for facilitators/catechists for teaching
     each events-centered learning program.   Yes / No

_____ All leaders participate in the training they need.   Yes / No

_____ We evaluate the effectiveness of the training with leaders.   Yes / No

PART 3. SUPPORTING LEADERS

_____ We authorize leaders to begin their service.   Yes / No

_____ We provide all leaders with the resources and information they need
     for their work.   Yes / No

_____ We gather information and evaluate the work of leaders.   Yes / No

_____ We express and celebrate the community's appreciation for leaders.   Yes / No

We need to strengthen or improve the following areas of our leadership system:

Leadership Tasks Listing

Program:_____

Leadership Tasks	**Leadership Positions**

Leadership Tasks

1._____

2._____

3._____

4._____

5._____

6._____

7._____

8._____

9._____

10._____

11._____

12._____

13._____

14._____

15._____

16._____

17._____

18._____

19._____

20._____

Leadership Positions

Position: _____
Leadership Tasks: _____
(Indicate numbers from column 1)

Position: _____
Leadership Tasks: _____
(Indicate numbers from column 1)

Position: _____
Leadership Tasks: _____
(Indicate numbers from column 1)

Position: _____
Leadership Tasks: _____
(Indicate numbers from column 1)

Position: _____
Leadership Tasks: _____
(Indicate numbers from column 1)

Position: _____
Leadership Tasks: _____
(Indicate numbers from column 1)

Position: _____
Leadership Tasks: _____
(Indicate numbers from column 1)

Position: _____
Leadership Tasks: _____
(Indicate numbers from column 1)

Position: _____
Leadership Tasks: _____
(Indicate numbers from column 1)

Position: _____
Leadership Tasks: _____
(Indicate numbers from column 1)

Leadership Role Description

1. **Program** _____

   Position _____

2. **Responsibilities: Leader Tasks to be Performed** (see Leader Tasks worksheet):

   1. _____ 5. _____
   2. _____ 6. _____
   3. _____ 7. _____
   4. _____ 8. _____

3. **Qualifications: Abilities Needed** (skills, attitudes, understandings):

   1. _____ 5. _____
   2. _____ 6. _____
   3. _____ 7. _____
   4. _____ 8. _____

4. **Length of Commitment**

   Length of Service (times/dates): _____

   When Ministry is Performed: _____

   _____

   _____

   _____

5. **Preparation/Training Provided** (what, how, where, when):

6. **Responsible To** _____

7. **Benefits of the Position**

   To the leader: _____

   _____

   To the community: _____

   _____

Completed by _____   Date _____

                                              Last Reviewed ____/____/____

Sample Leader Tasks and Responsibilities for an Intergenerational Learning Program

Program Director (or MC)
- guiding the whole group through the learning program
- welcoming all the participants and providing an overview of the learning program
- introducing each learning activity and the leaders
- keeping the program moving on schedule
- facilitating the whole-group sharing experience and at-home application

Lead Facilitator for Age-Based Learning Groups
- working with the team of catechists to prepare for the session
- working with team to conduct the learning activities
- directing learning activities
- giving presentations

Facilitators/Catechists for Age-Based Learning Groups (see sample job description)

Leaders for Intergenerational Opening Experience
- working with a team to lead the opening, large group experience
- leading a variety of large group activities such as drama, storytelling, and media

Hospitality Staff
- greeting people as they arrive
- registering/recording all participants
- distributing home kits
- directing people to meeting rooms

Child Care Staff
- providing child care for young children
- providing activities, such as reading story books

Prayer Leaders
- designing opening and closing prayer services
- leading opening and closing prayer
- leading the group in dramatic presentations

Sample Job Description: Facilitator/Catechist for Intergenerational Learning Program

Responsibilities: Leader Tasks to be Performed

- Participate in the preparation meetings for teaching the preparation program
- Engage in individual preparation for teaching
- Teach/facilitate the preparation program for your group
- Evaluate the learning program

Qualifications: Abilities Needed

- Willingness and ability to speak with conviction about his or her own Catholic faith
- Understanding the content of the learning program: Church year, sacraments, justice, prayer and spirituality, etc.
- Familiarity with the Generations of Faith approach to faith formation
- Familiarity with the learning styles and psychological development/faith growth of group(s) being taught.
- Ability to use experiential learning methods and activities.
- Ability to lead a group discussion and facilitate faith sharing activities
- Length of Commitment: 10 monthly sessions
- Service from September to May
- Meetings: One planning meeting per month (evening) and one monthly teaching session

Training Required:

- One orientation session
- Monthly preparation for teaching the program content by using the Generations of Faith Online Learning Center and reading background material
- Monthly planning meetings

Responsible to:

- DRE / program coordinator for monthly preparation program

Supervision/Support:

- Monthly preparation meetings
- Evaluation meeting twice year

Benefits of the Position to the Leader:

- Opportunity to share his or her faith, to guide people in their growth as Catholics, to enrich the faith experience of individuals and families, to grow as a Catholic, to receive the support of other adult leaders.

Sample Job Description: Art and Environment Ministry for Intergenerational Learning Program

Responsibilities: Leader Tasks to be Performed

- Attend orientation workshop to become familiar with the vision and practices of Generations of Faith.
- Participate in the training meeting to plan the environmental motif for the faith formation gathering.
- Create and/or build appropriate banners, table settings, decorative symbols, etc. that enhance the theme of the faith formation gathering.
- Recruit others as needed.

Qualifications: Abilities Needed

- Understanding of the content of the learning program for the season (e.g. Church year, sacraments, justice, liturgy, etc.)
- Familiarity with the Generations of Faith approach to faith formation
- Ability to visualize and articulate through the use of symbols using various art forms
- Appreciation and skill in decorative arts

Length of Commitment: minimum of 5 monthly sessions

- Ability to commit to a minimum of 5 of the 10 monthly faith formation gatherings held between September and June

Training Required:

- One orientation workshop
- One planning session/rehearsal for each faith formation gathering committed to
- Individual preparation for program content related to the art and environment

Responsible to:

- DRE / program coordinator for monthly preparation program

Benefits of the Position to the Leader:

- Opportunity to share one's creative talents in the form of visual arts, while enriching the faith experience of individuals and families.

Sample Job Description: Food Ministry
for Intergenerational Learning Program

Responsibilities: Leader Tasks to be Performed
- Order and/or prepare meal, including beverages and a vegetarian option for each faith formation gathering (budget to be determined).
- Recruit kitchen help and servers.
- Organize clean-up after the meal.
- Coordinate with parish staff regarding need for paper products and other non-food items.
- Collect cash donations and turn in to parish staff person

Qualifications: Abilities Needed
- Ability to organize a menu and feed a large group of people
- Ability to coordinate volunteers to prepare, serve, and clean-up

Length of Commitment:
- Ability to commit to a minimum of 5 of the 10 monthly faith formation gatherings held between September and June

Responsible to:
- DRE / program coordinator for monthly preparation program

Benefits of the Position to the Leader:
- Opportunity to share culinary and organizational skills, while contributing to the enrichment of the faith experience for individuals and families. A great way to meet other people in the parish and participate in menu selection for parish-wide events.

Other Comments
- This could be an ideal ministry for a small faith sharing group or for 2–3 families to work together.

Leader Profile and Interest Finder

Name_____

Street_____ Apt. #_____

City _____ State_____ Zip Code_____

Day phone_____ Evening phone_____

Email_____

Age group are you a member of: ❑ 14-18   ❑ 18-30   ❑ 31–55   ❑ 56-70   ❑ 71-100+

Occupation: _____

Marital Status: ❑ Single   ❑ Married   ❑ Separated   ❑ Divorced   ❑ Widowed

Ages of children (if applicable): _____

Availability (mark all that apply)
- ❑ Monday evening
- ❑ Tuesday evening
- ❑ Wednesday evening
- ❑ Thursday evening
- ❑ Friday evening
- ❑ Saturday morning   ❑ Saturday afternoon   ❑ Saturday evening
- ❑ Sunday morning   ❑ Sunday afternoon   ❑ Sunday evening

Leader Involvement Interests

❑ I would like to be part of the leadership team responsible for overall coordination of lifelong faith formation.

❑ I would like to help with planning learning programs.

❑ I would like to help with conducting the learning programs. (Please complete the interest finder on the next page.)

❑ I would like to help with support and/or office tasks, e.g., mailings, facility set-up, telephone calls. (Please complete the interest finder on the next page.)

Identify the skills, talents, and training you bring to church ministry leadership positions.

Our parish faith formation program needs your gifts and talents. You can select from a wide variety of leadership positions based on your interests and availability. Please review the list on the next page and indicate as many of the leadership positions that interest to you. We will contact you very soon about your choices.

Leader Profile and Interest Finder

Meal Preparation
- ❑ Develop menus and purchase food
- ❑ Prepare, serve, and clean-up meals for programs

Room Set-Up
- ❑ Set up meeting rooms for programs and clean up after programs

Hospitality
- ❑ Welcome and register participants for programs
- ❑ Provide childcare at programs

Learning Group Facilitators
- ❑ working with young children
- ❑ working with children
- ❑ working with teens in grades 9-12
- ❑ working with adults
- ❑ working with parents and children
- ❑ working with teens in grades 6-8
- ❑ working with young adults
- ❑ assist with activities

Music and Prayer
- ❑ Help prepare prayer services for programs
- ❑ Lead music at programs
- ❑ Play musical instrument: _____
- ❑ Sing as part of a choir or group
- ❑ Work on drama presentations
- ❑ Liturgical dance

Graphic Arts
- ❑ Create artwork, posters, etc., for programs
- ❑ Work on a newsletter
- ❑ Provide decorations for special events
- ❑ Take photos of events

Administration, Promotion, and Correspondence
- ❑ Write articles for the parish newsletter or bulletin, local and diocesan newspapers
- ❑ Design promotional materials (advertisements, brochures, etc.)
- ❑ Manage database and keep records
- ❑ Type and other clerical assistance
- ❑ Manage communication: correspondence, email, telephone
- ❑ Manage registrations and finances
- ❑ Assembling learning materials and home kits for participants

A Training Plan for All Leaders

Leadership Position	Training and/or resources necessary for this position	Approach/strategy for providing training and/or resources	Timeline for providing training and/or resources

Training Plan for Facilitators/Catechists

Part 1. Independent Learning

4 weeks prior to the learning program
Create an independent learning packet (see examples) for facilitators/catechists that provides the foundational knowledge they need to understand in order to teach the learning program.
- an online learning session at www.generationsoffaith.org
- short guided readings
- audio learning programs
- video learning programs

Your Independent Learning Plan

Part 2. Group Learning:
Facilitator/Catechist Meeting

2 weeks prior to the learning program,
2 to 2 1/2 hours
The Facilitator/Catechist Meeting is opportunity to help leaders prepare for and rehearse the learning program; and develop skills for teaching the learning activities.
Agenda:
- Distribution of the learning program.
- Walk-through of the learning program and individual age-appropriate learning activities.
- Demonstration of learning methods used in the learning program to familiarize leaders with how to conduct the methods
- Break-out into age-appropriate teaching teams (e.g., families with children, teens, adults) to prepare for teaching the age-appropriate session.

Your Date and Agenda for Meeting

Part 3. Group Learning: Evaluation

At the conclusion of the learning program
After the learning program concludes, gather the leaders to evaluate the program. The evaluation meeting has two purposes: (1) to identify the strengths of the program (content, methods, flow, etc.) and the areas for improvement; and (2) to guide the catechists in identifying their teaching strengths and areas they need to develop further.

Your Agenda for Evaluation Meeting

Sample Training Plan for Facilitators/Catechists

Here is an example of a training plan for facilitators/catechists who are to conduct an inter-generational learning program. Notice how this plan utilizes the various learning principles listed and explained above.

Part 1. Independent Learning Packet

Distribute four weeks prior to the intergenerational learning program.

Using the examples below, create an independent learning packet for facilitators/catechists that provides the foundational knowledge they need to teach the learning program:

- an online learning session from the Training Center at www.generationsoffaith.org
- short, guided readings, such as *Catholic Update* or excerpts from books and teaching manuals
- audio learning programs (cassette or CD), such as presentations from a conference on books on tape or CD
- video learning programs, such as *Echoes of Faith* or *Catholic Update* videos.

Part 2. Group Learning: Facilitator/Catechist Meeting

Held two weeks prior to the intergenerational learning program.

The facilitator/catechist meeting provides an opportunity to help leaders prepare for and rehearse the learning program. It is also a time to provide leaders with training that develops their skills for teaching the learning activities. A typical 2 to 2 1/2-hour meeting has the following agenda:

1. Distribution of the entire learning program to each facilitator/catechist.
2. Walk-through of each part of the learning program and the learning activities for families with children, teens, and adults.
3. Demonstration of teaching methods to be used by leaders during the learning program.
4. Meet in teaching teams to prepare for teaching a specific group (e.g., families with children, teens, adults).

Part 3. Group Learning: Evaluation Meeting

Held at the conclusion of the intergenerational learning program.

When the learning program concludes, gather the leaders to evaluate the program. The meeting has two purposes:

1. to identify the strengths of the program (content, methods, flow, etc.) and the areas for improvement;
2. to guide the catechists in identifying their teaching strengths and areas they need to develop further. The learning needs that are identified in the evaluation meeting can then become the focus of new training plans.

On the next page are three examples of independent learning plans and resources.

Sample Training Plan for Facilitators/Catechists

Independent Learning Plan: Baptism

1. Online learning session: "Baptism" (45-60 minute online program)
2. Guided reading:
   - *Infant Baptism*. Thomas Richstatter (*Catholic Update*)
   - *The Sacraments of Initiation: Sacraments of Invitation*. Thomas Richstatter (*Catholic Update*)
3. Video-based learning options:
   - *Echoes of Faith: Liturgy and Sacraments—3. Sacraments of Initiation* (RCL)
   - *Catholic Update Video: Adult Baptism* (St. Anthony Messenger Press)
   - *Catholic Update Video: Infant Baptism* (St. Anthony Messenger Press)
   - *The Sacrament of Baptism*. Kathleen Chesto (Twenty-Third Publications)
4. *Interview:* Develop a set of questions based on your study of baptism and interview the pastor or RCIA leaders in person or via e-mail or phone.

Independent Learning Plan: Eucharist

1. Online learning session: "Eucharist" (45-60 minute online program)
2. Guided reading:
   - *A Walk through the Mass*. Thomas Richstatter (*Catholic Update*,)
   - *Eucharist: Understanding Christ's Body*. William Shannon (*Catholic Update*)
3. Video-based learning options:
   - *Echoes of Faith: Liturgy and Sacraments—1. What is Liturgy* (RCL)
   - *Echoes of Faith: Liturgy and Sacraments—2. Liturgy and Christian Identity* (RCL)
   - *Catholic Update Video: A Walk through the Mass* (St. Anthony Messenger Press)
   - *The Sacrament of Eucharist*. Kathleen Chesto (Twenty-Third Publications)
   - *Why We Go to Mass*. Rev. J-Glenn Murray, S.J. (Loyola Press)
4. *Interview:* Develop a set of questions based on your study of the Eucharist and interview the pastor, liturgist, and/or parish staff in person or via e-mail or phone.

Independent Learning Plan: Reconciliation

1. Online learning session: "Reconciliation" (45-60 minute online program)
2. Guided reading:
   - *How to Celebrate the Sacrament of Reconciliation Today*. Thomas Richstatter (*Catholic Update*)
   - *The Gift of Reconciliation: Ten Tips for Better Confessions*. Thomas Richstatter (*Catholic Update*)
3. Video-based learning options:
   - *Echoes of Faith: Liturgy and Sacraments—4. Sacraments of Healing* (RCL)
   - *Catholic Update Video: The Church Celebrates the Reconciling God* (St. Anthony Messenger Press)
   - *Catholic Update Video: The God Who Reconciles* (St. Anthony Messenger Press)

Evaluation of a Ministry Position

Adapt this evaluation form to fit your particular ministry and programming.

Name: _____   Phone: _____

Name of ministry position: _____

Term of the position from: _____ to _____

1. This ministry position has been satisfying for me because:

2. The major frustrations in this ministry position have been:

3. I used the following skills in this ministry position:

4. The training I received for this position included:

5. I felt supported in this position in the following ways:

6. I received the following resources, which assisted me in this position:

7. I would have been able to complete this ministry more effectively if:

Evaluation of a Ministry Position

8. The highlights of this ministry for me have been:

9. The major accomplishments achieved through this ministry include:

10. A person following me in this ministry position needs to know:

Please indicate the degreee to which each of the following enabled you to complete this ministry effectively and faithfully. circle the appropriate response: 1=inadequate, 2=average, 3=outstanding.

11. The way in which the position was explained to me before I began   1 2 3

12. Opportunity to contribute to program planning   1 2 3

13. Satisfaction with the program design   1 2 3

14. Accuracy of your job description   1 2 3

15. Quality of the orientation to the ministry and its goals   1 2 3

16. Quality and extent of training prior to ministry involvement   1 2 3

17. Quality and extent of in-service training   1 2 3

18. Quality and extent of support provided   1 2 3

19. Quality of the supervision and feedback provided   1 2 3

20. Opportunity to express my opinions on how the program is going   1 2 3

21. Degree to which my volunteer work is recognized and properly appreciated   1 2 3

22. The challenge and responsibility I feel in doing my job   1 2 3

23. Factors that would influence my next volunteer ministry position:

CHAPTER 5
Designing a Learning Plan

► Task 1: Alignment of Learning for All Ages

Designing a learning plan provides a tool for *alignment* of learning throughout the parish. Remember that one of the important features of events-centered learning is that the whole parish is focused on an event—everyone is preparing for the same event with the same theological focus. This attention to alignment and focus creates parish-wide synergy.

In creating a plan, consider the different audiences that need to be included in preparation, e.g., children, adolescents, young adults, adults with grown children, older adults, the homebound, etc. Consider the current learning settings in the parish: classes (children, adolescents, adults), workshops, speaker series, parish missions, retreats, Bible study and faith-sharing groups, committees, leadership groups, RCIA, etc. The following are six questions to be asked in the process of developing a learning plan for the whole parish community. These questions also form the framework of the *Whole Parish Plan for Aligning Learning* worksheet on page 138.

1. *Who?* Identify current and potential audiences for faith formation: age groups, lifestyle groups, families, and the whole community. Write the names of these groups in the first column of your worksheet.

2. *How?* Identify the setting (i.e., program, small group, meeting, Sunday Mass, home) you will use to reach each audience in column 1. Write this information in the second column.

3. *What?* What learning program, strategy, or activity will you use to prepare each audience for the event? Write this information in the third column.

4. *When?* Identify the dates and times for implementing each program, meeting, strategy, and activity. Write the dates and times in the fourth column.

5. *Where?* Identify the location for each program, meeting, or gathering. Record the locations in the fifth column.

After completing the worksheet, you will be ready to develop the various activities for each group. Attention to the scope of the different audiences in the parish will help create alignment across it.

On the next two pages are two sample learning plans—one that includes a family learning program with age-specific learning groups, and one that includes an intergenerational learning program. The sample plans illustrate alignment and a comprehensive learning plan.

Sample Plan for Aligning Learning for All Ages

Event: Lent				
Focus: The three lenten practices of praying, fasting, and almsgiving				
Who?	How?	What?	When?	Where?
---	---	---	---	---
audience (current and potential)	program, small group, meeting, at home, Sunday assembly	learning program, strategy, activity	dates and times for implementation	locations for programs, meetings, gatherings
All ages and generations: • families with children • adolescents • young adults • adults • RCIA candidates	intergenerational learning model	parallel learning format	2nd Week of February Wednesday 6:00 -9:00 PM Friday 6:00 - 9:00 PM Saturday 9:00 AM - 12 noon Sunday 11:00 AM- 2:00 PM (after 10:00 AM Mass)	parish center, meeting rooms, and church
adults	adult Bible study	lenten Bible study, focusing on the Scriptures of Lent and the three practices	incorporated into weekly Bible Study sessions during February and March	parish meeting room
older adults	senior gathering and luncheon	guest speaker for Lent	45-minute presentation at the February gathering	parish center
homebound	at home	bulletin insert and Lenten Home Kit	distributed to the home by Eucharistic Ministers and family members	homes
parish leadership groups	committee meetings	opening prayer and Scripture reflection for Lent	all committee meetings and leadership groups during February	wherever leadership groups meet
men's groups and women's groups	monthly meetings	opening prayer and Scripture reflection for Lent	all groups in the parish during February	wherever groups meet
congregation as a whole	at Sunday Mass	• lenten newsletter of prayers, activities, and reflections • lenten *Catholic Update*	distributed on Ash Wednesday and the First Sunday of Lent	church

Whole Parish Plan for Aligning Learning

Event:_____ **Date:** _____

Catechetical-Theological Focus: _____

Who?	How?	What?	When?	Where?
Audience (current and potential)	Program, small group, meeting at home, Sunday assembly	Learning program, strategy, activity	Dates and times for implementation	Locations for programs, meetings, gatherings

▶ Task 2: Designing Intergenerational Learning Programs

1. Introduction to Events-centered Learning

Events-centered learning utilizes a catechetical process of preparing people of all ages and all generations for meaningful participation in Church events through a variety of learning programs, engaging them in Church events, and guiding them in reflecting on and applying the significance and meaning of the events to their lives as Catholics.

Preparation empowers people to participate meaningfully in the Church event, engaging them in its dynamic and providing the activities and resources that help people participate fully in the event. Preparation programs and activities are designed to help people of all ages and generations develop:

- *know-what,* that is, an understanding of the meaning of the event and its scriptural, doctrinal, and theological foundation;

- *know-why,* the ability to appreciate and value the meaning and significance of the event for their lives;

- *know-how,* the ability to participate competently in the event and then live out its meaning and significance.

The second movement in the events-centered methodology involves our *engagement* in the event. Events are at the heart of the learning process. By actively participating in the event, people transform their lives and they learn.

The events-centered methodology comes full circle with *reflection* on the meanings people draw from their engagement with the event, using the structure of the event and the preparation content and activities as guides. It also includes *application* of the learning to one's life as a Catholic today. Reflection and application activities and strategies are often packaged in kits for use by individuals and families at home.

Reflection helps people to

- *share* their experience of the event (storytelling);

- *assess* the significance or meaning they draw from their engagement in the event and connect it to the Scriptures and Catholic tradition (theological reflection);

- *apply* the meaning (beliefs, practices) to their daily lives (transfer of learning);

- *report* or "publish" their learning for others in the parish community (feedback).

2. Designing a Preparation Program

The following material is designed to guide you through the process of designing preparation programs for age-specific settings, family settings, and intergenerational settings. Use the *Intergenerational Learning Design* worksheet on pages 165-9 to record your design decisions.

Step 1. Identify the catechetical-theological theme.

Note: If you did not identify the theme when you created your curriculum plan, you will need to do so now.

The starting point for all design work is the indentification of one theme which emerges from an event. By carefully reviewing the event, several themes will emerge. It is essential to select one catechetical-theological theme to guide the preparation and reflection designs. Here are suggestions for discovering the themes embedded in the events:

- To identify themes in a Church year season (Advent, Christmas, Lent, Easter), reflect upon the lectionary readings for the season, the liturgies and rituals, the key symbols for the Sundays, and major celebrations within the season, etc.
- To discover themes in a sacramental celebration, explore and reflect upon the Rite or order of service, the introduction to the Rite (the theological foundation), and the lectionary readings, symbols, ritual actions, etc.
- To discover *themes* in a justice or service event, explore the focus and design of the project, the social issues being addressed and their impact on people, the causes of the situation, relevant Catholic social teachings, the reason for addressing the situation, the audience being served, the specific actions of those who are working for justice or serving those in need, etc.
- To discover *themes* in prayer and spirituality events, explore the history of the event or spiritual tradition, the prayer practices in the event, connection to a saint or Church tradition, and order of service, etc.

Be sure to review your parish's approach to the event. Every parish has its own style of celebrating feasts, seasons, and sacraments, of undertaking social justice and service projects, and of praying and celebrating community life. Review actual outlines for a worship service, sacramental celebration, justice/service project, prayer or spiritual practice, or community life program. For example, if you were researching the Advent season in your parish, you would consult the parish calendar to discover significant events in your parish's Advent celebration: the Sunday liturgies, celebration of the sacrament of reconciliation, prayer services, community events (caroling, making Advent wreaths), and service projects.

Use the following steps and questions to help you and your team surface several themes from the selected event. After reflection and discussion, select the theme that best reflects the sense of the group. Remember that one event can have many important themes, some of which you can utilize in subsequent years, e.g., Lent can be an annual event in your curriculum plan, with a different theme each year. Be sure to adjust the questions based on the event you have selected: Church year feast or season, sacrament, prayer and spirituality, justice and service, or community life.

1. Consult the Scriptures utilized in the event.
   - What Scripture texts are used in the event?
   - What images are central in the Scripture readings?
   - What is the context for the Scripture readings?
   - What do these Scripture texts teach us about God, Jesus, and the Holy Spirit?
   - What do they teach us about the Christian life?

2. Review the symbols, music, and artwork in the event.
   - What are the symbolic actions (e.g., Sign of the Cross) and elements (e.g. water, oil) used in this event?
   - Why are these actions/elements used in this event?
   - What music is used to celebrate the season/feast or sacrament/rite?
   - What art or environmental setting is used to celebrate the season/feast or sacrament/rite?
3. Review the prayer texts and Church teachings.

   For a sacrament/rite:
   - What is the theology of the rite according to the Introduction to the rite?
   - What images are used to describe the sacrament/rite in the Introduction to the rite and in the prayer texts of the rite?

   For a justice and service event:
   - What key principle(s) of Catholic social teachings are being addressed in this justice and service event?
4. Explore the tradition and history of the event.
   - What are the origins and history of the event?
   - Is it celebrated or conducted differently in particular cultures or countries?
5. Connect with the human experience in the event.
   - What are the human experiences that are being expressed in this event?
   - How does this event relate to the life of the community?

Use the *Scope of Church Events and Themes* in Chapter 2 to review potential themes for Church events. Several Church documents may also assist you in researching the Scriptural-theological foundation of an event.

Catechism of the Catholic Church (USCCB Publishing)

Communities of Salt and Light (USCCB)

Communities of Salt and Light—Parish Resource Manual (USCCB)

Lectionary for Mass (Catholic Book Publishing)

Lectionary for Mass—Study Edition (Liturgy Training Publications)

The Rites Volumes 1 and 2, Study Edition (Liturgical Press)

The Sacramentary (Catholic Book Publishing)

Sharing Catholic Social Teaching—Challenges and Directions and *Sharing Catholic Social Teaching, Leader's Guide* (USCCB)

Check online at www.generationsoffaith.org for additional resources.

Step 2. Develop learning objectives.

As mentioned previously, learning experiences designed for preparation programs need to address three important learning objectives: the know-what, know-why, and know-how of an event. These three outcomes combine the cognitive, the affective, and the behavioral. Specifically, we help the learners develop:

1. *Know-what*: understanding the meaning of the event and its Scriptural, doctrinal, and theological foundation. What will the learner now comprehend as a result of participating in the preparation program and household learning activities?
2. *Know-why*: appreciating and valuing the meaning and significance of the event for their lives as Catholics. What will the learner now value as a result of participating in the preparation program and household learning activities?

3. Know-how: acquiring the ability to participate competently in the event and to live its meaning in their lives as Catholics. What will the learner now be able to do as a result of participating in the preparation program and household learning activities?

Example: A Walk-Through of the Mass

A walk-through of the Mass guides learners of all ages to:

- develop a deeper understanding of the fourfold movement of the Mass: gathering, storytelling, meal sharing, and sending forth (*know-what*);
- utilize their understanding of the fourfold movement to participate more actively and more meaningfully in the celebration of the Eucharist (*know-how*);
- learn how to be the Body of Christ in the world (*know-how*);
- develop an appreciation for the significance of the Eucharist in their daily lives as Catholics (*know-why*).

Example: The Three Practices of Lent

The three practices of Lent guide learners of all ages to:

- develop a deeper understanding of praying, fasting, and almsgiving as well as their essential connection to the Lenten season (*know-what*);
- develop an appreciation for the significance of praying, fasting, and almsgiving in their daily lives as Catholics during Lent and throughout the year (*know-why*);
- live the practices of praying, fasting, and almsgiving during Lent and throughout the year (*know-how*).

Step 3. Design preparation programs.

▶ AN INTERGENERATIONAL LEARNING MODEL

In his book *Intergenerational Religious Education*, Robert White defines intergenerational religious education as "…two or more different age groups of people in a religious community together learning/growing/living in faith through in-common experiences, parallel learning, contributive-occasions, and interactive sharing." There are four major elements necessary for structuring an intergenerational learning model.

1. *All-Ages Experience/In-Common Experience.* Intergenerational religious education begins with a multigenerational experience of the theme that all generations share together. These in-common experiences are usually less verbal and more observational than those in the other three elements. In-common experiences equalize the group; people of different ages listen to music or sing, make an art project, watch a video, hear a story, participate in a ritual, pray together, and so on, at the same time and place, in a similar manner. Learning is at a level that allows all to fully participate. These shared experiences are absolutely critical for building intergenerational religious education.

2. *In-Depth Learning Experience.* Through structured learning activities and discussion, all generations explore the meaning of the event and develop the ability to participate meaningfully in the event. In-depth learning experiences can be designed in one of three formats:

Note: We recommend that families with children in grades one through five be treated as a learning group in all three formats. Intergenerational learning provides a marvelous opportunity to help the whole family learn how to learn together and share, celebrate, and live their faith. By learning together we can help parents develop skills to share faith with their children and make a significant difference in their home life. There may be times during the year when you separate parents from the children because of the content of the program. But as a general practice, we recommend that you keep families with children together in the intergenerational learning program.

❑ The *age-group format* provides age-appropriate learning for separate groups at the same time. Though groups are separated by age, each one focuses on the same topic, utilizing specific learning activities that are designed for their stage of the life cycle (e.g., families with children, adolescents, young adults, adult). Age-group sessions can be designed in a variety of ways: learning activity centers for the families-with-children group; integrated lesson plan for adolescents; faith-sharing groups or a guest speaker for adults.

We recommend that age groups be organized into the following learning groups, although the number of groups may vary depending on the number of participants. For example, if there are a small number of teens in grades six through twelve, you can group them together for large group presentations and activities and then divide them into separate groups (grades six through eight and grades nine through twelve) for reflection and discussion.

  • three-year-olds and younger: child care
  • four- and five-year-olds (including kindergarten): preschool program with one or more catechists in a separate meeting space
  • parents with children in grades one through five
  • middle school adolescents: grades six through eight
  • high school adolescents: grades nine through twelve
  • eighteen- through thirty-five-year-old young adults (single, married couples)
  • ages thirty-five and up adults.

❑ The *whole group format* provides a series of facilitated learning activities for everyone, using small groups or table groups. Groups can be organized in one of two ways: intergenerational (mixed ages in a group) or age groups (separate groups for families with children, teens, young adults, and adults). A lead facilitator or team guides the entire group through an integrated learning program, giving presentations, leading activities, etc. Catechists/facilitators can lead small group activities and discussions for groups without adults.

❑ The *learning activity center format* provides structured learning activities at a variety of stations or centers in a common area. Learning activity centers are usually facilitated by a leader, and provide background reading, instructions for the activity, and materials for engaging in the activity. Tables and chairs, or floor space, are essential so that individuals and families can learn, create, and discuss together. For example, an Advent-Christmas intergenerational preparation program might include activity centers for all ages: an Advent wreath or Jesse tree center, an Advent-service projects center, and other age-appropriate activity centers such as an adult faith-sharing center focused on the infancy narratives, or a families-with-children center focused on making an Advent calendar. Learning activity centers can be used with all age groups, and can be developed for an intergenerational audience or particular age groups (e.g., centers for families with children, teens, and adults). Activity centers work very well with families with children in grades one through five and can be used with families in the parallel format.

3. *Whole Group Sharing Experience.* The whole group reconvenes and each group briefly shares what it has learned and/or created during its in-depth experience. Whole group sharing provides an opportunity for each generation to teach one another. Groups can share the project or activity they created, using a verbal summary or symbol of their learning, a dramatic presentation, etc. Whole group sharing can also be conducted in intergenerational groups, sharing learning in small groups rather than using presentations to the entire group.

4. *Sharing Learning Reflections and Home Application.* To conclude the program, participants have the opportunity to reflect on what they learned and begin to apply it to their daily lives. The Home Kit provides individuals and families with a variety of practical tools for bringing the event home. After an explanation of how to use the Home Kit, individuals and families have time to create an at-home action plan for using the Home Kit. Participants can be organized into family groupings, intergenerational groupings, and/or kindred groups for reflection and application.

Design Template

Intergenerational learning models are designed for 2 1/2 to 3 hour programs with time for a meal included. The design format for an intergenerational learning program includes the following parts:

Registration and Hospitality

- Greeting
- Sign-in and name tag distribution
- Distribution of home kits and handouts
- Invitation to share a meal (depending on the time of day, the program may end with a meal instead)

Part 1: Gathering

- Welcome
- Overview of the event and theme
- A community-building activity and a forming-groups activity (if necessary)
- Opening prayer service with music on the theme of the event

Part 2: All-Ages Opening Experience

This is an activity designed to introduce the entire group to the theme of the program through an engaging activity that addresses the diverse ages of the participants.

- Conduct the activity, using dramatization, media/video, or storytelling to introduce the theme and help participants identify their own experience of the theme of the event.

Part 3: In-Depth Learning Experience

This part includes structured learning activities and discussion to engage participants of all ages in exploring the meaning of the event and to develop their ability to participate meaningfully in the event. In-depth learning experiences can be designed in one of three formats:

- Age-group format
- Whole group format
- Learning activity center format.

The learning format can vary from event to event. There is no need to set one format for an entire year. Let the event, the theme, the learning program content and activities, and your parish facility guide you in selecting the in-depth learning format.

Part 4: Sharing Learning Experiences and Home Application

Small groups share their insights and learning from the program by presenting projects to the entire group or by sharing in intergenerational groups.

- Determine what each group will share as a result of its learning.
- Determine how each group will share its report or project so that the entire group learns about the event and the theme.

This part of the program is designed to send people home ready to participate in the event and to utilize the home activities. Begin with reflection on the learning from the preparation program in family groups, age groups, or intergenerational groups. Then move on to explain the Home Kit and give families and individuals time to create an at-home action plan for using the Home Kit.

- Guide individuals and families in sharing their learning within family clusters, individual family units, and/or kindred groups (young adults, adults, older adults).
- Review the contents of the Home Kit: prayers, rituals, service projects, family enrichment, and learning activities.
- Review the reflection activities and how to use them.
- Guide participants in developing an individual- or family-action plan for celebrating/living the event, using the Home Kit and in planning for participation in the Church event.

Part 5: Closing Prayer Service

- Conclude with a prayer service and music on the theme of the event.

Role of the Home Kit in the Learning Program

The Home Kit is the resource centerpiece for both the home and the learning program. Distribute the Home Kit at the beginning of the program so that participants can work with the materials during the session. If we want people to feel confident, comfortable, and capable of using the home activities, then we need to use and model the activities in the session. If we want people to celebrate the home rituals included in the kit, they need to experience how to have a discussion in the session. If we want people to pray at home, they need to experience a prayer from the Home Kit during the session. By modeling what we want to happen at home during the session, we build the confidence of families and individuals so that they can share, celebrate, and live faith at home.

Facility Requirements

The parish facility (church, hall, meeting rooms) is a major influence on the choices that you will make as you design and structure the intergenerational learning program. Before you make choices about where you will hold large group gatherings, where you will serve the meal, and which in-depth learning format you will use, survey your facility. Remember that a parallel learning format requires break-out space, activity centers require one or more larger meeting rooms, and the learning-group format requires a large meeting room for table groups. Begin by making a facility inventory that considers the capacity of your meeting rooms. Consider the following meeting spaces:

- worship space
- large meeting spaces, e.g., parish hall, church basement, gathering space in the church
- medium-sized meeting rooms (twenty-five to fifty people), e.g., classrooms, conference rooms
- small-sized meeting rooms (under twenty-five people)

Next, determine what spaces you will need for intergenerational learning and how you will use your space. Sometimes you have to be very creative in the ways you use your space.

- Registration and hospitality: entrance to large meeting room, foyer, or gathering space
- Shared meal: large meeting room with tables and chairs
- Part 1. Gathering: large meeting room or worship space (Use the same space for the next part so as to reduce movement.)
- Part 2. All-ages learning experience: large meeting room or worship space (Depending on the type of learning activity, you may need movable chairs or tables.)
- Part 3. In-depth learning experience: needs vary, as indicated below:

    activity center format: large meeting room or separate meeting rooms for activity centers for families with children, adolescents, and adults

    age group format: large meeting room for families with children; meeting rooms forpreschool, young adolescents, older adolescents, young adults, and adults

    whole group format: large meeting room with tables and chairs

- Part 4. Sharing learning reflections and home application: large meeting room or worship space
- Part 5. Closing prayer service: large meeting room or worship space

    Check online at www.generationsoffaith.org for a sample intergenerational program. Also see the sample lenten intergenerational program outline in this chapter.

EXAMPLE: LENTEN INTERGENERATIONAL LEARNING PROGRAM OUTLINE

Event

Ash Wednesday and the lenten season

Catechetical-Theological Focus

Three Practices of Lent: praying, fasting, and almsgiving

Learning Objectives

This intergenerational preparation program guides learners of all ages to

- develop a deeper understanding of praying, fasting, and almsgiving and their essential connection to the lenten season (*know-what*);
- live the practices of praying, fasting, and almsgiving during Lent and throughout the year (*know-how*);
- develop an appreciation for the significance of praying, fasting, and almsgiving for their daily lives as Catholics during Lent and throughout the year (*know-why*).

Timing
2 1/2 to 3 hours, including time for a meal
Lenten Prayer Center
- Set-up a lenten prayer center (table) with the symbols of Lent: the lectionary or Bible, purple tablecloth, a thick white candle, clear glass bowl with water, a small clear bowl with olive oil, a loaf of bread on a plate, a clear glass with wine, a cross or crucifix, palms, ashes, and thorns.

Learning Design

Registration and Hospitality
- Sign-in participants and distribute name tags.
- Distribute Home Kits including the handouts for the session.
- Invite people to share a meal (depending on time of day, the program may end with a meal).

Part 1. Gathering (10-15 minutes)
- Environment: lenten prayer table
- Welcome the participants and provide an overview of the program and schedule.
- Conduct a community-building activity and if necessary, a forming-groups activity.
- Lead the participants in an opening prayer service on the theme. Use the Scripture reading for Ash Wednesday (Matthew 6:1–18), selected prayers from the Sacramentary for Ash Wednesday and the Sundays of Lent, and one or two hymns that will be used at the lenten liturgies.

Part 2. All-Ages Opening Experience (15–20 minutes)
This experience introduces the participants to the theme of the program. There are a variety of ways to conduct the opening experience. For a presentation to the large group, you can use drama, media, storytelling, or another interactive approach that works well with a large group.
Suggestions:
- Create a PowerPoint presentation that explains and illustrates each of the three practices.
- Create or find a drama to present praying, fasting, and almsgiving (Matthew 6:1–18) or, for younger groups, use an echo pantomime, e.g., "Ashes, Ashes" in *Echo Stories for Children* (Twenty-Third Publications).
- Invite a "Lenten Witness Panel" of parishioners of different ages to tell a story of Lent, e.g., a story of "conversion" or change, or a story of personal or family lenten traditions of fasting, service, or prayer.

Part 3. In-Depth Learning: Age-Group Format (75-90 minutes)
You can organize the learning activities in two ways. For activity centers: organize activity centers for each of the three activity plans in the meeting room with tables and chairs (or floor space) for children and families to learn, work, discuss. Each center is facilitated by a team of facilitators/catechists which guides the families through the activity plan. Each center has all of the materials necessary for conducting the activity. Be sure to keep the activity centers far enough apart so that people can focus on their activity.

For the table groups: organize the activities at tables for groups of two or more families. Make sure each table has the supplies, instructions, and learning materials necessary to complete the activities. A facilitator guides the families through each activity. Catechists move from table to table assisting families.

Method

Each activity plan is organized using the same methodology:

1. Introduce the practice.
2. Experience the practice.
3. Sharing ideas for living the practice.
4. Develop a "family lenten pledge" for living the practice as individuals and as a family.

Activity Plans

Activity #1: The Practice of Fasting

Activity #2: The Practice of Praying

Activity #3: The Practice of Almsgiving/Service

Adolescent Learning Plan

Use the following session plan with middle school and high school youth:

1. Explore the meaning of Lent.
2. Experience the three practices of Lent.
3. Share ideas for living the practices of Lent.
4. Develope a Lenten Pledge for living the practice.
5. Develop a group project for Lent.

Young Adult and Adult Learning Activities

Depending on the number of adult participants and your available meeting rooms, you can organize several young adult and adult program offerings.

Option 1: Video and Discussion

- Use a video presentation, *The Church Celebrates: Lent and Easter* (Catholic Update Videos, St. Anthony Messenger Press) as the centerpiece of learning activity. The video includes four segments: a story, witness (reflections from Catholics), teaching/presentation, and music video reflection. The study guide includes reflection questions and ways to use the video with groups.
- Follow the video with a presentation and discussion of the three practices of Lent. Conclude with the Lenten Pledge.

Note: You can begin either of the remaining two options with this video or weave it into the learning activity. This will provide a good context for any of the activities.

Option 2: Small Faith-Sharing Group

- Organize small groups of up to twelve participants and use the small group session plan on the three practices of Lent. Conclude with the Lenten Pledge.

Option 3: Guest Speaker

- Invite a guest speaker (parish staff or someone from outside the parish) to give a presentation on the meaning of Lent and the relevance of the three lenten practices for today. Allow time for discussion and completion of the Lenten Pledge.

Part 4. Sharing Learning Reflections and Home Application (25 minutes)

- Each group will share their reports or projects so that they "teach" the other groups about the event and theme. *Suggestion:* Each learning group can share ideas from the lenten pledge.

- Guide individuals and families in sharing what they learned during the program. Participants can be organized in family clusters, individual family units, and/or kindred groups (young adults, adults, older adults).

- Review the Lenten Home Kit containing prayers, rituals, service projects, family enrichment, and learning activities.

- Review the reflection activities or strategies to use in conjunction with the event.

- Guide everyone in using the Home Kit to develop an individual or family action plan for living at home, and planning for participation in the lenten season.

Part 5. Closing Prayer Service (5–10 minutes)

Note: For a free copy of the Lenten Intergenerational Learning Program go to www.generationsoffaith.org.

EXAMPLE: A LENTEN HOME KIT

Target Audience

Households of all ages (families and individuals) who are participating in the lenten intergenerational preparation programs.

Format and Contents

- Packaged in a purple gift bag
- Letter introducing the Home Kit
- Table of contents with titles of activities and their targeted audience

Adults

Annual *Daily Scripture Reflections, Prayers, and Activities* (Twenty-Third Publications)
Annual lenten *Catholic Update* (St. Anthony Messenger Press)
What Am I Doing for Lent This Year? (Liturgy Training Publications)

Youth

Youth Update: *One a Day During Lent* (St. Anthony Messenger Pres)
Catholic Teenager's Trip through Lent (Creative Communications for the Parish)

Children

Annual *Lent for Kids* booklet (Twenty-Third Publications)
Annual *Lenten Calendar for Children* (Creative Communications for the Parish)

Household

Annual Lent and Easter for Families booklets (Twenty-Third Publications)
Table Prayers during Lent (Liturgy Training Publications)
Daily Bible Readings for Lent (Creative Communications for the Parish)
Family lenten cross (wooden) with a guide for creating a lenten prayer space at home

EXAMPLE: LENTEN REFLECTION ACTIVITIES

1. Lenten Journal

Adolescents through adults, as well as families, can use journals to record their lenten experiences, including their thoughts, feelings, questions, hopes, dreams, faith practices, etc. Consider using a poster-journal designed for display on the refrigerator so that all family members can record their actions, thoughts, feelings, and what they have learned. Include the journal in the Lenten Home Kit.

2. Lenten Photo Collage

Provide each family with a disposable camera in their Lenten Home Kit. Ask individuals and families to take photos of their in-home experience of Lent, especially the three practices (e.g., a photo of the family at prayer, a photo of the family serving others, etc). Ask them to prepare a photo collage of their lenten experiences with descriptions or captions that explain their actions and provide a commentary on their feelings and/or thoughts about Lent.

Display the collages at Sunday Mass on a designated weekend or at a gathering during the week. Set up a gallery of collages and photos in the church gathering space as a way to publish what participants have learned. Be sure to take photos of the display for the parish scrapbook. After the display at church is taken down, encourage participants to display their photos at home.

3. Lenten "Recipe for Living" Cards

Ask individuals and families to identify practical strategies that they can use during Lent. Distribute 3" 3 5" file cards and ask people to record a practical strategy on each one. Ask them to return the cards during the offertory collection on a particular Sunday or during the week at a gathered program. Consider creating a lenten or annual parish "cookbook" of recipes for living the Catholic faith during Lent. Publish the book and distribute it to individuals and families. Include pre-printed file cards in the Lenten Home Kit so that families can record their experiences.

4. Lenten Scrapbook

Provide individuals and families with a small scrapbook in their Lenten Home Kit. Ask participants to document their lenten journey, from Ash Wednesday to Easter Sunday. The scrapbook can be filled with photos, artwork, prayers, and reflections documenting the in-home experience of Lent. Incorporate storytelling into your next meeting of the whole community so that individuals and families can share their scrapbooks and document their learning and growth.

Step 4. Evaluate a Preparation Program

An essential step in programming is program evaluation. Evaluation is a systematic and objective process that compares what the program intended to do with what the program actually accomplished in order to determine how it can be improved. Program evaluation needs to be regularly scheduled, and evaluations should be conducted at the end of each individual program and the program year. Is the evaluation process really worth the time and effort? Yes! An evaluation can provide affirmation and legitimization for your efforts. Through an evaluation process, programming can be altered. Program plans can be reviewed and redefined. New needs and interests can come to light and be addressed.

Following an evaluation, the results and findings should be reported to all who participated in the program, to the program leaders, to the parish staff, and to appropriate committees. These findings should give details about the decisions that program leaders have made and describe the actions that have been taken since the evaluation.

Here is an evaluation process you can adapt to address your particular situation.

1. Develop a participant evaluation form, using the sample evaluation forms on pages 170-4.
2. Conduct a participant evaluation of the preparation program and reflection activity.
3. Review the results of the participant evaluation with your leaders or planning team for this event.
4. In light of the evaluation results, review your original program plans for this event, using the following questions:
   - How well did we accomplish our goals for this event?
   - How effective were the preparation program and reflection strategies for this event?
   - Did we select an appropriate scheduling model, date, time, and place for the preparation program? What could we do differently next time?
   - Did our events-centered plan work effectively? What should be modified?
   - Did we have enough leaders? Were their jobs clearly defined? Were leaders properly trained? Did they conduct the preparation programs effectively? How could their performance be improved or strengthened?
   - Did we have adequate resources and funds?

Based upon the results of your discussion, determine how you will make adjustments or modifications in your events-centered plan. Then make any necessary changes in your design.

▶ Task 3: Designing Home Activities

The Generations of Faith approach integrates home and parish into a comprehensive model of faith formation. Empowering and equipping individuals and families to live their faith at home and in the world is key to this approach. Generations of Faith views the family as the Church of the home, and as a community of learning and practice. The events-centered approach provides a focus and a support structure to build a partnership between the home and parish. It overcomes the isolation many families feel when they are asked to engage in home-based activities and faith-sharing. The parish-wide support structure enhances family participation in the process because "everyone is doing it."

The catechetical task is to provide individuals and families with the resources and tools they need to *extend* and *expand* their learning from a preparation program and their experience of the event to their lives and home. Event-specific home materials help families and individuals celebrate traditions and rituals, continue their learning, pray together, serve others and work for justice, and enrich their relationships and family life. Attention to home resources and tools is as important as the parish preparation program.

Home activities assist families and individuals in developing know-what, know-why, and know-how, and seek to:

- *extend* and *expand* the learning that has taken place through participation in the preparation program and in the actual event;
- *engage* families and individuals in living the event at home through traditions and celebrations, rituals, symbols, prayers, service, learning activities, and enrichment activities by providing a variety of activities and resources for nurturing faith;
- *create a pattern* of faith-sharing that becomes integral to home life and is woven into the fabric of daily life.

Home activities need to address the primary ways that families share faith. Research by the Search Institute and noted in the book, *The Teaching Church*, has identified five key factors that nourish faith maturity in families:

1. family faith conversations—talking about faith at home;
2. family devotions and worship—prayer, rituals, celebrations, Scripture reading;
3. family service projects—family involvement in helping others;
4. family education—parent education, family-centered or intergenerational catechesis;
5. parental relationships and parental faith.

These five factors can be translated into a framework for promoting faith at home and designing home activities. Home activities for an event should include as many of the following five elements as possible:

- Learning: helping families and individuals to develop the know-what and know-why of Church events, to explore the Scriptures and the Catholic tradition, and to apply faith to daily life as a follower of Jesus Christ
- Celebrating rituals: helping families and individuals to develop patterns of ritual celebrations (daily, weekly, seasonally, annually) and to celebrate Church events in a family way at home through a variety of ritual experiences for Church year feasts and seasons (e.g., Advent, Lent), for weekly Sunday worship, for sacraments (e.g., baptism, Eucharist), for calendar year events, and for milestones (birthdays, anniversaries, graduations, retirements), etc.
- Praying: helping families and individuals to develop their prayer life and live the Church event through a variety of prayer experiences, such as morning and evening prayer, daily prayers for the season, table prayers, and traditional Catholic prayers
- Enriching relationships: helping families strengthen family life by developing skills for family living, deepening the marriage relationship, and participating in family activities that build family strengths and celebrate family life
- Serving and working for justice: helping families and individuals connect their involvement in Church events with the call to act justly and serve those in need, relate the Scriptures and Catholic social teaching to community and global social issues, engage in service to others and actions for social justice, and develop lifestyles based on Gospel values.

Designing and Selecting Home Activities

It is important to think like the families and individuals who will use the home activities when selecting them, and to select activities that are user-friendly in content, format, style, and delivery. All design decisions should make it easy for people to use the activities. Make families feel comfortable and confident about using an activity. Create content that is inviting and accessible for family members. Create formats for activities that families will find familiar and easy to use. Create formats that can be integrated into the flow of everyday home life. Create delivery systems that utilize existing and new ways to distribute activities and get them into the home. As you begin to design and select home activities, here are some suggestions to keep in mind:

- *Keep it simple.* Home Kits and activities do not need to be complex. In fact, it is actually better to focus on making it easy for individuals and families to actually use the activities. For example: create lenten booklets with a page for each Sunday in Lent that includes a prayer for the week, a justice response, a fasting option, and a suggested G-rated movie with discussion questions.

- *"If they create it, they will use it."* Households are more likely to use activities that they have created at a preparation program or for which they have received instructions on how to create them at home. There are a variety of "create-your-own" activities,— e.g., Advent wreaths, decorated journal books, laminated table placemats with prayers and activities, magnets decorated with a symbol for the season, and decorated posters with the symbols of the Triduum—that are ideal for at-home use.

- *Provide a variety of age-appropriate activities.* Some parishes have had good success in stocking tables with activities resources from which individuals and families can select materials to create their own Home Kits. All resources are marked to indicate whether they are appropriate for an all-ages activity or a specific age group. Leaders can guide people in making good choices for their Home Kits.

- *Packaging is important.* There are a variety of ways to package the Home Kits so that individuals and families can carry the resources home, such as colored gift bags, two-pocket folders, printed paper bags (some paper bags fit easily into a standard copier), and small boxes decorated with the symbols of the season or the parish logo.

- *Give households the tools and resources they need.* If you have invited households to read Scripture make sure that they have copies selected passages or a Bible to use at home. If you have invited people to pray certain prayers for a season, provide them with copies of the prayers and necessary resources (e.g., a rosary). If you have invited people to create a project at home, make sure they have the necessary resources at home or supply them with what they need.

- *Provide a "user's guide" for the Home Kit.* Include a letter and table of contents with the guide so that individuals and families can feel confident and comfortable with the activities. If you have given households several things to accomplish in a season, provide them with a guide indicating what needs to be accomplished and when. For example, one parish that collected different supplies for local justice agencies throughout Lent included a list of items that households needed to bring to Mass each Sunday. Another parish asked families to create a variety of symbols for each Sunday of Advent, so they provided this information on the Advent calendar that was included in the Home Kit.

- *Carefully evaluate the costs of resources.* It may initially seem that it is cheaper to create resources than to purchase them. However, when factoring in staff time and equipment use, you may find it cheaper to purchase the resources. (See the list of publishers of home materials on page 157.)

The following guide will assist you with the process of designing and selecting home activities for an event. In addition, there are two worksheets in the Appendix that will help you: Creating a Home Kit is a worksheet for recording all of the materials you are including in the Home Kit; the Home Activities Planning Form is a worksheet for recording your parish-wide home activities plan for all ages, e.g., home activities distributed at the weekend Masses, targeted home materials for young adults, or home materials for homebound older adults.

Step 1. Identify target audiences.

The design process for the Home Kits begins with deciding on the target audience(s) for the home activities. Remember that even if people receive activities that do not relate directly to their needs and interests or age, they can share these materials with other family members or neighbors. Every Church event is an opportunity to nurture the faith of the entire family—grandparents, parents, and children. Oftentimes the grandparent generation has great leverage in nurturing the faith of the entire family system across generations. The are several options for targeting audiences that will use home activities:

- Target the entire congregation, producing home activities that address the learning needs of all ages and generations in the parish.
- Target specific groups at one or more stages of the life cycle, producing home activities that address their particular needs and interests:
  —Family life-cycle stages: new couple, families with young children, families with older children, families with young adolescents, families with older adolescents, families with young adults, families with married children and grandchildren, families in later life
  —Life-cycle stages and groupings: children, adolescents, young adults, adults, older adults
- Target participants in preparation programs.
- Target parishioners who do not participate in preparation programs but do attend Sunday Mass and other services.

Step 2. Design or select home activities.

To determine the kinds of home activities you will need to design or select, ask yourself the following questions:

- How will the activities help families and individuals to develop the know-how, know-what, and/or know-why of an event?
- How will the activities incorporate the five ways of nurturing faith—learning activities, rituals, prayers, service projects, and enrichment activities?
- How will the activities extend and expand the learning that has taken place through participation in the preparation program and/or the actual event?
- Will we produce individual activities or combine several activities into a kit, booklet, or newsletter?

Here are two examples of the different types of activities that can be included in a Home Kit:

Baptism Home Kit

- *Learning*: Scripture passages to read as a family, a guide to exploring the symbols of baptism, a *Catholic Update* on baptism, list of children's storybooks and Bible stories, video and music suggestions for learning more about baptism.
- *Family enrichment*: resources for parenting children—skills, tools, information; family-life activities—making meal time special, family projects, family trips.
- *Ritual*: the symbols of baptism—a small cross, bottle of holy water, candle, bottle of oil; ideas for creating a family baptism prayer space (home altar), using the symbols and and other objects, such as family baptism pictures, garment, candle; a ritual for celebrating the anniversary of a baptism.
- *Prayer*: table prayers for the anniversary of a baptism, table prayers for the symbols of baptism (water, light, oil), a week of prayers before meals on the themes of baptism.
- *Service*: suggestions for developing a stewardship lifestyle, a guide to getting involved in parish ministries, ideas for community service (e.g., preparing and serving a meal at a soup kitchen, donating food and clothes for children in need, visiting the elderly, recycling, planting trees or a garden).

Advent-Christmas Home Kit

- *Prayer*: morning and nighttime prayers for December, prayers for every day of Advent, table prayers for Advent and the Christmas Season, a guide to praying the Joyful Mysteries of the Rosary, weekly prayers for the Advent wreath.
- *Rituals*: a blessing before the Christmas meal and the Christ candle, a blessing for a Christmas crèche, a blessing for a Christmas tree, a blessing upon opening gifts, a ritual for Our Lady of Guadalupe and Dia de los Reyes Magos (Three Kings Day, January 6).
- *Learning*: background, instructions, and materials for the Jesse Tree activity and/or creating an Advent wreath (provide the candles); day-by-day Advent calendars for children, teens, and adults; Advent reflections books for the family, for teens, and for adults; a list of Advent-Christmas storybooks and videos; a guide to reading and exploring the Advent and Christmas lectionary.
- *Service*: a guide to Advent-Christmas service projects (e.g., collections of toys, food, or clothing, "adopt-a-family" project; alternative gift-giving suggestions; a list of charitable organizations for making donations.
- *Family enrichment*: recipes for family baking activities; ideas for making gifts; meal-time activities for the Advent-Christmas season.

Step 3. Choose a format for each activity.

To determine the format for an activity consider the following questions:

- What is the purpose of the activity? How will people at home use the activity?
- Is the format user-friendly—inviting, accessible, attractive, simple, easy-to-use?
- Will the format make families and individuals feel comfortable and confident about using the activity?
- Does the format fit into the flow of everyday home life?
- Will individual family members and the family as a whole use this activity in this format?
- Will several activities be packaged in a Home Kit, newsletter, or booklet?

There are a variety of formats you can choose:

note cards	calendar	music CD
one-fold stand-up card	poster	video
newsletter	prayer card	e-mail
booklet	bookmark	web site
magnet	poster	artwork
journal	placemat	symbols and images
bumper sticker	door hangers	

You can package the activities into a Home Kit in a variety of ways:

- two-pocket folders
- gift bags
- file folders
- large envelopes
- boxes.

Step 4. Determine delivery methods.

Choose the way you will deliver activities to the home. Be creative and find new ways to reach families and individuals. Consider the following delivery methods:

- at the preparation programs for an event
- at gathered parish programs for children, youth, and adults
- at Sunday Mass
- at meetings of parish social groups, committees, and leadership/ministry groups
- through a parish newsletter or as an insert in the newsletter
- through the Sunday bulletin or as an insert in the bulletin
- through the parish web site
- through e-mail distribution to targeted audiences
- through home distribution to the elderly and homebound

To determine and design the delivery system for activities consider the following questions:

- What is the best delivery system for each audience and its activities?
- How will you utilize the existing delivery systems to reach people? Among those you need to reach, who may be excluded from the current delivery systems?
- How can you create or utilize new delivery systems, such as the web and e-mail?

Step 5. Develop a timeline and implementation plans.

Here are several suggestions that may be helpful to you in implementing your design plan. Use those that are appropriate for your plan.

- Develop a step-by-step implementation plan and timeline, including all of the major tasks that must get done in order to implement the home activity successfully. Be sure to give yourself enough time to order and/or create your home activities.
- Develop evaluation and follow-up procedures that provide families and individuals with opportunities to evaluate the effectiveness of the activity, recommend how to improve it, and suggest ideas to build on its success. Consider evaluative methods such as postcard evaluations, phone surveys, success stories, focus groups of families who have participated in the activity, etc.
- Identify the resources you will need to implement the activity.

EXAMPLES OF HOME ACTIVITY KITS

A Eucharist Home Kit (Easter Season)

Target Audience

Households of all ages (families and individuals) who are participating in the Eucharist intergenerational preparation program, families with a child receiving First Eucharist, and adults in the RCIA receiving first Eucharist at the Easter Vigil.

Format and Contents

- Packaged in a colored gift bag or two-pocket folder
- Letter introducing the Home Kit
- Table of contents with titles of activities and their intended audiences

Adults

Catholic Update: *A Walk through the Mass–A Step-by-Step Explanation.* (St. Anthony Messenger Press)

Catholic Update: *Eucharist: Understanding Christ's Body.* (St. Anthony Messenger Press)

Catholic Update: *Participating Fully at Sunday Mass.* (St. Anthony Messenger Press)

Youth

Catholic Update: *A Walk through the Mass—A Step-by-Step Explanation.* (St. Anthony Messenger Press)

Youth Update: *The Top 10 Reasons for Going to Mass.* (St. Anthony Messenger Press)

Children

We Say Thanks: A Young Child's Book for Eucharist. (St. Anthony Messenger Press)

Parents of Children Receiving First Communion

Your Child's First Communion. (St. Anthony Messenger Press)

Household

Scripture reflections on Eucharist

Meal rituals on Eucharist

Guidelines for celebrating at a family meal

Family meal traditions

Baking bread (recipe and activity)

Feeding the hungry of our world—ideas for individual and family activities

Delivery Method

Distribution at the intergenerational preparation programs, RCIA class, and first Eucharist program.

Sources for Home Activities

Home activities for an event may be found at a variety of sources:

Creative Communications for the Parish produces a wide variety of Church year resources for families and individuals of all ages in a variety of designs and formats (print, media). Contact them at 800-325-9414 or www.creativecommunications.com.

Liturgy Training Publications produces a variety of Church year and sacramental resources for parish and home. Contact them at 800-933-1800 or www.ltp.org.

St. Anthony Messenger Press produces Catholic Updates on the Church year, sacraments, and a variety of theological themes, as well as sacrament booklets and resources for home. Contact them at 800-488-0488 or www.AmericanCatholic.org.

Twenty-Third Publications produces a variety of Church year and sacrament booklets and resources for families and individuals of all ages. Contact them at 800-321-0411 or www.23rdpublications.com.

Web Sites

www.AmericanCatholic.org (St. Anthony Messenger Press)

www.blestarewe.com (Silver Burdett Publishing Company)

www.cyberfaith.com (Sadlier Publishing Company)

www.faithfirst.com (RCL Publishing Company)

www.harcourtreligion.com (Harcourt Religion Publishing Company)

www.homefaith.com (Claretian Publications)

www.mhschool.com/benziger/activity (Benziger Publishing Company)

United States Conference of Catholic Bishops

New American Bible: www.usccb.org/nab/bible/index.htm

Daily Readings: www.usccb.org/nab/index.htm
Publications: www.usccb.org/publishing/index.htm

Check online at www.generationsoffaith.org for other examples of home activities.

▶ Task 4: Designing Reflection Activities

The events-centered methodology comes full circle with reflection on the meanings people draw from their engagement in the event. The final element in the prepare-engage-reflect/apply methodology is designed to help people reflect on their experience of the event or season, using the structure of the event and the preparation content/activities as guides. It also includes application of what was learned at the preparation program and event to living as a Catholic today. Reflection and application activities and strategies are often packaged in kits for use by individuals and families at home.

Reflection helps people to:

- *share* their experience of the event (storytelling);
- *assess* the significance or meaning they draw from their engagement in the event and connect it to the Scriptures and Catholic tradition (theological reflection);
- *apply* the meaning (beliefs, practices) to their daily lives (transfer of learning);
- *report* or "publish" their learning for others in the parish community (feedback).

The next section presents a guide to assist you with the process of designing reflection activities for an event. A worksheet is included to record your reflection activities.

Step 1. Identify target audiences.

The design process begins with identifying the target audiences for the reflection activities by reviewing all of the learning settings used in the preparation programs and by the participants in the event. Activities need to be developmentally appropriate so that they address the particular needs of a family or age group.

Given the scope of participation in the preparation programs and the actual event, a parish might develop reflection activities for the following audiences:

- the entire congregation
- families who participate in the preparation programs and utilize home materials
- age groups
    young children
    grade-school children
    young adolescents
    older adolescents
    young adults
    adults
    older adults

Step 2. Design reflection strategies and activities.

Reflection activities are designed around the content of the preparation program and the event. To determine what kinds of strategies and activities you will design, consider the following questions:

- Will you incorporate an opportunity for participants to share their experience of the event and their insights on the reflection activity? How will you design the reflection strategy and activity to encourage in-home sharing? You can incorporate time for sharing reflections into the next program or session that occurs after the event. You can also incorporate time for reflection and sharing right after the event, perhaps with refreshments. All reflection strategies and activities should be designed to promote in-home sharing, whether or not there is an opportunity for a parish gathering.

- What age-appropriate or family-appropriate activities will you develop to help people reflect on the know-what, know-why, and know-how of the event? How will you help them reflect on the significance or meaning they draw from their engagement in the event and connect it to the Scriptures and Catholic tradition? How will you engage the participants in connecting the content of the preparation program to the event?

- What practical strategies and resources will you give participants to apply the meaning of the event to their daily life? How will you help them transfer learning from the preparation program and event into their daily lives? Many home activities can help to transfer what has been learned into daily life.

- Will you provide opportunities for individuals and families to report or "publish" their learning for others in the parish community? Will you invite participants to "bring back" to the parish community an expression of their learning and reflection as individuals and families? For example, if families and individuals created a lenten pledge (fasting, prayer, and almsgiving ideas) during their preparation program, ask them to bring back their completed pledge to the Holy Thursday or Good Friday liturgies. Many of the suggested reflection activities that follow lend themselves to bringing a creative expression of learning back to the parish community.

Step 3. Determine delivery methods.

Design ways that you can distribute reflection activities to the different audiences you have selected. You can use the ideas found on page 000. To design the delivery system for an activity, consider the following questions:

- What is the best delivery system for each audience and its activities?
- How will you utilize the existing delivery systems to reach people? Among those whom you need to reach, who may be excluded from the current delivery systems?
- How can you create or utilize new delivery systems, such as the web and e-mail?

Reflection Activities and Strategies

The following written strategies can be used alone or incorporated into other formats (see art and media reflection strategies on page 162). To provide feedback using written strategies, incorporate time into large or small group sessions following an event or season. You can also use feedback strategies such as postcards, e-mail, and a web site. For example, create a postcard with reflection questions and ask people to send it back to you after the event or season. Be sure to include the parish's return address and a business reply stamp (you pay only for the postcards that are returned).

Use e-mail to send people a written reflection strategy and ask them to reply by completing the questions. You can also post the written reflection strategy on the parish web site and ask people to complete it and e-mail it to you. Be sure to compile and post a summary of the feedback on your parish web site or publish it in the bulletin or as an insert.

1. Written Reflection Activities

Unfinished Sentences

This strategy can be incorporated into all reflection activities. It provides unfinished sentences that participants are asked to complete. You can add specific content that you want people to reflect upon. Here is a sample list to get you started.

- I learned…
- I discovered…
- I was surprised…
- I was moved by…
- I felt…
- I wonder about…
- I need to know more about…
- I was reminded that…
- I'm excited by…
- I'm challenged by… or challenged to…
- I need to remember… or remember to…

Reflection Questions/Learning Journal

Have participants complete a worksheet or journal page that includes the following instructions:

To reflect on what you have learned, identify the insights you have gained and the potential application to your life.
- Insights (what I've learned)
- Applications (how I'll use what I've learned)
- Questions (what I need to learn or explore further)

Seasonal Journal

Individuals as well as families can use journals to record their experience of an event (or the events of whole year): their thoughts, feelings, questions, hopes, dreams, and faith practices. Provide journals along with guidelines for keeping a journal, and sample questions for an event (or in the case of a Church year season, for each day or week). You may also want to include seasonal Bible passages and prayers.

Structured Reflection

Create a reflection questionnaire that uses the structure or outline of the event or the "calendar" of a season as the categories for reflection questions. If the event is a liturgy, use the readings, ritual actions, special prayers, etc., to structure the questionnaire. Then for each category, ask participants to record their thoughts, feelings, insights, how the event applies to their life, etc. For a season such as Advent-Christmas, use the parish calendar of events to structure the questionnaire (e.g., liturgies, service projects, prayer services, sacrament of reconciliation, community life events).

Include questions designed to surface participants' experience of the season (thoughts, feelings), what they have learned about the meaning and significance of the season, and their application of the meaning to their lives (new awareness, new faith practices, etc.). On page 177 is an example of a structured reflection questionnaire on the four movements of the Mass and people's experience of Sunday Mass.

2. At-Home Application Strategies

Action Plan

Have participants complete a worksheet or journal page that includes the following instructions for creating an action plan:

1. List three actions you would like to undertake as a result of your participation in the preparation and event.
2. Choose and record the action that you would like to plan to do first.
3. List the potential roadblocks to implementing this action.
4. Discuss with another person or your small group how you might overcome these roadblocks. Record your solutions.
5. Describe in writing the specific action you will undertake and the steps you will take to ensure that the action is accomplished.

A second version of an action plan worksheet uses a three-column format:

Actions	Potential Roadblocks	First Steps
List several actions that you will undertake	List potential roadblocks to implementing your chosen action.	List the steps you need to take to accomplish the action.

Practice Plan

Create a worksheet or journal page (with room for writing) that helps people identify new practices for living the Catholic faith that they learned from participating in the preparation program and event.

I want to use_____ (practice) in this situation:

_____.

The roadblocks that could get in the way:

_____.

Sample script or plan for using the skill:

_____.

I will make my first attempt by (date):

_____.

To-Do List

Create a worksheet that helps people list new practices for living the Catholic faith that they learned during their participation in the preparation program and event. You can begin the "to-do" list with: "Remember to...." You can also modify the "to-do" list as reminder cards (file cards) that people can place on their desks, post at work, or display at home on the refrigerator. Provide each person or family with a pack of reminder cards preprinted with "Remember to..." that can be personalized.

Resolution Letter

At the conclusion of a preparation program and/or event, ask the participants to write letters to themselves indicating what they (personally) are taking away from the experience and what steps they intend to take to apply what was learned. Ask each participant to seal his or her letter in a self-addressed envelope and attach a self-adhesive note indicating the date on which he or she wants the letter mailed. Send the letters to the participants on the dates specified.

3. Art and Media Reflection Strategies

Art and media reflection strategies help people express their learning in creative, "hands-on" ways and provide opportunities to publish the results of people's learning. Each strategy below includes an idea for feedback. Adapt the idea for your parish, or create your own feedback technique. Art and media strategies are excellent for families—as the family creates its project, they talk, discuss, and reflect on the event and its meaning for them.

Bumper Sticker

Use a bumper sticker as a reflection tool. Provide write-on bumper stickers (available at crafts shops, party/novelties stores, office supply stores, or in crafts catalogs) or posterboard cut in the shape of a bumper sticker. To capture the experience of an event, invite individuals or families to draw a picture or symbol or to create a phrase by completing an unfinished sentence such as

> I learned…
>
> In the future, I will remember…
>
> An action step I will take…

Ask participants to bring their bumper stickers to Sunday Mass on a designated weekend or to a gathered program during the week. Be sure participants' names appear on the back of the bumper stickers. Set up a gallery of bumper stickers as a way to publish what participants have learned. *Be sure to take photos of the display for the parish scrapbook.* After the display at church, encourage participants to display their bumper stickers at home.

Collage/ Poster

At the conclusion of an event or season invite individuals and families to create a collage or a poster. Supply magazines and ask participants to cut out words and images that describe their experience of the event (feelings/thoughts), what they have learned from the event, and the ways in which they will live as Catholics because of their participation in the event. Have participants paste the words and images onto a poster and write or draw additional words and images to complete their collage. As an alternative, each family member can contribute one drawing to the poster. Then the entire family creates and adds a family symbol or image of the event or season.

Ask the families to bring their poster to Sunday Mass on a designated weekend or to a gathered program during the week. Be sure they put their name on the back of the collage. Develop a gallery or bulletin board of collages that is placed prominently in a parish gathering space as a way to publish people's learning. Be sure to take photos of the display for the parish scrapbook. After the display at church is taken down, encourage people to display their posters at home.

"Recipe for Living" Cards

In the weeks following an event or season, invite individuals and families to identify practical strategies that they have actually tried for living the meaning of the event or season. Distribute 3" x 5" file cards and ask people to write practical strategy on each card. Ask them to return the cards during the offertory collection on a particular Sunday or during the week at gathered programs. Consider creating a parish "cookbook" of recipes for living the Catholic faith. Publish the book and distribute it to individuals and families. This might also be a good fundraising project.

Photos

Invite individuals and families to take photos of their at-home experience of a season or an event. Ask them to bring their photos to Sunday Mass on a designated weekend or to a gathered program during the week. Be sure they put their name on the back of the photo. Develop a gallery or bulletin board of photos in a parish gathering space to display the photos. After the photos taken down, encourage families to display their photos at home.

Quilt

At a preparation program or event, provide each person with a square piece of cloth, colored construction paper, or posterboard that can be assembled into a "quilt" that shows what the whole community has learned about particular event or season. Ask individuals and families to add a symbol, image, or key words to their square that reflect what they have learned. Ask everyone to bring their "quilt" piece to Sunday Mass on a designated weekend or to a gathered program during the week. Be sure they put their name on the front of their piece. Assemble the quilt, and display it in a prominent place within the church.

Bring Something Back

At the end of an event or season, invite people to bring evidence of their at-home experience back to church. For example, if children and adolescents made Advent wreaths during the preparation program for Advent, or if you distributed Advent wreaths to parishioners, invite everyone to bring back the used candles after Christmas. Consider melting the candles into four Advent candles for next year's parish Advent wreath; if you used white candles with colored ribbon for the Advent wreath, consider melting the candles to create the parish's paschal candle.

4. Integration Strategies

An integration strategy is a way to publish reflections, ideas, and reports from individuals and families about how they are living out a particular event or season. It is also a great way to engage members of the whole parish in teaching each other.

Newsletter

Create a seasonal newsletter with stories, reports, activities, etc., from individuals and families that describe their experience of the season or events. The newsletter provides a way to publish what people are learning *and* share new ideas and strategies for growing in faith. You can use the newsletter as a means to publish summaries of reflection strategies, or the results of many of the other strategies, for example, the recipes for living out the Catholic faith. Consider publishing the newsletter electronically on the parish web site and/or sending it to parishioners via e-mail.

"Faith Through the Year" Scrapbook

Give individuals and families an annual "Faith Through the Year" scrapbook that they can use to document their journey through the events and seasons of the year. The scrapbook can be filled with photos, artwork, prayers, reflections, etc., that document their at-home experience (e.g., photos of their Advent wreath or times of prayer or service to others, copies of prayers used during Advent-Christmas, or copies of completed reflection strategies). Design an annual gathering for storytelling and celebration at which individuals and families can share their scrapbooks and celebrate their year of learning and growth.

Parish Web Site

A parish web site is an excellent tool for sharing activities, resources, and feedback with everyone in the parish. A web site can contain all of the home activities, as well as activities from parish preparation programs. It can also provide a means for individuals and families to share their real-life stories of living the Catholic faith, experiences with home activities, reflections on participating in the event or season, and ways to apply what they have learned to daily life. The web site can provide a way to publish what the community is learning and to share new ideas and strategies created by parishioners for growing in faith.

Intergenerational Learning Design

There are four major elements necessary for structuring an intergenerational learning model.

1. *All-Ages Experience/In-Common Experience.* Intergenerational religious education begins with a multigenerational experience of the theme that all generations share together. These in-common experiences are usually less verbal and more observational than those in the other three elements. In-common experiences equalize the group; people of different ages listen to music or sing, make an art project, watch a video, hear a story, participate in a ritual, pray together, and so on, at the same time and place, in a similar manner. Learning is at a level that allows all to fully participate. These shared experiences are absolutely critical for building intergenerational religious education.

2. *In-Depth Learning Experience.* Through structured learning activities and discussion, all generations explore the meaning of the event and develop the ability to participate meaningfully in the event. In-depth learning experiences can be designed in one of three formats:

   Note: We recommend that families with children in grades one through five be treated as a learning group in all three formats. Intergenerational learning provides a marvelous opportunity to help the whole family learn how to learn together and share, celebrate, and live their faith. By learning together we can help parents develop skills to share faith with their children and make a significant difference in their home life. There may be times during the year when you separate parents from the children because of the content of the program. But as a general practice, we recommend that you keep families with children together in the intergenerational learning program.

   ❑ The *age-group format* provides age-appropriate learning for separate groups at the same time. Though groups are separated by age, each one focuses on the same topic, utilizing specific learning activities that are designed for their stage of the life cycle (e.g., families with children, adolescents, young adults, adult). Age-group sessions can be designed in a variety of ways: learning activity centers for the families-with-children group; integrated lesson plan for adolescents; faith-sharing groups or a guest speaker for adults.

   We recommend that age groups be organized into the following learning groups, although the number of groups may vary depending on the number of participants. For example, if there are a small number of teens in grades six through twelve, you can group them together for large group presentations and activities and then divide them into separate groups (grades six through eight and grades nine through twelve) for reflection and discussion.

   - three-year-olds and younger: child care
   - four- and five-year-olds (including kindergarten): preschool program with one or more catechists in a separate meeting space
   - parents with children in grades one through five
   - middle school adolescents: grades six through eight
   - high school adolescents: grades nine through twelve
   - eighteen- through thirty-five-year-old young adults (single, married couples)
   - ages thirty-five and up adults.

Intergenerational Learning Design

- ❑ The *whole group format* provides a series of facilitated learning activities for everyone, using small groups or table groups. Groups can be organized in one of two ways: intergenerational (mixed ages in a group) or age groups (separate groups for families with children, teens, young adults, and adults). A lead facilitator or team guides the entire group through an integrated learning program, giving presentations, leading activities, etc. Catechists/facilitators can lead small group activities and discussions for groups without adults.

- ❑ The *learning activity center format* provides structured learning activities at a variety of stations or centers in a common area. Learning activity centers are usually facilitated by a leader, and provide background reading, instructions for the activity, and materials for engaging in the activity. Tables and chairs, or floor space, are essential so that individuals and families can learn, create, and discuss together. For example, an Advent-Christmas intergenerational preparation program might include activity centers for all ages: an Advent wreath or Jesse tree center, an Advent-service projects center, and other age-appropriate activity centers such as an adult faith-sharing center focused on the infancy narratives, or a families-with-children center focused on making an Advent calendar. Learning activity centers can be used with all age groups, and can be developed for an intergenerational audience or particular age groups (e.g., centers for families with children, teens, and adults). Activity centers work very well with families with children in grades one through five and can be used with families in the parallel format.

3. *Whole Group Sharing Experience.* The whole group reconvenes and each group briefly shares what it has learned and/or created during its in-depth experience. Whole group sharing provides an opportunity for each generation to teach one another. Groups can share the project or activity they created, using a verbal summary or symbol of their learning, a dramatic presentation, etc. Whole group sharing can also be conducted in intergenerational groups, sharing learning in small groups rather than using presentations to the entire group.

4. *Sharing Learning Reflections and Home Application.* To conclude the program, participants have the opportunity to reflect on what they learned and begin to apply it to their daily lives. The Home Kit (see page 000) provides individuals and families with a variety of practical tools for bringing the event home. After an explanation of how to use the Home Kit, individuals and families have time to create an at-home action plan for using the Home Kit. Participants can be organized into family groupings, intergenerational groupings, and/or kindred groups for reflection and application.

Facility Requirements

The parish facility (church, hall, meeting rooms) is a major influence on the choices that you will make as you design and structure the intergenerational learning program. Before you make choices about where you will hold large group gatherings, where you will serve the meal, and which in-depth learning format you will use, survey your facility. Remember that a parallel learning format requires break-out space, activity centers require one or more larger meeting rooms, and the learning-group format requires a large meeting room for table groups.

Intergenerational Learning Design

Begin by making a facility inventory that considers the capacity of your meeting rooms. Consider the following meeting spaces:

- worship space
- large meeting spaces, e.g., parish hall, church basement, gathering space in the church
- medium-sized meeting rooms (twenty-five to fifty people), e.g., classrooms, conference rooms
- small-sized meeting rooms (under twenty-five people)

Next, determine what spaces you will need for intergenerational learning and how you will use your space. Sometimes you have to be very creative in the ways you use your space.

- Registration and hospitality: entrance to large meeting room, foyer, or gathering space
- Shared meal: large meeting room with tables and chairs
- Part 1. Gathering: large meeting room or worship space (Use the same space for the next part so as to reduce movement.)
- Part 2. All-ages learning experience: large meeting room or worship space (Depending on the type of learning activity, you may need movable chairs or tables.)
- Part 3. In-depth learning experience: needs vary, as indicated below:

  activity center format: large meeting room or separate meeting rooms for activity centers for families with children, adolescents, and adults

  age group format: large meeting room for families with children; meeting rooms forpreschool, young adolescents, older adolescents, young adults, and adults

  whole group format: large meeting room with tables and chairs

- Part 4. Sharing learning reflections and home application: large meeting room or worship space
- Part 5. Closing prayer service: large meeting room or worship space

Role of the Home Kit in the Learning Program

The Home Kit is the resource centerpiece for both the home and the learning program (see more about creating a Home Kit on page 00). Distribute the Home Kit at the beginning of the program so that participants can work with the materials during the session. If we want people to feel confident, comfortable, and capable of using the home activities, then we need to use and model the activities in the session. If we want people to celebrate the home rituals included in the kit, they need to experience how to have a discussion in the session. If we want people to pray at home, they need to experience a prayer from the Home Kit during the session. By modeling what we want to happen at home during the session, we build the confidence of families and individuals so that they can share, celebrate, and live faith at home.

Registration and Hospitality

- Greeting
- Sign-in and name tag distribution
- Distribution of home kits and handouts
- Invitation to share a meal (depending on the time of day, the program may end with a meal instead)

Intergenerational Learning Design

Event

_____

Catechetical-Theological Theme

_____

Session Dates and Times

_____

Location and Facilities

_____

Learning Objectives

- _Know-what:_ understanding of the meaning of the event and its scriptural, doctrinal, and theological foundation. _What will the learner now comprehend as a result of participating in the learning program and household learning activities?_

- _Know-why:_ the ability to appreciate and value the meaning and significance of the event for their lives as Catholics. _What will the learner now value as a result of participating in the learning program and household learning activities?_

- _Know-how:_ acquiring the ability to participate competently in the event and then live out its meaning and significance. _What will the learner now be able to do as a result of participating in the learning program and household learning activities?_

Intergenerational Learning Design

Part 1: Gathering

- Welcome
- Overview of the event and theme
- A community-building activity and a forming-groups activity (if necessary)
- Opening prayer service with music on the theme of the event

Part 2: All-Ages Opening Experience

This is an activity designed to introduce the entire group to the theme of the program through an engaging activity that addresses the diverse ages of the participants.

- Conduct the activity, using dramatization, media/video, or storytelling to introduce the theme and help participants identify their own experience of the theme of the event.

Part 3: In-Depth Learning Experience

This part includes structured learning activities and discussion to engage participants of all ages in exploring the meaning of the event and to develop their ability to participate meaningfully in the event. In-depth learning experiences can be designed in one of three formats:

- Age-group format
- Whole group format
- Learning activity center format.

The learning format can vary from event to event. There is no need to set one format for an entire year. Let the event, the theme, the learning program content and activities, and your parish facility guide you in selecting the in-depth learning format.

Part 4: Sharing Learning Experiences and Home Application

Small groups share their insights and learning from the program by presenting projects to the entire group or by sharing in intergenerational groups.

- Determine what each group will share as a result of its learning.
- Determine how each group will share its report or project so that the entire group learns about the event and the theme.

This part of the program is designed to send people home ready to participate in the event and to utilize the home activities. Begin with reflection on the learning from the preparation program in family groups, age groups, or intergenerational groups. Then move on to explain the Home Kit (see page 000) and give families and individuals time to create an at-home action plan for using the Home Kit.

- Guide individuals and families in sharing their learning within family clusters, individual family units, and/or kindred groups (young adults, adults, older adults).
- Review the contents of the Home Kit: prayers, rituals, service projects, family enrichment, and learning activities.
- Review the reflection activities and how to use them.
- Guide participants in developing an individual- or family-action plan for celebrating/living the event, using the Home Kit and in planning for participation in the Church event.

Part 5: Closing Prayer Service

- Conclude with a prayer service and music on the theme of the event.

Sample Evaluation Form 1

One thing I found most helpful during this program...

One way I can use what I learned or experienced in my life...

One concrete suggestion for improving this program...

I feel that this program was... (circle one)

   very helpful   somewhat helpful   not very helpful   not at all helpful

I was pleased by/with...

I was disappointed by/with...

I learned...

Please rate your overall feeling after participating in this program. (Circle the one(s) that most apply.)

   Enthusiastic   Astounded   Satisfied   Indifferent   Angry
   Ambivalent   Irritated   Uneasy   Threatened   Discouraged

How do you feel about the amount of presentation/activities/discussion in this session?

   ❏ Too much presentation   ❏ Too much discussion
   ❏ Too many activities   ❏ Good mixture

Please rate the environment or physical facilities...

   ❏ Fine   ❏ Good   ❏ Okay   ❏ Poor

Please rate the length of the program...

   ❏ Fine   ❏ Good   ❏ Okay   ❏ Poor

Please rate the scheduling (time, day, month) of the program...

   ❏ Fine   ❏ Good   ❏ Okay   ❏ Poor

How did you find out about the program?

Why did you decide to participate in this program?

Sample Evaluation Form 2

What is your overall feeling after participating in this session? (Circle all that apply.)

Enthused   Astounded   Satisfied   Indifferent   Ambivalent   Encouraged
Uneasy   Threatened   Discouraged   Affirmed   Challenged   Enriched

What did you hope to gain from participating in this session?

How well were your expectations fulfilled?

❏ Completely   ❏ Mostly   ❏ Partially   ❏ Not at all

How do you feel about the amount of presentation and the amount of activities/discussion in this session?

❏ Too much presentation   ❏ Too much discussion   ❏ A good mixture

Benefits and learning that you gained from this session include:

Disappointments and dissatisfactions you experienced in this session:

How do you rate the physical facilities?

❏ Fine   ❏ Good   ❏ Okay   ❏ Poor

How do you rate the scheduling and length of the session?

❏ Fine   ❏ Good   ❏ Okay   ❏ Poor

Some suggestions you would like to make to improve this session:

New learning needs you discovered through this session:

Sample Evaluation Form 3

What did you find most helpful during this session?

List three specific ways this workshop has increased your knowledge of the topic.

List three ways in which you can apply the learning from this workshop.

List your concrete suggestions for improvement of this session.

List new learning needs you discovered through this session.

Sample Evaluation Form 4

I feel that this session was: (circle one)

     very helpful   somewhat helpful   not very helpful   not at all helpful

I was pleased by/with...

I was disappointed by/with...

I learned...

New learning needs I discovered through this session...

Creating a Home Kit

Event: _____ Catechetical-Theological Focus: _____

Packaging: _____

☐ **User's Guide (letter, overview of activities, suggestions for use)**   ☐ **Listing of all activities**

TYPE OF ACTIVITY	AUDIENCE	ACTIVITY DESCRIPTION	FORMAT
Learning			
Ritual			
Prayer			
Enrichment			
Justice and Service			

Home Activities Planning Form

Event:_____

Catechetical-Theological Focus: _____

Who?	What?	How?	How?	When?	How Well?
Audience	Activity	Format	Delivery	Date	Evaluation

Reflection Activities and Strategies

1. Written Reflection Activities

Unfinished Sentences

This strategy can be incorporated into all reflection activities. It provides unfinished sentences that participants are asked to complete. You can add specific content that you want people to reflect upon. Here is a sample list to get you started.

- I learned…
- I discovered…
- I was surprised…
- I was moved by…
- I felt…
- I wonder about…
- I need to know more about…
- I was reminded that…
- I'm excited by…
- I'm challenged by… or challenged to…
- I need to remember… or remember to…

Reflection Questions/Learning Journal

Have participants complete a worksheet or journal page that includes the following instructions:

> To reflect on what you have learned, identify the insights you have gained and the potential application to your life.
> - Insights (what I've learned)
> - Applications (how I'll use what I've learned)
> - Questions (what I need to learn or explore further)

Seasonal Journal

Individuals as well as families can use journals to record their experience of an event (or the events of whole year): their thoughts, feelings, questions, hopes, dreams, and faith practices. Provide journals along with guidelines for keeping a journal, and sample questions for an event (or in the case of a Church year season, for each day or week). You may also want to include seasonal Bible passages and prayers.

Structured Reflection

Create a reflection questionnaire that uses the structure or outline of the event or the "calendar" of a season as the categories for reflection questions. If the event is a liturgy, use the readings, ritual actions, special prayers, etc., to structure the questionnaire. Then for each category, ask participants to record their thoughts, feelings, insights, how the event applies to their life, etc. For a season such as Advent-Christmas, use the parish calendar of events to structure the questionnaire (e.g., liturgies, service projects, prayer services, sacrament of reconciliation, community life events).

Include questions designed to surface participants' experience of the season (thoughts, feelings), what they have learned about the meaning and significance of the

Reflection Activities and Strategies

season, and their application of the meaning to their lives (new awareness, new faith practices, etc.). Here is an example of a structured reflection questionnaire on the four movements of the Mass and people's experience of Sunday Mass.

Structured Reflection: Living the Mass All Week

Reflect on these questions, alone or with your family, each week after Mass.

What did I see this week?

- Look at the colors, decorations, and artwork used at Mass this week. What do these colors and decorations mean to you? How do the colors and decorations help you to experience the season of the Church year?

What did I hear this week?

- Think of the songs you sang this week. What was the mood of the music this week? What message in the music stood out?

- Think of the Scripture readings this week—First Reading, Psalm, Second Reading, and Gospel. What message in the Scriptures stood out for you this week? What do you want to keep in mind and/or share with others this week?

- Think of the homily this week. What do you want to keep in mind and/or share with others this week?

How did I pray this week?

- Think of the prayer petitions this week. For whom did we pray and how can you keep these intentions in prayer all week?

- Think of the Eucharistic Prayer and receiving Holy Communion. How did you experience Jesus today? How did receiving Jesus' body and blood nourish you? How did you give thanks and praise to God?

How will I live this week?

- What is this week's Mass calling you to do? How can you live the Mass all week—at home, at work or school, in the community?

2. At-Home Application Strategies

Action Plan

Have participants complete a worksheet or journal page that includes the following instructions for creating an action plan:

1. List three actions you would like to undertake as a result of your participation in the preparation and event.
2. Choose and record the action that you would like to plan to do first.
3. List the potential roadblocks to implementing this action.
4. Discuss with another person or your small group how you might overcome these roadblocks. Record your solutions.
5. Describe in writing the specific action you will undertake and the steps you will take to ensure that the action is accomplished.

Reflection Activities and Strategies

A second version of an action plan worksheet uses a three-column format:

Actions	Potential Roadblocks	First Steps
List several actions that you will undertake	List potential roadblocks to implementing your chosen action.	List the steps you need to take to accomplish the action.

Practice Plan

Create a worksheet or journal page (with room for writing) that helps people identify new practices for living the Catholic faith that they learned from participating in the preparation program and event.

I want to use_____ (practice) in this situation:

_____

_____

_____

_____

_____

The roadblocks that could get in the way:

_____

_____

_____

_____

_____

Sample script or plan for using the skill:

_____

_____

_____

_____

_____

I will make my first attempt by (date):

_____

_____

_____

_____

Reflection Activities and Strategies

To-Do List

Create a worksheet that helps people list new practices for living the Catholic faith that they learned during their participation in the preparation program and event. You can begin the "to-do" list with: "Remember to...." You can also modify the "to-do" list as reminder cards (file cards) that people can place on their desks, post at work, or display at home on the refrigerator. Provide each person or family with a pack of reminder cards preprinted with "Remember to..." that can be personalized.

Resolution Letter

At the conclusion of a preparation program and/or event, ask the participants to write letters to themselves indicating what they (personally) are taking away from the experience and what steps they intend to take to apply what was learned. Ask each participant to seal his or her letter in a self-addressed envelope and attach a self-adhesive note indicating the date on which he or she wants the letter mailed. Send the letters to the participants on the dates specified.

3. Art and Media Reflection Strategies

Art and media reflection strategies help people express their learning in creative, "hands-on" ways and provide opportunities to publish the results of people's learning. Each strategy below includes an idea for feedback. Adapt the idea for your parish, or create your own feedback technique. Art and media strategies are excellent for families—as the family creates its project, they talk, discuss, and reflect on the event and its meaning for them.

Bumper Sticker

Use a bumper sticker as a reflection tool. Provide write-on bumper stickers (available at crafts shops, party/novelties stores, office supply stores, or in crafts catalogs) or poster-board cut in the shape of a bumper sticker. To capture the experience of an event, invite individuals or families to draw a picture or symbol or to create a phrase by completing an unfinished sentence such as

> I learned…
> In the future, I will remember…
> An action step I will take…

Ask participants to bring their bumper stickers to Sunday Mass on a designated weekend or to a gathered program during the week. Be sure participants' names appear on the back of the bumper stickers. Set up a gallery of bumper stickers as a way to publish what participants have learned. *Be sure to take photos of the display for the parish scrapbook.* After the display at church, encourage participants to display their bumper stickers at home.

Collage/ Poster

At the conclusion of an event or season invite individuals and families to create a collage or a poster. Supply magazines and ask participants to cut out words and images that describe their experience of the event (feelings/thoughts), what they have learned from the event, and the ways in which they will live as Catholics because of their participation

Reflection Activities and Strategies

in the event. Have participants paste the words and images onto a poster and write or draw additional words and images to complete their collage. As an alternative, each family member can contribute one drawing to the poster. Then the entire family creates and adds a family symbol or image of the event or season.

Ask the families to bring their poster to Sunday Mass on a designated weekend or to a gathered program during the week. Be sure they put their name on the back of the collage. Develop a gallery or bulletin board of collages that is placed prominently in a parish gathering space as a way to publish people's learning. Be sure to take photos of the display for the parish scrapbook. After the display at church is taken down, encourage people to display their posters at home.

"Recipe for Living" Cards

In the weeks following an event or season, invite individuals and families to identify practical strategies that they have actually tried for living the meaning of the event or season. Distribute 3" x 5" file cards and ask people to write practical strategy on each card. Ask them to return the cards during the offertory collection on a particular Sunday or during the week at gathered programs. Consider creating a parish "cookbook" of recipes for living the Catholic faith. Publish the book and distribute it to individuals and families. This might also be a good fundraising project.

Photos

Invite individuals and families to take photos of their at-home experience of a season or an event. Ask them to bring their photos to Sunday Mass on a designated weekend or to a gathered program during the week. Be sure they put their name on the back of the photo. Develop a gallery or bulletin board of photos in a parish gathering space to display the photos. After the photos taken down, encourage families to display their photos at home.

Quilt

At a preparation program or event, provide each person with a square piece of cloth, colored construction paper, or posterboard that can be assembled into a "quilt" that shows what the whole community has learned about particular event or season. Ask individuals and families to add a symbol, image, or key words to their square that reflect what they have learned. Ask everyone to bring their "quilt" piece to Sunday Mass on a designated weekend or to a gathered program during the week. Be sure they put their name on the front of their piece. Assemble the quilt, and display it in a prominent place within the church.

Bring Something Back

At the end of an event or season, invite people to bring evidence of their at-home experience back to church. For example, if children and adolescents made Advent wreaths during the preparation program for Advent, or if you distributed Advent wreaths to parishioners, invite everyone to bring back the used candles after Christmas. Consider melting

Reflection Activities and Strategies

the candles into four Advent candles for next year's parish Advent wreath; if you used white candles with colored ribbon for the Advent wreath, consider melting the candles to create the parish's paschal candle.

4. Integration Strategies

An integration strategy is a way to publish reflections, ideas, and reports from individuals and families about how they are living out a particular event or season. It is also a great way to engage members of the whole parish in teaching each other.

Newsletter

Create a seasonal newsletter with stories, reports, activities, etc., from individuals and families that describe their experience of the season or events. The newsletter provides a way to publish what people are learning and share new ideas and strategies for growing in faith. You can use the newsletter as a means to publish summaries of reflection strategies, or the results of many of the other strategies, for example, the recipes for living out the Catholic faith. Consider publishing the newsletter electronically on the parish web site and/or sending it to parishioners via e-mail.

"Faith Through the Year" Scrapbook

Give individuals and families an annual "Faith Through the Year" scrapbook that they can use to document their journey through the events and seasons of the year. The scrapbook can be filled with photos, artwork, prayers, reflections, etc., that document their at-home experience (e.g., photos of their Advent wreath or times of prayer or service to others, copies of prayers used during Advent-Christmas, or copies of completed reflection strategies). Design an annual gathering for storytelling and celebration at which individuals and families can share their scrapbooks and celebrate their year of learning and growth.

Parish Web Site

A parish web site is an excellent tool for sharing activities, resources, and feedback with everyone in the parish. A web site can contain all of the home activities, as well as activities from parish preparation programs. It can also provide a means for individuals and families to share their real-life stories of living the Catholic faith, experiences with home activities, reflections on participating in the event or season, and ways to apply what they have learned to daily life. The web site can provide a way to publish what the community is learning and to share new ideas and strategies created by parishioners for growing in faith.

Reflection Activities and Strategies

Example: Four Lenten Practices

1. LENTEN JOURNAL

Adolescents through adults, as well as families, can use journals to record their experience of Lent—their thoughts, feelings, questions, hopes, dreams, faith practices, etc. Journals or poster-journals can record the actual Lenten practices of individuals and families. Consider a poster-journal designed for the refrigerator so that all family members can record their actions and thoughts, feelings, and learning. Include the journal in the Lenten Home Kit.

2. LENTEN PHOTO COLLAGE

Give each family a disposal camera in their Lenten Home Kit. Ask individuals and families to take photos of their "in-home" experience of Lent, especially the three practices of Lent (e.g., a photo of the family at prayer, a photo of the family serving others, etc). Ask them to pre-pare a photo collage that presents their experience of Lent with descriptions or captions that explain their actions and commentary on their feelings and/or thoughts about living Lent.

Ask them to bring their photos to Sunday Mass on a designated weekend or to a gath-ered program during the week. Be sure they put their name on the back of the photo. Develop a gallery or bulletin board of photos (in the church gathering space) as a way to publish people's learning. Be sure to take photos of the display for the parish scrapbook. After the display at church, encourage people to display their photos at home (on the refrig-erator).

3. LENTEN "RECIPE FOR LIVING" CARDS

During Lent ask individuals and families to create practical strategies for living Lent that they have actually practiced. Distribute 3x5 file cards and ask people to write down one practical strategy on each recipe card. Ask them to return the cards on a particular Sunday during the offertory collection or during the week at gathered programs. Consider creating a Lenten or annual parish "cook book" of recipes for living the Catholic faith. Publish the book and dis-tribute it to individuals and families. Include pre-printed file cards in the Home Lenten Kit.

4. LENTEN SCRAPBOOK

Give individuals and families a small scrapbook in their Lenten Home Kit. Ask everyone to doc-ument their 40-day journey from Ash Wednesday to Easter Sunday. The scrapbook can be filled with photos, artwork, prayers, reflections, etc. documenting the "in-home" experience of Lent (e.g., photos of their times of prayer or involvement in serving others, copies of prayers used during the year such as Lenten daily prayers, copies of completed reflection strategies, etc). Incorporate storytelling in the next gathered program so that individuals and families can share their scrapbooks and their learning and growth.

Reflection Activities Planning Form

Event:_____ Catechetical-Theological Focus: _____

Who?	What?	How?	When?	When?	How Well?
AUDIENCE	ACTIVITY	DELIVERY	DISTRIBUTION DATE	RETURN DATE	EVALUATION

CHAPTER 6

Planning and Facilitating Meetings

▶ Part 1: Meeting Outlines

The following meeting outlines are offered as a guideline for using the planning steps in the Resource Manual. They are intended to assist your parish in creating a plan and timeline for moving from vision to implementation of your own lifelong, intergenerational, events-centered plan for parish faith formation. Each meeting is designed as 2 to 2 1/2-hour session. The meeting outlines refer to a particular chapter in the Resource Manual that contains the description of the process and the worksheets. Be sure to make copies of worksheets that you are going to need for each session.

It is recommended that each core team member have a copy of the Resource Manual. In this way every team member has access to all of the information and the planning processes. This will make facilitation much easier. Order additional copies from Twenty-Third Publications by calling 800-321-0411 or by going online to www.23rdpublications.com.

Meeting 1:   Introduction to Lifelong, Intergenerational, Events-Centered Faith Formation

Meeting 2:   Fashioning a Lifelong Curriculum

Meeting 3:   Implementing a Lifelong Curriculum

Meeting 4:   Leadership Development: Inviting, Preparing, and Supporting Leaders

Meeting 5:   Designing an Events-centered Learning Plan

Meeting 1. Introduction to Lifelong, Intergenerational, Events-Centered Faith Formation (Chapter 1)

The first meeting introduces your team to the vision and practices of lifelong, intergenerational, events-centered faith formation. Use the workshop in Chapter 1 as the design for your meeting. Be sure to order the video.

Resources

- Resource: Chapter 1
- Workshop: "Introducing Generations of Faith" in Chapter 1
- Video: *Introducing Generations of Faith* (available free from the Center for Ministry Development; call 203-723-1622.)
- Participant Handout: *Generations of Faith: Vision and Practice* in Chapter 1 (for those who want a more detailed presentation, refer them to the essay in Chapter 1)
- Participant Handout: *Our Hopes and Dreams for Faith Formation*

Your Meeting Notes

_____

_____

_____

_____

_____

_____

_____

_____

_____

_____

_____

_____

_____

_____

_____

_____

_____

Meeting 2. Fashioning a Lifelong Curriculum (Chapter 2)

During the second meeting, the team begins the process of fashioning a curriculum plan. There are three tasks, which are described in Chapter 2:

Task 1:   Determining your curriculum approach: primary or blended

Task 2:   Developing a multi-year curriculum plan

Resources

- Resource: Chapter 2
- Participant Handout: *Church Events Profile*
- Participant Handout: *Lifelong Curriculum Plan of Events*
- Generations of Faith Online (www.generationsoffaith.org): For this session review the examples of parish stories, parish curriculum plans, and the sample intergenerational program.

Meeting Outline

1. Introduction: Provide an overview of the fashioning process.

2. Determine your curriculum approach: primary or blended. (Task 1)

Using Chapter 2 of this manual, review the two curriculum approaches: primary and blended. Be sure to spend time exploring the curriculum examples in Chapter 2 (see pages 000-000). Remind the team that some parishes begin with a blended approach and move to a primary approach over several years.

Take time as a team to discuss the two approaches and decide on the approach that will work best in your parish in the coming year and over the next several years. Use the sidebar on the next page to guide your decision making.

3. Develop a multi-year curriculum plan. (Task 2)

For the whole parish community, the goal of this task is to develop a six-year curriculum plan for lifelong, events-centered catechesis around the six major content areas that reflects the people, cultures, character, traditions, and history of your parish community. Guide your parish team through the steps in the following process. This process will most likely not be completed at the meeting. However, it is recommended that several team members take the initial work of the team and develop a first draft that the entire team can review at its next meeting.

- Begin by developing a *Church Events Profile*, adding events that are particular to your parish community, local area, and/or diocese. Use the *Church Events Profile* worksheet on page 000. Remember that your curriculum plan is tailored to the unique needs of your parish community. Determine if your parish will have special events, e.g., parish anniversary, dedication of a new church, or a diocesan-wide event during your first six-year plan. These events should be included on the list.

- Review the task of creating a six-year curriculum plan and the two basic organizing principles: a *single focus*, using one of the six core-content areas (e.g., sacraments) for each year of the six-year plan or an *integrated focus*, which incorporates the six core-content areas each year—Church year, sacraments, justice and service, prayer, morality, and Creed. Share with the team actual examples of parish curriculum plans based on each organizing principle.

- Discuss which of the two organizing principles your parish will use to fashion the curriculum plan.

- Review how to select events for each year of the plan and the ways to sequence events within a year. Select events for each year of their plan, using the completed *Church Events Profile* and the *Scope of Events and Themes*. Use the *Lifelong Curriculum Plan of Events* worksheet to record your selections and create your six-year plan. You do not need to complete the column for preparation program dates. This will be done during meetings.

Task 1: Planning Decisions

There are a number of factors your parish needs to consider when determining your curriculum approach. Remember, the goal of all three approaches is to develop a lifelong, events-centered curriculum for the whole parish community. You need to select the approach that will work best for your parish. Here are several factors that parishes have used to determine where they will start:

1. *Parish vision.* The culture and character of the parish and the vision of faith formation are important factors in determining your curriculum approach. It is also important to consider the long-term vision for faith formation and which approach—primary or blended—best matches the parish's vision, now and in the future.

2. *Dedication to age-group catechesis.* Many parishes have a long tradition of age-group catechesis that is working effectively. They want to maintain a strong age-group catechesis while building a lifelong curriculum for everyone. On the other hand, many parishes have found that their age-group catechesis is not working effectively and they are seeking another approach to faith formation.

3. *Character of the parish.* Many parishes have found that adopting the primary approach consolidates, focuses, and simplifies their faith formation curriculum, while building a greater sense of community spirit.

4. *Staffing.* Many parishes have found that they do not have enough paid and volunteer leaders to support the blended approach. For these parishes, moving to the primary approach focuses their leadership and energy on events-centered, intergenerational learning.

Discuss the strengths of each approach—primary, blended, and blended-toward-primary—and select the approach that your parish will initiate in the coming year, as well as the approach that your parish will be working toward in future years.

Your Meeting Notes

Sample Follow-Up Report Format

Date:_____ Meeting:_____

Task:_____

1. **Results Achieved**: What do you regard as the major outcomes of the meeting?

```



```

2. **Work Outstanding**: Which action items do you still need to complete? What's the time frame for these activities?

```



```

3. **Next Steps**: Are there any steps that the whole group needs to take in order to help you complete your action items? Are there any further discussions that need to take place?

```



```

Meeting 3: Implementing a Lifelong Curriculum (Chapter 3)

During the third meeting, the team begins the process of implementing a curriculum plan. There are three tasks described in Chapter 3:

Task 1:   Developing a calendar and scheduling preparation programs

Task 2:   Determining a budget and participant fees

Task 3:   Developing promotional and registration strategies and materials

Resources

- Resource: Chapter 3
- Participant Handout: *Implementing a Lifelong Faith Formation Curriculum*
- Participant Handout: *Blended Curriculum Calendar* (if your team chose the bBlended approach)
- Participant Handout: *Sample Implementation Calendar*
- Participant Handout: *To Do List*
- Generations of Faith Online (www.generationsoffaith.org): For this session review the implementation tools: brochures, flyers, promotion strategies, registration forms, etc.

Meeting Outline

1. Review the Curriculum Plan.

Review the first draft of the curriculum plan to determine how well it addresses the six essential content areas of catechesis: Creed, sacraments, morality, justice and Catholic social teachings, prayer, and the Church year (and the lectionary). Determine if content areas or themes are missing or have not been fully addressed, and make sure that the theme is embedded in the event (emergent catechetical content). Make revisions as necessary.

2. Introduction: Provide an overview of the implementation process.

At this meeting, you will address three implementation tasks: 1) scheduling, 2) budgeting, and 3) promotion and registration. This meeting is a decision-making meeting. There will be homework, e.g., creating promotional materials.

Use the *Implementing a Lifelong Faith Formation Curriculum* worksheet to record your decisions for each implementation task.

Task 1: Scheduling

Review the process for developing a schedule of preparation programs (external calendar) and a schedule for planning (internal calendar). Move through each step in the process and record the team's decisions on the *Implementing a Lifelong Faith Formation Curriculum* worksheet. Use *To-Do List* worksheet to record items that need furthur action.

1. Identify the number of times you will offer your preparation program and the days of the week on which it will be offered.
   - Determining the timeframe for the intergenerational learning program
   - Surveying your meeting spaces
   - Determining the number of program offerings
   - Determining the days of the week for program offerings
2. Develop a calendar for the year with dates for preparation programs and events.
   - For primary curriculum parishes: Will you designate a set week or weeks for preparation programs (e.g., 2nd week of month), offer preparation on multi-

ple weeks during the month, or adjust the preparation program dates based on the date of the event?

- For blended curriculum parishes: Will you schedule events and age-specific programs on a monthly or annual cycle?

3. Develop a planning timeline for designing preparation programs and for training leaders.

Task 2: Budget and Fees

Review the process for developing a budget and program fees. Move through each step in the process and record your decisions on the *Implementing a Lifelong Faith Formation Curriculum* worksheet. Use the *To-Do List* worksheet to record items that need further action.

1. Determine a budget for preparation programs and home materials.
   - Determining fixed expenses for organizing and conducting the program
   - Determining variable per-household expenses
   - Determining variable per-person expenses
2. Determine registration/material fees for households and individuals.
   - Annual fee
   - Per-program fee

Task 3: Promotion and Registration

Review the ideas for promotion and registration. Discuss and decide on the strategies you will use for promotion and registration. Record your decisions on the *Implementing a Lifelong Faith Formation Curriculum* worksheet. Use the *To-Do List* worksheet to record items that need furthur action.

1. Develop a plan and materials for promoting your lifelong faith formation curriculum to the parish community.
   - Who will you include in the promotion?
   - What will you use for promotion?
   - What information will you include in a letter or printed material?
2. Develop a registration procedure and form.

Check Generations of Faith Online (www.generationsoffaith.org) for examples of registration forms and promotional materials, such as brochures.

3. Review tasks to be completed.

Conclude the meeting by reviewing the work that needs to be done and assigning tasks to be completed before the next meeting.

Your Meeting Notes

_____

_____

_____

_____

_____

_____

_____

_____

_____

_____

_____

_____

_____

_____

_____

_____

_____

_____

_____

_____

_____

_____

_____

_____

Sample Follow-Up Report Format

Date:_____ Meeting:_____

Task:_____

1. **Results Achieved**: What do you regard as the major outcomes of the meeting?

[   ]

2. **Work Outstanding**: Which action items do you still need to complete? What's the time frame for these activities?

[   ]

3. **Next Steps**: Are there any steps that the whole group needs to take in order to help you complete your action items? Are there any further discussions that need to take place?

[   ]

To Do List

TASK (scheduling, promotion, budgeting, leadership)	COMPLETION DATE	PERSONS RESPONSIBLE

Meeting 4: Leadership Development: Inviting, Preparing, and Supporting Leaders (Chapter 4)

The fourth meeting focuses on developing leaders. There are three stages described in Chapter 4:

Stage 1: Inviting people into leadership
Stage 2: Preparing and training leaders
Stage 3: Supporting leaders

Resources

- Resource: Chapter 4
- Participant Handout: *Leadership System Checklist*
- Participant Handout: *Leadership Tasks Listing*
- Participant Handout: *Leadership Role Description*
- Participant Handout: *Sample Leader Tasks and Responsibilities for an Intergenerational Learning Program*
- Participant Handout: *Sample Job Descriptions*
- Participant Handout: *Leader Profile and Interest Finder*
- Participant Handout: *Training Plan*
- Participant Handout: *A Training Plan for Facilitators/Catechists*

Meeting Outline

1. Review the Curriculum Plan.

Review progress on the implementation steps, especially promotional efforts. Identify work that needs to be done and establish a timeline for its completion.

2. Develop an Empowerment Mindset.

- Take time to read/review the four principles of an empowerment mindset in Chapter 4. Emphasize that these four principles are the theological underpinning of the leadership system. Review the five key practices of an empowerment approach.

- Discuss the importance of an empowerment mindset—principles and practices—for your church. How does it compare with your current approach? How could it influence the way you invite people into leadership, prepare and train them for leadership, and support them in their leadership responsibilities?

3. Introduction to Leadership Development.

Introduce the three stages of a leadership development system:

1. inviting people into leadership
2. preparing and training leaders
3. supporting leaders

4. Inviting People into Leadership.

Step 1. Identify the leaders you need.

Step 2. Develop job descriptions for each leadership position.

- Using the process and the worksheets on pages 119-127, review the sample leadership positions for an intergenerational learning program and the sample job descriptions.

- As a team, identify leadership positions responsible for conducting preparation programs (e.g., intergenerational learning program) and for administering the programs (logistics, finances, registration).
- After leadership positions have been identified and clarified, assign each person on the team the responsibility of developing a job description for one leadership position. Share drafts of each job description, make revisions, and finalize the job description.

Step 3. Search for people with leadership potential.

Step 4. Develop a database of potential leaders.

- Review the recruitment strategies and invite the team to share ideas for recruiting leaders to fill the jobs whose descriptions you have developed. Decide on the strategies you will use and who will be involved in recruiting.

Step 5. Secure needed leaders.

Step 6. Meet with each prospective leader.

- Decide how you will accomplish these two tasks once you have developed a pool of prospective leaders.

5. *Preparing and Training Leaders.*

Review the five key insights about adult learning as they apply to preparing and training leaders for their ministry. Discuss the value of this approach for preparing and training leaders for your church. How does it compare with your current approach? How could it influence the way you prepare and train people for leadership positions?

Step 1. Provide an orientation workshop.

- Review the importance of providing an orientation workshop to help leaders become familiar with the principles and practices of Generations of Faith. Review the key components of an orientation workshop and discuss how you want to orient leaders.

Step 2. Develop a training plan.

- Using the information in Chapter 4, review how to determine the leadership positions that require training. Identify which of your positions need training. Then, review the four learning approaches.
- Review the training plan for catechists/facilitators and the use of multiple formats. Explain how training can be made "user-friendly" for catechists/facilitators (independent learning, reducing the number of meetings). Point out that the training plan is a good example of targeted, "just-in-time" training that respects the key adult learning principles. Review the independent learning plans.
- Since facilitators/catechists will require the most preparation for an events-centered learning program, create a training plan for them. Select your first event and preparation program, and develop your training plan.

6. *Supporting and Nurturing Leaders.*

Step 1. Authorize leaders to begin service.

Step 2. Provide the information and resources that leaders need.

Step 3. Gather information and evaluate the effectiveness of leaders.

Step 4. Deal with problems.

Step 5. Express and celebrate the Church's support of volunteer leaders.

- Review the strategies for supporting leaders. Discuss ways that your parish is currently supporting leaders and new approach it can adopt to strengthen this aspect of the leadership development system. Decide on specific strategies your parish will use to support leaders in lifelong faith formation.

7. Review Tasks to Be Completed.

Conclude the meeting by reviewing the work that needs to be done and assigning tasks to be completed before the next meeting.

Your Meeting Notes

_____

_____

_____

_____

_____

_____

_____

_____

_____

_____

_____

_____

_____

_____

_____

_____

_____

_____

Sample Follow-Up Report Format

Date:_____ Meeting:_____

Task:_____

1. **Results Achieved**: What do you regard as the major outcomes of the meeting?

[ ]

2. **Work Outstanding**: Which action items do you still need to complete? What's the time frame for these activities?

[ ]

3. **Next Steps**: Are there any steps that the whole group needs to take in order to help you complete your action items? Are there any further discussions that need to take place?

[ ]

Meeting 5: Designing an Events-Centered Learning Plan (Chapter 5)

The fifth meeting focuses on designing an events-centered learning plan for one event in your curriculum plan. In this meeting, the team will complete some of the design work and brainstorm ideas for continuing the design work after the meeting. In most cases the team will develop the basic structure of the learning plan and then assign individuals or small groups the work of completing the learning program and Home Kit.

This meeting begins the work of the design team which has primary responsibility for creating the learning designs for a Church event. The design team has primary responsibility for creating the learning designs for Church events. The design team consists of members of the core team, especially parish staff and other faith formation leaders, who are invited to work on the design team because of their expertise with particular age groups (e.g., preschool children or teenagers) or particular tasks (e.g., creating home materials). The team's major tasks include:

- designing the preparation programs by selecting and/or creating the learning activities for an intergenerational, family-centered, and/or age group program;
- creating Home Kits and activities for a variety of ages and settings (e.g., participants in preparation programs, parishioners at Mass);
- designing reflection activities;
- preparing the learning materials.

Several months prior to a preparation program, the design team meets to begin design work around the event and theme that was selected by the core team when it created the curriculum. In parishes that offer monthly family or intergenerational preparation programs, the design team meets regularly. In other parishes the work of the design team is integrated into regular staff meetings or committee meetings.

You can use this meeting design each time you need to design a learning plan for an event. Task 1 will be completed as the final task so that it reflects the design work that you have completed.

Task 1: Aligning learning for all ages
Task 2: Designing parish preparation programs
Task 3: Designing and selecting home activities
Task 4: Designing reflection activities

Resources

- Resource: Chapter 5
- Home Kit samples: Purchase or collect a variety of sample home activities for the design meeting. See the listing of sources of home activities in Chapter 5.
- Participant Handout: *Whole Parish Plan for Aligning Learning* worksheet
- Participant Handout: *Intergenerational Learning Design* worksheet
- Participant Handout: *Creating a Home Kit* worksheet
- Participant Handout: *Home Activities Planning Form*
- Participant Handout: *Reflection Activities Planning Form*

Meeting Outline

1. Review the Implementation and Leadership-Development Plans.

Review progress on implementation and leadership development tasks. Identify work that needs to be done and establish a timeline for its completion.

2. Introduction: Provide an overview of the process of designing an events-centered learning plan.

Identify the four tasks in designing a learning plan for an event listed above. In this meeting, the team will create the alignment plan as the concluding activity.

Review the events-centered learning process. Identify the three catechetical components of the process that the team will be designing: preparation programs, home activities, and reflection activities. The team will *not* be designing the event! That is already in place. The team will build the learning process around the event.

3. Designing a Preparation Program.

Select your first event in the coming year. Guide the team, step by step, through the design process for intergenerational learning, using the *Intergenerational Learning Design* worksheet. (If you are using a family-centered learning model and/or age group learning model, adapt the following process.)

Step 1: Identify catechetical-theological theme.

- Review the process for choosing a catechetical-theological theme. Using the reflection questions in Chapter 5, identify the catechetical-theological theme for your event.
- Review the *Scope of Church Events and Themes* in Chapter 2 for suggested themes. Record your theme, using the *Intergenerational Learning Design* worksheet.

Step 2: Develop learning objectives.

- Review the process for developing learning objectives and the examples in Chapter 5. Develop learning objectives—*know-what*, *know-why*, and *know-how*— for your event and theme. They should just brainstorm, no need to decide on learning objectives. They need to experience how to develop them. Record your learning objectives on the *Intergenerational Learning Design* worksheet.

Step 3: Design the intergenerational preparation program, using the design process.

- Review each part (component) of the intergenerational design found in Chapter 5. Review the Lenten Intergenerational Program in Chapter 5 for an example of how to program each part. As a team, move step by step through the intergenerational design, brainstorming ideas for each part. Use the worksheet and the information in Chapter 5 to guide your work. Be sure to explore the different formats for the in-depth learning experience (activity centers, parallel, learning group).

After the team has brainstormed ideas for each part, assign responsibilities for continued development of the design. In most cases the team develops the basic structure of the learning plan and then assigns an individual or small group the work of completing the learning program. Schedule a follow-up meeting to review the work of the designers and finalize the learning program.

4. Designing and Selecting Home Activities.

Begin by reviewing the suggestions to keep in mind when designing Home Kits in Chapter 5. Review the five design steps below. Then review examples of Home Kits in Chapter 5.

Step 1. Identify target audiences

Step 2. Design or select home activities

Step 3. Choose a format for each activity

Step 4. Determine delivery methods

Step 5. Develop a timeline and implementation plans

Using the designated event, theme, and learning objectives, guide the team in brainstorming ideas for Steps 1-4 of the design process. Use the *Creating a Home Kit* worksheet on page 174 to record the team's ideas.

Assign responsibilities for continued development of the Home Kit. Delegate the work of completing the Home Kit to an individual or small group. Schedule a follow-up meeting to review the work of the designers and finalize the Home Kit.

5. ***Designing Reflection Activities.***

Begin by reviewing the importance of reflection and application in the learning process. Review the design process examples of the four types of reflection activities and strategies in Chapter 5.

Step 1. Identify target audiences

Step 2. Design reflection strategies and activities

Step 3. Determine delivery methods

Reflection activities and strategies:
- Written reflection activities
- Back-home application strategies
- Art and media reflection strategies
- Integration strategies

Using the designated event, theme, and learning objectives, guide the team in brainstorming ideas for reflection activities. Use the *Reflection Activities Planning Form* on page 000 to record the team's ideas. Assign responsibilities for continued development of reflection activities. Delegate the work of completing the reflection activities to an individual or small group. Schedule a follow-up meeting to review the work of the designers and finalize the activities.

6. ***Aligning Learning for All Ages.***

Using the design process in Chapter 5, create an overall plan for aligning learning for the event. The plan ensures that all audiences are being reached and that there is alignment across all ages and generations in the parish. Review the example in Chapter 5. Then, step by step, guide the team in completing the plan using the design process.

Use the *Whole Parish Plan for Aligning Learning* worksheet on page 183 to record your strategies.

7. ***Review Tasks to be Completed.***

Conclude the meeting by reviewing the work that needs to be done and assigning tasks to be completed before the next meeting.

Your Meeting Notes

Sample Follow-Up Report Format

Date:_____ Meeting:_____
Task:_____

1. **Results Achieved**: What do you regard as the major outcomes of the meeting?

2. **Work Outstanding**: Which action items do you still need to complete? What's the time frame for these activities?

3. **Next Steps**: Are there any steps that the whole group needs to take in order to help you complete your action items? Are there any further discussions that need to take place?

Part 2: Tools for Facilitating Meetings

1. The Role of a Facilitator

Facilitators contribute to the success of meetings by:

- helping the group define its overall goal, as well as its specific objectives;
- providing processes that help members make high-quality decisions;
- guiding group discussion to keep it on track;
- making accurate notes that reflect the ideas of members;
- helping the group understand its own processes in order to work more effectively;
- making sure that assumptions are surfaced and tested;
- using consensus to help a group make decisions that take all members' opinions into account;
- providing feedback to the group so that members can assess their progress and make adjustments;
- managing conflict, using a collaborative approach;
- helping the group communicate effectively;
- creating an environment in which members enjoy a positive, growing experience while they work to attain group goals;
- fostering leadership in others by sharing the responsibility for leading the group.

2. Planning a Meeting

Planning a meeting is a common function of a facilitator. Here are seven key ingredients in an effective meeting plan:

1. *Objective:* What results do you want to achieve? List the top three.
2. *Timing:* How long should the meeting last? When is the best time to hold it?
3. *Participants:* Who should attend? List the names. Check again—have you included those who have the authority to make decisions, those whose commitment is needed, and those who need to know?
4. *Agenda:* What items do you think should be included? What items do participants want to see included? Who is responsible for preparing and distributing the agenda?
5. *Physical requirements:* What facilities and equipment are needed for the meeting? How should the equipment be arranged in the meeting room?
6. *Meeting assignments:* Who will be the recorder, the timekeeper, and the discussion moderator?
7. *Follow-up action items:* Have tasks been assigned with deadlines for completion? Who is accountable to whom?

3. Facilitating a Meeting

The facilitator should attend to or monitor a number of things before, during, and after a meeting. The following is a partial list of points to consider. You may want to add others.

- The leader prepares an agenda prior to the meeting.
- Participants have an opportunity to contribute to the agenda.
- The leader provides advance notice of the meeting time and place.
- The leader makes sure all materials and supplies are ready for the meeting: handouts, extra pens, pencils, markers, newsprint pad, masking tape, handouts, etc.

- Meeting facilities and equipment are reserved in advance and are comfortable and adequate for the number of participants.
- Coffee, ice water, and snacks are available.
- The meeting begins on time.
- The meeting has a scheduled ending time.
- Everyone is made to feel welcome, comfortable, and part of the group. With new groups, conduct an ice-breaker activity to help participants get acquainted.
- The facilitator introduces and explains the objectives and process for the session.
- Designated participants monitor time and take notes throughout the meeting.
- Everyone has an opportunity to present his or her viewpoint.
- Participants listen attentively to each other.
- No one dominates the discussion.
- The chosen decision-making process is appropriate for the purpose and size of the group.
- Everyone has a voice in decisions made at the meeting.
- The facilitator paces the session and determines how much time to spend on each agenda item in order to finish the session on time.
- The group defines and delegates follow-up action items and sets dates for their completion.
- The meeting ends with a summary of the group's accomplishments and a review of the action items that need to be completed before the next meeting.
- The leader ensures that each participant receives minutes of the meeting.
- The leader stays in touch with participants, following up on action items agreed upon during the meeting.

4. Guiding the Group through the Stages of Development

There are many factors that contribute to the effectiveness of a group and the quality of its experiences. The effectiveness of a group, however, does not need to be left to chance. All groups develop and interact in a similar manner. During each stage in the process, members have characteristic interactions and associated feelings. When the group leader understands the process of group development and the dynamics of group interaction, he or she enables the group to function at its best. The role of a leader is to tend to the needs of group members at each stage and encourage the group to grow together as it moves toward the next stage. Below is an overview of four typical stages in group development and the role of the leader at each stage.

Stage 1: Forming (Gathering and Orientation)

The move from being an individual to being a member of a team can be stressful. As individuals take on new roles, it is normal to have conflicting feelings—fear and anxiety, excitement and anticipation, as well as pride at being chosen for the team. The team's first order of business includes attempts to define tasks and work through group dynamics. Experts note that at this stage many abstract discussions about concepts and issues are likely to occur. Discussions irrelevant to the team and complaints about the organization are common. Because of the many distractions, it is normal for the team to accomplish little regarding its goals.

Some common characteristics of a group at this stage are:

- initially, members don't know one another

- general sense of politeness and curiosity
- members check each other out
- feelings of anxiety about the unknown, insecurity about degree of acceptance/rejection.

Here, the leader's role is to
- lessen anxieties by clarifying the expectations and purpose of the team
- identify guidelines for participation
- encourage questions and include everyone.

Stage 2: Storming (Making Connections)

Once team members begin a task, they may realize it is different from what they expected and perhaps, more difficult than they thought. They are likely to become impatient with the lack of progress, yet they are too new to the task to be able to make decisions. Team members may want to draw on their own experiences rather than collaborate with the other members.

Some common characteristics of a group at this stage are:
- arguing among members, even when they agree on real issues
- defensiveness and competition
- establishing unrealistic goals
- tension and jealousy
- questioning of leader
- questions about how they work together, what they are doing, whom they have to influence.

At this point the situation may seem hopeless and team members wonder if the team can succeed. This is normal. In fact, it is how the members are getting to know and understand each other. Here, the leader's role is to
- affirm the value of each person and focus on what team members have in common rather than on how they differ
- emphasize shared responsibility and cooperation toward a common goal as well as commitment to work through any conflicts that arise
- deal with tension when it surfaces, but help the team to move through it and then on to the next stage.

Stage 3: Norming (Establishing an Identity)

More time and energy are spent on goals during this stage since this is the point at which members come to accept the team, the team ground rules, their roles on the team, and each other as individuals.

Some common characteristics of a group at this stage are:
- competitive relationships becoming more cooperative
- members being able to express criticism constructively
- more friendliness and personal sharing
- a sense of cohesion, common spirit, and goals
- a sense of relief that everything is going to work out
- members beginning to work together as a group
- roles and responsibilities defined and delegated.

Here, the leader's role is to
- avoid over-reliance on yourself

- encourage members to take responsibility for the work
- fosters confidence and a sense of accomplishment
- provide appropriate praise and encouragement for individuals and the team as a whole.

Stage 4: Performing (Getting the Job Done)

At this stage, individuals begin to function as a team. With relationships and expectations established, team members work at constructive self-change and prevent or work through group problems. Members feel a close attachment to the team, which has become an effective, cohesive unit.

Some common characteristics of a group at this stage are:
- group is cohesive and confident, working toward goal
- shared pride and mutual respect
- feelings include relaxed sharing, trust, and acceptance
- much more work is accomplished.

Here, the leader's role is to
- maintain the comfort level and keep the team moving toward its objective
- focus on acknowledging, supporting, and encouraging collaborative efforts.

When the team finishes its work, people may feel the anxiety and grief associated with transition and saying good-bye. It is important to discuss transition issues and needs. Provide a way for people to celebrate what they have accomplished, to be thanked for their work, and to put closure on the experience through an appropriate ritual. Some common characteristics of a group at this stage are
- transition and disbursement
- bringing closure to the experience together
- feelings of anxiety and grief associated with saying good-bye
- depth of relationships will determine intensity of feelings.

Here, the leader's role is to
- provide ways to celebrate efforts and acknowledge accomplishments and losses
- provide a way to say good-bye and show appreciation for contributions.

Remember that when new members come into the team or if the leadership changes, your team may revert to an earlier stage. This should be temporary. Relax and remember that team building takes time and effort before it takes hold.

5. Balancing Group Functions

Group dynamics are the interactions among group members while the group is working. One responsibility of group leadership is maintaining relationships within the group; the other is helping members accomplish the group's goals and tasks. The balance between how the group works together (relationship) and what members accomplish as a result of the work (task) is crucial. If members focus too much on their relationship they will grow close but get little done. If they spend all their time on the task, they will get the job done, but probably will not feel connected to each other. A balance must be struck.

Relationship Functions

There are several ways to maintain good relationships among the members of a group. The maintenance of these relationship functions is important to morale and creates the kind of atmosphere that allows each person to contribute to his or her full potential. Here are six essential relationship behaviors of effective group leaders *and*, eventually, of group members themselves:

- *Encouraging*: Be friendly, warm, and respectful to others: "I am glad to see everyone here today."
- *Expressing group feelings*: Try to sense feelings within the group and share them with the other members: "I'm sensing some reluctance on this issue. Is there a problem?" or "I think we all need a break."
- *Harmonizing*: Reduce tension and try to get people to explore their differences: "There's no need to be defensive. These are all good ideas."
- *Compromising*: When your opinion is involved in a conflict, offer a compromise that will bring resolution: "I would prefer that we support the city council plan to provide summer programs for inner-city kids, but Charlie makes a strong case for standing against it because of where the money will be taken from. Unless someone has a third option, let's take another look at Charlie's idea."
- *Gate-keeping*: Keep the lines of communication open and invite everyone to participate in the conversation: "I think Maria is trying to say something important. Let's hear her out."
- *Process observing*: Watch how the group is operating and share what you see with the group: "These are interesting observations, but we've drifted off course. Let's get back to our agenda."

Task Functions

Group members also have a job to do—there are goals that direct the group and its work that must be achieved. Here are six essential task behaviors of effective group leaders and, eventually, of group members themselves:

- *Initiating*: Start the discussion. Propose tasks, goals, and actions. Suggest a procedure: "Let's write the ideas on the flip chart and analyze them. Who will be our recorder?"
- *Information or opinion-seeking*: Request facts or information about group concerns or opinions: "Whom should we invite to the workshop?" or "What do you think about...?"
- *Information-giving*: Provide facts or information about group topics or concerns. Group members can concentrate on what they are doing if they know what is going on: "We had to cut the budget by ten percent in that area. If we want to keep the program at this level we will have to do some fund-raising or find a grant."
- *Consensus-testing*: Check with the group to see how much agreement has been reached: "Could we go around the table quickly and let each member share one sentence describing where they stand on this question?"
- *Summarizing*: Pull together related ideas. Offer a decision or conclusion for group members to consider: "What I hear the group saying is this...."
- *Clarifying*: Interpret ideas or suggestions. Clarify issues before the group: "I think what she means is that we do not know if we can afford that program."

6. Leading Effective Group Discussions

Good discussions allow participants the chance to think about a question and decide how they feel about the topic. An effective leader keeps the discussion going like a volleyball player keeps the ball in the air. Use the following ideas to help you lead a successful group discussion:

- *Become familiar with the subject matter and the process.* Prepare the process in advance and plan the kinds of questions you want to ask.
- *Address everyone in the group by name.*
- *Ask focused or specific questions.*
- *Invite participation.* Give each person a chance to speak. Develop some novel ways to encourage non-participating members and to redirect those who may be sharing too much. Always respect a participant who chooses to pass on a particular question.
- *Encourage participants to ask questions of one another.* This technique will avoid having the focus continually shift back to you and will maintain the conversational tone of the discussion.
- *Explore how and why participants feel as they do about the topic.* This strategy will keep the discussion interesting and meaningful and avoid having it deteriorate into a simple reporting of facts.
- *Avoid questions that require yes or no for an answers.* If questions of this type are necessary, follow up by asking why or why not. The best tactic is to ask open-ended questions such as, If you had to..., What do you think the most effective way..., If it were up to you, how would you have handled..., or What do you think or feel about this?
- *Understand and be comfortable with silence.* This might seem contradictory to maintaining a good discussion, but there will be times when participants fall silent. Know that this often happens because they might be taking time to think about their response. At other times, participants may not have understood what you asked. Be aware and alert to participants' body-language and facial expressions in order to respond properly. Clarify when necessary.
- *Avoid evaluating responses with comments like "good answer," "nice point," etc.* Help participants understand why responses should not be evaluated. This will serve to keep the atmosphere open and objective.
- *Ask questions in non-confrontational ways so as not to put anyone on the spot.*
- *Do not take disagreements personally.* These are simply opportunities for the group to think about a variety of views on an issue.
- *Be orderly and stay on topic.* Avoid getting off on tangents. Participants should eventually be able to call the group to task when it strays from the topic or when it becomes distracted and too noisy.
- *Give everyone a chance to talk, but don't exhaust the topic.* Watch for signs of boredom.
- *During the discussion, and particularly at the end, summarize what was said to determine if the subject was covered thoroughly and everyone had an opportunity to have their say.* A variation on this idea is to ask if there are any participants who would like to summarize. Be prepared when needed to provide a brief report for a larger group.

7. Making Group Decisions

There are several ways to make decisions, especially when working with groups. Because every group is different, decide which of the following methods of decision making is best for your group.

▶ *Voting*: This method works well in very large groups. For a "simple majority" the choice with the most votes wins. A "true majority" requires the support of fifty percent of the voters plus one (e.g., six out of ten people). Arriving at a decision with a true majority will probably require more than one vote as the group eliminates low-scoring choices.

- Benefits: This is seen as a "fair" way of making decisions.
- Drawbacks: Group members may feel like winners or losers. This can affect if or how much they buy into the decision.

▶ *Consulting*: This method works well in large groups and/or at times when it would help to have an expert's guidance on a decision. One person has the authority to make the decision, but he or she invites group members to give input before making it. This method works best when a group clearly understands its role and how the decision will be made.

- Benefits: If the leader informs group members of the decision and the reasons behind it, they will know that their opinions were taken into consideration. This will help them accept the decision, even if they do not agree with it.
- Drawbacks: As the leader, you must be sincere in consulting with the group. If a decision has already been made, and you are only going through the motions of seeking opinions and information, group members may feel betrayed and lose trust.

▶ *Consensus*: This method works well in groups of any size, especially small groups. A group can use consensus-building at any stage of the problem-solving process. When group decisions are preferred, it is often the most effective method. Everyone expresses his or her ideas and opinions without feeling judged or threatened. The group reaches consensus when each member can support, or at least live with, the decision.

- Benefits: This method takes time, but it is a wonderful way to create a sense of ownership and support. The group welcomes differing views as a means of getting more information, clarifying issues, or seeking the best alternative. There are no losers with this method, only winners.
- Drawbacks: It is possible to reach a "false" consensus. This happens when the group interprets silence as consent. You must be careful to get a clear response from each member of the group to make certain the group hears all thoughts.

As a leader you play an important role in bringing a group to consensus, since you set the tone for how things will get done. You can help team members most by

- emphasizing fact over opinion;
- giving team members an appropriate amount of time to work through an issue;
- reminding team members that conflict is an inevitable part of the process;
- letting them know that negotiation and collaboration are expected;
- making certain team members do not give in just to avoid conflict.

Sometimes a group will not achieve consensus. This is a reality of group interaction and it is no one's fault. When this happens, take these steps to get the group moving again.

- *Agree to disagree.* Move to a related issue. Return to the original issue at another time.
- *Change topics for a while.*
- *Call a recess.* Allow things to settle and take up the issue again later.
- *Work toward a compromise decision.* It may not be the best decision, but it keeps the issue in play.
- *Consider alternatives.* Voting, for example, can quickly reduce a large number of options while retaining team commitment. Establish these alternatives at the beginning of the process.